RED FLAGS

George Magnus is an associate at the China Centre at Oxford University, research associate at the School of Oriental and African Studies and former chief economist at UBS. He was featured in the *Telegraph* as 'the man widely acknowledged to have predicted that the US sub-prime mortgage crisis would trigger a global recession'. Magnus has written extensively about China in print media including for the *Financial Times*, Bloomberg View and *Prospect* magazine, and is regularly asked to speak on radio and TV.

Further praise for *Red Flags*:

'Compelling, ominous and thought-provoking, George Magnus has written a book that should be essential reading for anyone trying to make sense of what is happening in China – and why it will have a global impact.' Peter Frankopan, author of *The Silk Roads*

'For insight into the dilemmas and decisions China's leaders, notably Xi Jinping, will face in the next decades, it would be hard to beat *Red Flags*.' Diane Coyle, author of *GDP: A Brief but Affectionate History*

'An excellent, tightly argued and fluently written analysis of the challenges that lie behind the China Dream.' Jonathan Fenby, author of *Will China Dominate the 21st Century?*

'An immensely important and powerful book from one of our premier commentators on economics.' Rana Mitter, author of *China's War with Japan, 1937–1945*

'A nuanced, historically informed and highly readable account of why we should never be complacent about the People's Republic.' Kerry Brown, author of *CEO, China*

RED FLAGS
WHY XI'S CHINA
IS IN JEOPARDY

GEORGE MAGNUS

YALE UNIVERSITY PRESS
NEW HAVEN AND LONDON

For information about this and other Yale University Press publications, please contact:
U.S. Office: sales.press@yale.edu   yalebooks.com
Europe Office: sales@yaleup.co.uk   yalebooks.co.uk

Set in Adobe Caslon Pro by IDSUK (DataConnection) Ltd
Printed and bound by CPI Group (UK) Ltd, Croydon, CR0 4YY

Library of Congress Control Number: 2018947835

ISBN 978-0-300-23319-3 (hbk)
ISBN 978-0-300-24663-6 (pbk)

A catalogue record for this book is available from the British Library.

10 9 8 7 6 5 4 3 2

To Lesley, Daniel, Kerri and Elias, Jonathan, Rachel and Ben

CONTENTS

PREFACE TO THE PAPERBACK EDITION

According to Chinese folklore, the year of the Pig is associated with wealth. However else 2019 is remembered, though, it will be for other, less auspicious things. The economy, the deterioration of the relationship with the US and the political situation in both Hong Kong and Taiwan will all have given cause for concern in Zhongnanhai, the central headquarters of the Communist Party and the State Council in Beijing.

Amid these and other concerns, plans for the celebration in October of the seventieth anniversary of the founding of the People's Republic of China will have been a welcome distraction because it is a moment to commemorate triumphs and reflect on the lessons learned from history, both of which the Party likes to do.

The way in which anniversaries are celebrated or observed is quite revealing, informing us how countries have either integrated and come to terms with their history, or otherwise chosen to ignore or rewrite it, burying things they don't want people to discuss or remember. The first is a sign of maturity and confidence, the second isn't. China does both.

The fortieth anniversary exhibition of Deng Xiaoping's policy of 'Reform and Opening Up' at the end of 2018 certainly paid homage to China's great accomplishments since 1978, but neither the political leader that kicked it all off, nor significant reformers that followed him, featured significantly. The exhibition did, however, shower praise on the contribution made by President Xi Jinping, who only came to power in 2012, and whose contribution to 'Reform and Opening Up', if we are to be generous, has been patchy.

The centenary of the May Fourth Movement, formed in 1919 to protest both China's treatment at the Treaty of Versailles and its own government, was rather subdued. Recalling the protest movement, from which the Communist Party emerged formally two years later, Xi Jinping urged today's youth to be loyal to the Party, to be patriotic and to resist foreign influence, but no large or open celebrations were permitted. Marxist students, who see themselves as the embodiment of their May Fourth antecedents and who had also been campaigning since 2018 for workers' rights, were not able to organise for the centenary, and several were detained or went missing before the 4 May. The Party can hardly ignore the May Fourth Movement, but it remembers à la carte. It doesn't want to remind people that the 1919 protestors were both loyal citizens and strongly critical of their government, wanting to be rid of autocracy just like their successors in Tiananmen Square in 1989.

The Tiananmen Square crackdown on the night of 3–4 June 1989 has never been remembered or commemorated in mainland China. It features fleetingly as a disturbance or not at all in school history books and there is nothing in the square or anywhere else to remind us of what happened. In 2019, ahead of the thirtieth anniversary of the night the tanks rolled into the square, the authorities detained people, shut down discussion and even blocked global source information, for example on Wikipedia.

Inspired by their May Fourth Movement heroes, students agitated early in 1989 against rising inflation, inequality and corruption, and for new reforms. They professed loyalty to their country and anticipated the fortieth anniversary of the founding of the People's Republic later that year, but they were also driven to protest. The death of Hu Yaobang, general secretary of the Party, who had been forced to resign in 1987 over pro-democracy reforms, served as a catalyst for the protestors who then elevated him to a sort of martyr for the cause of liberal reform.

We still don't know how many people were killed on the night of 3 June. Government estimates that 241 were killed and 7,000 wounded were always thought to have been too low. In a secret diplomatic cable declassified in 2017, the then UK Ambassador to Beijing, Sir Alan Donald, estimated that as many as 10,000 may have been killed.

Tiananmen has nevertheless left a contentious legacy. There is a school of thought in China, and also among some China-watchers, that while the crackdown was brutal, it cemented the dominance of the Communist Party and kicked off three decades of a rising China that has brought us to the current day. Crudely, the argument goes, Chinese autocracy worked, and still works.

The people of Hong Kong, or Taiwan would beg to differ and, more generally, we should not dismiss so lightly what happened in 1989, the airbrushing of history or such simplistic reasoning.

Before Tiananmen, as I emphasise later in the book, China had already enjoyed a decade of considerable economic progress under autocratic rule, but from a government that was keen to experiment with a more liberal approach to ownership structures and market mechanisms. After Tiananmen, Deng Xiaoping was eventually able to re-energise the drive for significant and highly effective reforms, passing the baton to his successors. While an autocratic one-party state owned the initiatives and the consequences, the narrative had little to do with a one-party state, autocracy or top-down industrial strategy. Rather, the real narrative was about the incorporation of markets in goods, the encouragement of entrepreneurship and private firms, and learning best practice from the rest of the world.

The enduring legacy of Tiananmen is also different from the formal narrative linking autocracy with phenomenal economic success. At the time, Party leaders were consumed by three things that now resonate loudly in Xi's China, even if they were subdued for long periods of time in the interim. First, that the Party was under threat from enemies within and meddling from outside China. Second, that discipline and social control were more important than economic reform. Third, that the Party's integrity can only be preserved by suppressing internal divisions.[1]

President Xi Jinping has taken these lessons to heart, and emphasised even before he came to power the importance of the primacy and purity of the Party in all walks of life. Yet for China, this could one day prove to be a double-edged sword. On the one hand, President Xi is a strong leader who has centralised power around himself, demanding loyalty and suppressing dissent. On the other hand, there is now no provision for an orderly succession, either for his role as Party general secretary and chair of the Central Military Commission, or as president, since the abandonment of presidential term limits in 2018. Even if opposition to the president can be stifled, there is no way to eliminate it or to guarantee that the president himself will not falter over something that might provide opponents with the catalyst to resist. The trade war between China and the US may be just such a phenomenon, as we shall see later in the book, especially if the political and economic climate in China were to deteriorate.

As stated at the outset, though, there are other less-sensitive anniversaries in which China excels, and which feature pomp and circumstance, big public displays of military might and a myriad of ways to celebrate the Communist Party's historic achievements. An example of this is the October 2019 commemoration of the seventieth anniversary of the founding of the People's Republic of China; Mao's proclamation of the republic is described at the start of Chapter 2.

After 2019, China's next big event occurs in 2021 with the much anticipated centenary of the founding of the Communist Party, an event that will doubtless be celebrated as a core part of President Xi's 'Chinese Dream of the great rejuvenation of the Chinese nation'. And while not an anniversary as such, 2021 is also the year in which the Party will have been in power for seventy-two years, rivalling the longevity of the Soviet Communist Party, in power from the Bolshevik Revolution to the revolutions of 1989 that presaged the collapse of the Soviet Union.

Bearing in mind the lessons China has drawn from the experience of its Soviet peer, notably the need to continuously strengthen Party discipline and dominance, its leaders will take considerable comfort from the knowledge that in modern China, the Communist Party's own longevity is under no apparent threat.

Perhaps so.

Yet the arguments in this book invite readers to reflect on the nature of and challenges to Xi's China with an open mind. The paperback edition, including a new Afterword, offers an opportunity to bring readers up to date with some of my additional thinking about China since the manuscript of the hardback was completed in the spring of 2018, in particular because of the flurry of economic and political developments that have unfolded since that time.

While China is in many ways strong and powerful, the Party's preoccupation with centralised control and negation of sensitive discussion and debate contribute to policies that I think speak to other interpretations. China's governance system under Xi Jinping, for example, may be nurturing policy instability and incoherence. Xi's government may be more powerful than any since Mao, but its governance system could easily make China and the stability it craves more brittle than they appear.

Straws in the wind

In the past year, for example, President Xi Jinping's government has encountered, unusually, some criticism at home over its management of the economy and its approach to the United States over the trade war, in which it has been wrong-footed by the persistence with which the US has prosecuted trade and commercial conflict. Moreover, in his biggest political climbdown since coming to power in 2012, President Xi doubtless had to bite his bottom lip and acknowledge the success of street politics in Hong Kong in June 2019, when an estimated 2 million protestors forced the Hong Kong government to suspend a controversial Extradition Bill seen as further undermining of civil liberties and the rule of law in Hong Kong.

For decades, China enjoyed and benefited from a largely benign global system in which it wanted to and was allowed to integrate. In the heyday of Chinese economic growth, when the world economy and world trade were booming, it was able to ride the surf of accelerating globalisation along with other countries. However, these days have gone and the picture today could not be more different as China and the US stand off against each other in a geopolitical and existential crisis that is the biggest the world has seen since the Cold War. This makes it all the more important to try to understand what is going on in the Chinese economy, the governance structure at home and, if possible, the Party itself.

The trade war looks to have not only accentuated a weakening economy in China but also spawned dissent or disquiet. Some Sinologists think that opposition to Xi Jinping certainly exists in the Party following six years of his anti-corruption campaign and ideological shifts, though no one is prepared to break cover as things stand. Xi's position, however, is not without risk were he to be blamed for, for example, losing China's most important external relationship – that is, with the United States.

Other sources of criticism, while of no material political consequence currently, are nonetheless noteworthy. They have come from intellectuals and, now and again, former policymakers who have criticised the external policies of China's government, especially as they affect the US, trade and the Belt and Road Initiative (BRI). Some criticism has also been directed at the popular narrative that places the Party at the heart of the country's past success and bright future. An important debate has also been going on about the relative importance of and attitudes to the state sector, seen by the government as the core of the economic system, versus the private sector, still viewed by many as the most dynamic part of the economy and responsible in the main for China's economic eruption.

The economic slowdown that developed in and especially after the autumn of 2018 highlighted the sensitive situation of private firms. As the economy lost traction, private sector firms flagged even as state firms prospered, and employment became the number one issue in policy meetings and strategy documents. The government was obliged to reverse, at least in part, important economic and financial policies that it pursued with serious intent in 2017 and 2018. It backed away from some of the tougher deleveraging policies and turned to fiscal stimulus, more infrastructure spending, and even faster credit growth so as to stabilise the economic downturn.

Because of the government's sensitivity to pushback and criticism, the rhetoric surrounding two core strategic policies was toned down considerably. Made in China 2025, the industrial programme that seeks to establish China's self-sufficiency and dominance in key advanced sectors, remains an essential part of the government's strategy but came to be seen as a catch-all for numerous industrial and technological policies to which the US and other western countries and firms are strongly opposed, and as an example of chauvinism, spurring them to act against China. The phrase 'Made in China 2025' is barely mentioned nowadays, if at all. Yet we should not be misled by what is a tactical silence: China is now four years into the Made in China strategy and implementing more and more of it. It is a highly significant upgrading of China's industrial and technological capacity, and seen by Beijing as a means of boosting self-reliance and averting the middle income trap.

The Belt and Road Initiative, President's Xi's signature foreign policy, which entails large-scale financing of infrastructure projects in over 100 countries, has also been the subject of complaints ranging from ineptitude, inefficiency and poor governance to debt diplomacy. The problems are almost certainly more about the former, and the pushback may well have contributed to a softer rhetoric when Xi Jinping addressed the second Belt and Road Forum in Beijing in 2019. He acknowledged that some elements in the implementation of Belt and Road projects could change. It could now be scaled back and other countries, global financial institutions and financial centres might become involved. How far it might be recalibrated, though, remains a moot point: in many ways, the Belt and Road is an extension of the domestic model of how banks, state enterprises and local governments do infrastructure business in China. What critics complain about are features, not unforeseen errors, that might otherwise be fixed around a negotiating table.

The most striking development over the past year, however, was how the volatile Sino–US relationship became the biggest geopolitical challenge to stalk the world since the Cold War. After the initial tit-for-tat tariffs implemented in 2018, the two sides came together at the G20 Summit in Buenos Aires in November and agreed to try and negotiate a deal. The US suspended tariff increases that were due to take effect at the start of 2019 and for a few months the mood surrounding the talks seemed constructive and optimistic.

Yet in May they broke down with both sides accusing the other of bad faith and reneging on previously agreed commitments. In a marked escalation, both sides took actions designed to target the other's companies. The US sought to withhold the sale of microchips and other key components to the Chinese telecommunications giant Huawei, its subsidiaries and other technology firms deemed to be security risks. China said it would blacklist and punish US firms and individuals that acted for non-business interests to harm Chinese firms, and ban the export of certain materials.

The trade war, ostensibly about trade but always about the struggle for technological dominance and the rules of industrial policy, took a more ominous form. It threatened to ensnare companies all over the world, which were part of the global technology supply chain and force them to choose to subscribe to US or Chinese laws and regulations, with the risk of punishment by the other. What started off as a row over common-or-garden agricultural and manufactured goods now embraced the risk of a balkanised and less efficient global technology industry, and of still wider conflicts between the world's two biggest economies.

The global technology industry could not be less like, say, steel and soybeans when it comes to trade and connectivity. It is a genuinely global industry featuring high levels of integration and extensive supply chains that cross national boundaries. It connects companies all over the world. In some important respects, it has systemic features not unlike the global financial sector, which we learned about to our cost in and after 2008.

The escalation in the summer of 2019 of the trade war that spread out from punitive tariffs to the targeting of companies and the integrity of the global technology sector marked a serious deterioration in China's relations with the US, and by implication with the West. It seems we have crossed the Rubicon, and that there will be no going back to the relationships that formed in the last decades.

While there are those on both sides calling for 'decoupling' and greater 'self-reliance', we have to hope that China and Western nations may yet be able to rebuild some trust, and new forms of engagement and cooperation where they share common interests, even if in other respects, irreconcilable differences will persist.

It is not pre-ordained that China and the US will come into overt conflict, but it will take a lot of effort and political goodwill to stabilise and improve the relationship. Hopefully, this book will help us all understand a little more about what makes Xi's China tick and the challenges it now faces on many fronts.

ACKNOWLEDGEMENTS

While writing this book, I was driven to emphasise at various points that President Xi Jinping's China was turning out to be different from the China that most of us have known for the last twenty to thirty years. None of us can know now whether he will be the equivalent of a good or bad emperor, but the one thing we can say with some certainty is that the outlook for Xi's China cannot be drawn with lines from the past: it has reached the end of extrapolation. In a rather curious way, then, I feel I owe a small debt of gratitude to President Xi, because he has inadvertently added some frisson to my title. It is his China, and he will take all the credit or shoulder all the blame for whatever happens on his now extended watch.

I wanted to write an accessible book about the prospects for and challenges facing Xi's China because, as the twenty-first century matures, I think we all need to understand more about the Middle Kingdom. Regardless of what happens, it will certainly play a prominent role in shaping the world and affecting our lives and those of our progeny. It all came together thanks to some important recent developments in China, and two meetings.

In 2015–16, China succumbed to significant financial and economic turbulence. Until then Xi Jinping hadn't paid much attention to economic matters, but in the spring of 2016 I was visiting China when the now well-known 'authoritative person' front-page interview in the *People's Daily* appeared, warning that China had to change course. Speculation about the person's identity centred on Liu He, then head of the National Reform Development Committee, and now vice premier and in charge of economic and financial affairs overall. Everyone knew the intervention was important. At the same time, speculation about the following year's 19th Party Congress was starting. It felt at the time as though important changes in China were afoot. And so it has proven to be.

The decision to get on with drafting emerged during a typically convivial lunch with HSBC's senior economic adviser, Stephen King. Stephen is a wise and thoughtful economist, and when he revealed the title of his forthcoming book, *Grave New World* (published by Yale University Press in 2017), I thought this was one of the most inspired non-fiction titles I'd ever come across. I had a chronic case of title envy, and try as I did to find a comparable play on great titles applied to a China book, it eluded me. Nevertheless, it spurred me to get on with the organisation of my own ideas and start writing.

Soon after, I had a meeting with Taiba Batool, commissioning editor at Yale University Press, who approached me to discuss the possibility of writing something that would slot into the company's economic book series. The last piece of the jigsaw fell into place, and the die was cast.

At various points in the drafting, I sent longer or shorter parts of the book for comment to a few people, who kindly responded with helpful suggestions, reminders and corrections. Guy de Jonquières, former Asia and trade editor of the *Financial Times*, and now senior fellow at the European Centre for International Political Economy, ploughed through the whole of an early draft. Victor Shih, political economist at the School of Global Policies and Strategy at the University of California, San Diego, and Chris Balding, formerly associate professor at the HSBC Business School in Shenzhen, also provided useful comments and tips on considerable sections of the book. Taiba Batool also laboured through the later drafts of the book offering her own expertise and suggestions to improve the content, flow and sequencing. A draft of the book was also sent out to three expert readers, who were anonymous to me, but who all reverted with comments that gave me cause for thought, and the opportunity to sharpen up. Thanks are also due to Rachael Lonsdale for her editing labours, and Ruth Killick for her work on promotion.

I would also like to acknowledge some of the many people whose thinking has contributed to the formation of my own understanding of China's politics and economics. I am deeply grateful to Rana Mitter, director of the China Centre at Oxford University, and Steve Tsang, director of the China Institute at the School of Oriental and African Studies (SOAS), both inspirational academics who took me on as a research associate. Also Bob

Ash at SOAS, still imparting wisdom and who taught there when I was doing my MSc many years ago.

Others whose work, thinking and counsel I have always held in the highest esteem merit an important mention. Jon Anderson, a former colleague at UBS, who was the China, later emerging markets economist, runs the Emerging Advisors Group out of Shanghai. Simon Ogus, who was the head of Asian economics at Swiss Bank Corporation when it and UBS merged in 1997, was briefly a colleague before leaving to do a doctorate and then run DSG Asia out of Hong Kong. I never tire of reading and listening to Michael Pettis, a former trader turned professor of finance at Peking University's Guanghua School of Management, whom I have met at events in fancy hotels and in his hutong in Beijing. Joerg Wuttke, permanent representative of BASF in China, and former head of the EU–China Chamber of Commerce in Beijing, has been a never-ending source of business and political insight.

It has also been and remains my privilege to attend a regular series of China lunches in a private upstairs room in a Chinese restaurant in Soho, which is much less clandestine than it sounds, organised by Guy de Jonquières. The assembled wisdom of the attendees, who include Mick Cox, Jonathan Fenby, Roger Garside, Isabel Hilton, Christopher Hum, Nigel Inkster, Charles Parton, James Richards, Stein Ringen, Geoffrey Yu and Jie Yu is humbling and highly informative.

To all of these individuals, I would like to record my thanks for sharing their China acumen with me at various times and in different ways. I have benefited enormously from our exchanges and interactions, and absolve each and every one from any errors or misunderstandings in the book, which are, of course, mine entirely.

Finally, I should like to thank Lesley, my wife, for her love and unswerving support, especially during the researching and writing of the book, and my children, Daniel, Jonathan, Rachel and Ben, for their love and humour, often at my expense. I am sure I am not the only author to succumb to phases of tedium when the going gets tough, and when social skills become rather blunt. Lesley fully deserves my thanks for her endearing irreverence, and for keeping her head while I may have been losing mine.

London, June 2018

INTRODUCTION

In less than forty years, China has quintupled its share of global output, and transformed itself from a poor country and source of cheap toys and textiles to a fierce competitor in high-end manufacturing, advanced technologies and military might. It is the dominant power in Asia and a rival and adversary of the United States. Xi Jinping, who is general secretary of the Communist Party, chairman of the Central Military Commission, and president of China, is now one of the most powerful political leaders in the world. He insists that the primacy of the Party is indispensable to developing China in the twenty-first century and managing its growing footprint overseas. If his health holds and his opponents stay subdued, he could remain a strongman president for life.

Whilst economists and China-watchers have been well aware of the global consequences of a rising China for some time, Xi's China is going to resonate much more for all of us in future. If, as several Chinese thinkers now assert, China stood up under Mao Zedong and got rich under Deng Xiaoping, it is becoming powerful again under Xi Jinping, who articulates that China's troubled twentieth century now lies firmly in the past as the Communist Party under his leadership pursues the great rejuvenation of the Chinese nation, based around 'socialism with Chinese characteristics'. Under Xi, China has become more controlling, more confident and more assertive. Driven by its own sense of and pride in millennia of history, it is determined to 'take back' its place in Asia and the world, and consign to history forever what it calls its 'century of humiliation'. This was the period from roughly 1840 to 1949 during which imperial powers fought wars and settled in

China, imposing what the Chinese argue to have been harsh economic punishment.

Now economically strong enough to leverage geopolitical power, China's cause has been aided and abetted by President Trump, who is pulling the United States back from the liberal economic order it created and championed for the last seventy years. It has also been helped by a world in which political change is more aligned with its own autocratic and nationalistic tendencies. Winding up the National People's Congress in 2018, Xi Jinping reminded delegates of China's history, and insisted that it would not tolerate 'separatism', a not so vague reference to Hong Kong, the two provinces of Tibet and Xinjiang, and importantly, Taiwan, which it sees as an inalienable part of China. We should expect Xi's China to make waves in the world in ways we may not anticipate, and for which we may not be properly prepared.

There is no question that Xi's ascent has been extraordinary, and this book aims to put into context what it means for China, and for the rest of the world. From our Western bunker, there is unmistakable fawning and awe, which is understandable to a degree. Yet it is also misplaced and plays to China's own carefully crafted narrative about itself. Remember, the last time confident assumptions about China were doing the rounds, the gist was that reform would lead to China's becoming a liberal state.

Xi could become a benevolent dictator, but such individuals are few in number, and have generally run small countries. He might go on to become omnipotent and unassailable, but in Xi's China, lacking institutions of constraint and consensus, one of the main surprises as the years roll by is likely to be policy or political instability. This could emanate from unchallenged personal errors and miscalculations, inertia or fear of change among bureaucrats, eventually impatient or resentful opponents or, quite simply, events that go wrong or are mishandled and for which he must now shoulder total responsibility.

Nothing is assured, and we have to learn much more about the domestic politics of China and the consequences of Xi Jinping to integrate better our understanding of its prospects, and how to interact with both him and it.

Looking back, it is curious to reflect that Xi's path to the Chinese presidency in 2012 was shrouded in political intrigue. With only days to go before new leaders would be unveiled at the Party's 18th Congress, he disappeared for two weeks. To this day, no one knows why, or with what or whom he was engaged. After he became president, he launched a Leninist crusade to reshape and gain control of the Party, the military and the internal security apparatus. He embraced a virulent anti-corruption campaign, which was aimed as much at ensuring the obedience of Party members as at disposing of enemies. He transferred much decision-making from technocrats and ministries into the hands of Party officials and committees, known as Leading Small Groups, which are anything but small.

At the Party's 19th Congress in 2017, 'Xi Jinping Thought on Socialism with Chinese Characteristics for a New Era' was incorporated into the Party's constitution to sit alongside that of only Mao Zedong, and Deng Xiaoping. The Congress was remarkable for this outcome, and it is important to understand that this allows the pursuit of communism and Marxism to achieve a great unity in the Chinese tradition where everyone's needs are addressed and met; for the Party under Xi to be at the forefront of achieving a socialist modernity and establishing a model to help other nations eliminate the dependency imposed by capitalist modernity; for putting the Party at the heart of the state governance system; and for the engagement in 'struggle' to define the Party's realisation of the coming revolutions in science and technology. Xi Jinping Thought, therefore, occupies a special place in modern China.

In 2018, the state constitution was changed to remove the requirement, introduced in 1982 to institutionalise the orderly succession of leaders, for the president to be limited to two five-year terms. It also incorporated a new National Supervision Commission, which, reversing decades of formal separation, unifies the power of the Party and the basic elements of the justice system, and extends its authority to all public servants, whether or not they are Party members. This was part of the biggest overhaul of state institutions since 2003. Ostensibly designed to improve China's governance structure, these changes also served to tighten the Party's grip on and takeover of the state, a theme which runs through this book.

Xi Jinping's power and long-term influence are assured by his Party posts, which are not subject to term limits, but the audacious move to abandon presidential limits means that he is now, in effect, a dictator with more personal authority than anyone since Mao Zedong. He will certainly remain in power beyond 2022 when his second term would have expired, but we can only speculate for how long. In the meantime, Xi will continue to articulate to citizens the 'Chinese dream of the great rejuvenation of the Chinese nation'. Couched in general terms of the spirit of the nation, patriotism and innovation, his ambition is for the Party to lead China towards greater prosperity, a better quality of life, and dominance in modern industries and technologies.

The consequences of Xi Jinping will be significant for people all over the world as they affect both China and its international relations and foreign policy. Xi sees the opportunity of America's retreat from global leadership and the West's laboured recovery from the financial crisis as an opportunity to press China's claims for recognition, respect and a bigger role in the global system. He is pitching to an insecure and rudderless world a China that is the new leader of globalisation and an open trading system, even though this rhetoric contrasts starkly with the reality of the alternative model of governance China is championing, which is authoritarian and protectionist. He evokes China's ancestors who connected Asia, Europe and Africa by the Silk Road as a segue to his personal recreation of it as the 'Belt and Road Initiative'. It is nothing less than the modern battleground for influence and advantage across Eurasia and beyond.

The divergence between China and the West is manifesting itself in two interlocking but separate universes in which economic decision-making, social change and technological advances are being shaped. How is this all going to end?

It is a question to which no one knows the answer but it is self-evident that China and the West are now pursuing quite different paths when it comes to the values that matter for economic and social development, and for their own systemic economic viability. We need to ask questions of China, in much the same way as we do of ourselves, and not simply nod to the assertions of those who judge, sometimes self-servingly, that the future belongs to China.

The core of the book is about the four economic traps which I think China faces. These comprise, in the next few years, the debt trap, and, related to it, the Renminbi trap; and, over the medium term, the demographic or ageing trap, and the middle-income trap. Each of these would represent a considerable challenge in isolation. China has to confront them more or less simultaneously. The debt problem in China is the most pressing, but China is also ageing faster than any other country on earth, and is already at the point where the quality of institutions and governance matter to future growth prospects, as well as to the resolution of more immediate economic challenges.

The book then takes on a geo-economic and geopolitical sweep. Guided by the phrase coined by Edward Luttwak that geo-economics is the logic of conflict in the grammar of commerce, it examines economic and policy issues surrounding China's trade relations in the world, especially vis-à-vis the US, and the Belt and Road Initiative. In the final chapter, I present some closing thoughts about Xi's China, especially the two main sources of divergence between it and the West, in technology and international relations, which seem likely to define the Sino-Western relationship for years to come.

China matters

My first visit to China in 1993 was to pitch economic research for S.G. Warburg's foreign exchange business at the People's Bank of China and the still secretive State Administration for Foreign Exchange. Beijing was a rather humdrum city that lived up to its image: people in drab and monotonous clothing, bicycles galore, and minimalist hotels. It was in the throes of preparing expressways and infrastructure for the 2000 Olympics bid, but by the time it actually held the 2008 Games, it was already a different country.

I have visited China nearly every year since that first trip, sometimes on multiple occasions, and have watched a unique national transformation unfold at unprecedented speed. As the chief economist of Warburg and later UBS for nearly twenty years, and senior economic adviser for a further decade, I spent a lot of time researching many aspects of China's economic surge and its global consequences. In more recent years, my more academic associations with China-related institutions have provided an opportunity for deeper learning and understanding. Over time, my primary interest has become the sustainability of China's economic progress. In a nutshell, I think China has reached the end of extrapolation, and Xi's China, in particular, is unquestionably a new phenomenon.

Nowadays, visitors flock to China's cities and are wowed by their size, sophistication and skyscrapers. Interestingly, there is a bit of folklore about skyscrapers – or at least the topping-out process – and subsequent economic mishaps. The Shanghai World Financial Centre, for example, was topped out at 492 metres in 2007 to become the nation's biggest building, about a year before the financial crisis rolled into China. The Shanghai Tower was topped out at 632 metres in 2016, coinciding with a period of home-grown financial instability. In 2018, China is expected to complete the world's second highest building, the Wuhan Greenland Tower, comprising 636 metres of luxury offices and apartments, designer shops and a high-end hotel. Will this portend a tipping point in the Chinese economy? And how would that manifest itself in the rest of the world economy?

China obviously matters. This is well understood, but let us look at why this is so in a more holistic perspective, first tracing a few signposts along

China's path to current prosperity, and then considering how China's economic challenges might affect the rest of us.

In 1990, China was not on most people's radar screen, except perhaps for China experts and expats who were watching it change from inside its borders. To the outside world, China's economy, accounting for just over 2 per cent of world GDP, was of little consequence. Most of its limited amount of trade was with Hong Kong, and to a much lesser extent some other Asian countries such as Malaysia and Indonesia.

China's relative backwardness at the time was suitably illustrated by the inspirational but ageing Deng Xiaoping, who had been dismissed and then rehabilitated by the Party in earlier years, and who was trying to revive reforms that had been put on hold in the wake of the Tiananmen Square disturbances in 1989.[1] He urged citizens to strive to match the economic growth rates of China's Asian neighbours, and, as Henry Kissinger recalled, he extolled the 'four big items' it was essential to make available to consumers in the countryside: a bicycle, a sewing machine, a radio and a wristwatch.[2]

Under the slogan 'Reform and Opening Up', Deng articulated and inspired China to become modern, to prioritise science and technology, to encourage intellectuals to return home, and possibly to become a 'moderately developed country' within a hundred years. Under his leadership, the 1980s brought significant reforms of agriculture, measures to help spur the growth in private firms, and the creation of special economic zones (SEZs) in rural backwaters, such as Shenzhen, designed to attract foreign investment and bolster private enterprise and financial liberalisation.[3] Based on these experiences and on opening up to both the US and other countries for political and economic exchanges, China kicked on in the 1990s, now under the leadership of Deng's successors, Party General Secretary and President Jiang Zemin and his able premier Zhu Rongji.

Jiang and Zhu presided over an unprecedented and rapid rise in income per head – a compound rate of 9.4 per cent per year between 1993 and 2003 – a negotiated return of Hong Kong to the mainland, and a reboot of China's relations with the US and other leading countries. They steered China successfully through the Asian financial crisis in 1997–98, albeit not without incident. Some territories adjoining Hong Kong, especially Guangdong, witnessed serious financial difficulties and obliged Beijing to send a fixer, Wang Qishan, to oversee bankruptcies and restructuring.[4] Wang became a close associate of President Xi Jinping, ran his anti-corruption campaign, and became vice-president in 2018.

Under Jiang, China joined the World Trade Organization (WTO) in 2001. This proved to be an important institutional catalyst in China's economic development – perhaps the biggest in the last four decades. The lure of membership was every bit as important as the consequences. Together they gave succour and substance to the political arguments for economic reform, and locked China into internationally enforceable obligations, which made it more difficult for more conservative and anti-reform factions of the Party to resist.

In the 2000s, optimism about China became intense and infectious. In a now well-known 2001 economic research paper called 'Building Better Global Economic BRICs', the US investment bank Goldman Sachs argued, in the immediate aftermath of the 9/11 terror attacks in the US, that the structure of the global economy was going to change radically over the next fifty years, courtesy of sustainably faster growth in Brazil, Russia, India and China (later South Africa too) than in advanced economies.[5] The bank embraced the acronym, which became a major marketing coup, and common parlance around the world for about a decade or so.

The concept was catchy, but inherently flawed. China is the only BRICS country to have enjoyed steady economic success. Its economy has wobbled from time to time, and it has had moments of extreme financial instability, but so far it has managed to stay on a broadly even keel. It is already the world's biggest export nation, the largest or second largest economy in the world, depending on the choice of measurement, and the only country to have raised its share of world output by a significant amount, by a factor of five to be precise, to about 15 per cent.

In the global system, China now presents to the world a form of economic and political governance that is the antithesis of the so-called neoliberal version that held sway until the financial crisis. Many countries are now weighing up not whether the state should play a more active role in the economy, but how much intervention is desirable, and where. The doctrines of free trade and capital movements are being reconsidered, not always for good reasons, but even the IMF and World Bank are no longer wedded totally to laissez-faire ideas. China's authoritarian government and state-driven economic management is no longer an outlier. State enterprises and intervention in the economy are commonplace in Asia, for example, and several countries, including Hungary, Poland, Russia, Turkey and Venezuela, have embraced autocratic government. Politicians even in Trump's America and Brexit Britain have borrowed attitudes and behaviour normally associated with autocracies.

The potential for rising tensions between China and the West is high. There is conflict surrounding trade regulations and practices, and about the race for leadership in new and advanced technologies. Rumblings previously restricted to the conditions under which foreign firms operate in China have migrated into a frostiness towards China's direct investment abroad in the US and the EU. China's maritime goals in the South and East China Seas, and the Belt and Road Initiative, are incubating frictions with other Asian countries, notably India and Japan, as well as with the US and Europe. The Belt and Road is hailed as an alternative means of promoting economic development in poorer countries, and winning friends worldwide, but can equally be seen as a China-centric strategy designed to spread China's political and commercial footprint. Larger and richer countries don't need the infrastructure, and will compete with or oppose China. Poorer nations will want infrastructure, but some may suffer commercially and financially. Like any power, China wants to build its influence abroad, but by interfering in foreign countries it is crossing lines, including those of legality.

Swings in the Chinese economy send out strong ripple effects into its manufacturing supply chains in Asia and further afield, and into commodity and other financial markets. China may not impact the global economic system the way that the US does, but it's worth remembering that the increase in the US dollar value of China's GDP in 2017 was the equivalent of Mexico's or Indonesia's GDP. Developed economies may be relatively more insulated from the gyrations in China's economy, but many industries worldwide, and emerging and developing countries, feel the effects of problems in China quickly and sensitively. All countries were affected by the instability and volatility in China's exchange rate and financial markets in 2015–16. It was always said that when America sneezes, the rest of the world catches a cold, and it is certainly increasingly true of China.

Although the Chinese home market in many goods and services is highly protected, its rising middle class and enterprise opportunities remain a magnet for foreign companies. Just consider that a decade ago, few people took the Chinese car market seriously. Now it is the world's largest, selling about 25 million units a year and with roughly 149 million privately owned passenger vehicles on the road in 2016. In a measure of economic connectivity linked to growth and productivity between 2010 and 2016, China's metro and urban light-rail track length more than tripled to 4,000 kilometres. Its high-speed rail network quintupled to 25,000 kilometres, and its motorways expanded by 77 per cent to 131,000 kilometres. China is a leader in e-commerce and mobile payments, is currently rolling out facial recognition technology, and aims to be a global leader in artificial intelligence. Without much regard for privacy and individual rights, it is making waves in the use of big data and the exploitation of information gathered from its large population.

So what's not to like? Well, as the title of this book implies, there are also warning signs of threats to China's economy. Its leaders have been cognisant of them for a while. In 2007, former premier Wen Jiabao said at the National People's Congress that the Chinese economy was becoming unstable, unbalanced, uncoordinated and unsustainable.[6] Wen was worried by a long list of concerns including over-investment, unbalanced trade, inequality of incomes between cities and the countryside, wasteful and inefficient use of energy and other resources, and environmental damage. A decade on, most of these problems are still awaiting effective solutions.

In May 2016, the *People's Daily* published an 11,000-word, front-page interview with an 'authoritative source' – widely believed but never confirmed to be Liu He, a close economic adviser to President Xi Jinping – that warned that China was on a dangerous and unstable path, and needed to extensively reform its economic model with urgency.[7] The interview appeared in the wake of a turbulent economic and financial period in China, encompassing a 40 per cent plunge in the value of the Shanghai composite stock market index, an unexplained, albeit minor, devaluation of the Renminbi, and capital flight that contributed a loss of about $1 trillion to China's prized foreign exchange reserves.

When Xi Jinping addressed the 19th Party Congress in 2017, he too spoke to this theme, saying the economy was unbalanced and inadequate to meet the 'people's needs for a better quality of life'. This emphasises a long-standing goal of Chinese leaders to 'rebalance' the economy, lower its dependence on credit and investment, and strive to build a more innovative, service-oriented and equal society.

There is no doubt that the economy is in the process of a long-term slowdown. Its long-run sustainable growth rate at the moment is probably around 3–4 per cent, or roughly half the rate suggested by official statistics. Getting there could happen in a smooth and uneventful way, or in a disruptive fashion that would shake the world considerably. It is important to try and understand the circumstances under which this slowdown will occur.

It is also worth noting that China's manicured, official GDP data reveal very little about the sometimes volatile nature of what's going on in the economy. Systemic bias in the collection of data arises from the practice of setting annual GDP growth targets. Once set, state and local government authorities are duty-bound to hit the target even if, as in recent years, this involves misallocated investment and the rapid accumulation of debt. Reported steady growth of 6.5–7 per cent, therefore, includes misallocated or uncommercial investment, and overstates GDP. By contrast, GDP in most other economies is the end-product of a plethora of spending decisions rather than a target that has to be met. Western economies make bad investments too, but these tend to be written down or written off with costs allocated to creditors or owners much more quickly by accounting and legal conventions, and so-called hard budget constraints. The government in China has suggested it may de-emphasise growth targets after 2020. It would be a positive step if this happened, but, as we shall see, stated intentions and actual implementation are often worlds apart in China.

Where bulls and bears clash

I am conscious that in the voluminous literature about modern China over the last ten to twenty years economists, political scientists, China commentators and well-known people in the finance industry have periodically expected China's economy to falter or crash, and its political system to fail. So far, we can say that while the bearish China view has had occasional gratification, those predicting economic collapse or the end of Communist Party rule have had no hint of vindication. China has had political crises, and episodes of economic instability, but time and time again, the Communist Party's pragmatism and ability to craft state-driven, top-down solutions and use a wide array of tools and policy instruments have succeeded in avoiding worst-case economic scenarios. While there certainly has been a groundswell of rising social and worker unrest over corruption, environmental issues and labour conditions, there has been no proliferation of grassroots political instability, and certainly no 'street' threat to the Party.

The main reason that China has managed to get to where it is today is because it has managed change rather well. Its economic eruption over the last forty years can be traced to the policies of 'Reform and Opening Up' pursued in the 1980s and the 1990s, and then to the more rapid integration of China into the global system following its accession to the World Trade Organization in 2001.

When Xi Jinping came to power, though, he knew that the Party had to reboot and restrengthen and China had to change. Consequently, the Party has become more powerful and controlling, and China is now pulling its weight in the world as never before. By 2021, the Party will have ruled China for as long as the Soviet Communist Party ruled the former Soviet Union, and Xi's mission is to keep the Chinese Communist Party away from the liberalisation and openness that are deemed to have driven its Soviet counterpart into oblivion. He may still be president, and will still be influential in 2035, halfway between the 19th Congress and the centenary of the founding of the People's Republic.

We are now at an inflection point. China has changed beyond recognition from the type of economy and country it was under Deng Xiaoping and Jiang Zemin, whose economic reforms did so much to propel their country forward. Xi Jinping has inherited a more prosperous but also much more complex economy that also needs reforms to push it forward again. The future, though, cannot be drawn in straight lines from the past. Many of the things China did to overcome obstacles in the past could only be done once. Like joining the WTO, or moving people from low-productivity rural life to high-productivity urban manufacturing, or enrolling all children in secondary schools. What worked in the past has been overtaken by the circumstances of development and economic maturity.

Reform in Xi's China, though, is not going to be about liberalisation and the extensive use of markets to determine resource allocation and patterns of economic development. China uses the slogan 'a more decisive role for markets' but to all intents and purposes, that's all it is, a slogan. China's reforms will focus on prices, tariffs and taxes, organisational and administrative changes, and regulations to influence supply and demand, but only according to the Party's top-down narrative.

Reform will also hinge on the centralisation of power around the president in the Party, the Party in the state, and Beijing in the country. It is interesting to speculate why this is all happening at this time. It is certainly related to the state of the Party and the economy that Xi inherited, and to China's alternative to the Western model of development. Yet these explanations don't go far enough. Centralisation of power can speak to pressing demands in the face of perceived threats for either military preparedness or economic reorganisation. The latter seems overwhelmingly likely, and so it is plausible that China's main purpose is economic transformation in the face of perceived insecurity from the economic, technological and trade challenges coming from the US, Japan and the EU.

China's industrial policies, and the now clear pursuit of leadership in a broad range of manufacturing and technological sectors, fit this narrative.

They also present the world with an intriguing question. Are the stifling effects of autocracy and repression in a big data and machine intelligence economy, or what we can call digital authoritarianism, compatible with a burst of productivity growth and enduring economic and commercial success? We know that authoritarian regimes historically have certainly come up with inventions, new products and processes, and scientific and engineering successes. The China of dynasties itself was an example. In other respects, of course, they failed. Yet, do artificial and machine intelligence and their complementary technologies break the mould? Is it going to be different this time? In this book, I will try to frame this discussion, and suggest how we should think about the answers.

How the book is organised

The book is divided up into three main sections.

The first, comprising three chapters, considers a little bit of China's economic history from the nineteenth century through to the founding of the People's Republic and then traces some of the main way-markers and changes in the organisation and performance of the economy up to the present day. Chapter 1, Echoes, looks at the main characteristics of the Chinese economy before foreign powers arrived and traces key developments in what China calls its 'century of humiliation' from roughly 1840 to 1949. Chapter 2, From Mao to Modernity, examines the economic achievements and developments under Mao, Deng Xiaoping, Jiang Zemin and Zhu Rongji, and then Hu Jintao and Wen Jiabao, with a strong focus on the liberalising economic reforms that began under Deng and petered out in the 2000s. In Chapter 3, The End of Extrapolation: Rebalancing and Reform, the focus is on why China's economic model needs a makeover, and where the reform agenda has worked, and where it has stalled or been stifled.

The second part of the book is about China's four traps: debt, the Renminbi, demographics, and middle income. Chapter 4 looks at the debt trap, the role of banks and shadow banks, and some of the riskier products and structures that regulators are now trying to address. Ultimately, China will have to inflate or deflate its way out of debt, but both options raise penetrating questions about its capacity to absorb both the economic and social consequences. Chapter 5 reviews the Renminbi trap, asking whether China can keep its currency stable in the wake of the debt problem. It also considers the structural shortcomings that will prevent the Renminbi becoming a truly global reserve currency. Chapter 6 considers the demographic trap in the fastest ageing country on earth. Ageing is occurring substantially faster than it has done in the West, and at lower levels of income per head, giving rise to the question of whether China will get old before it gets rich. Chapter 7 focuses on the middle-income trap, a condition which is primarily about the quality and effectiveness of governance and institutions. In Xi's China, politics may again become a headwind, when previously they were unequivocally a tailwind.

The third section of the book comprises three chapters that look more broadly at China's position in the global system. Chapter 8, Trade Dogs of War, considers China's position in what has become a more fractious and difficult environment for world trade, especially given China's pitch to be a new leader of globalisation, which is largely rhetorical. Misunderstanding or miscalculation could lead to much greater friction affecting trade and investment. The US fusses about its trade deficit with China, but China has a trust deficit that ideally must also be resolved. Chapter 9 runs the rule over Xi Jinping's signature international relations and foreign policy project, the Belt and Road Initiative, asking whether it is more a Eurasian development programme or a China-centric economic project, with real benefits, but also shrouded in hype. In Chapter 10, Xi Jinping's China, I lay out some concluding ideas about how to think about China in the future. Xi's intention is to show that an authoritarian, even dictatorial China can switch its economic agenda seamlessly away from high growth and malinvestment towards greater equality, a better environment, financial stability, OECD-type wealth status, and global technological leadership. To do this, China will have to accept the low economic growth implicit in this agenda but also strive to find the key to sustained productivity growth. If it happened, China would be the first authoritarian country or dictatorship to do so.

Xi Jinping's China is a wake-up call for us to rethink, collectively, the ways in which we engage with China politically and commercially. Our best strategic and diplomatic thinkers should evaluate where we think we can cooperate with China, where we have to draw lines, and where we can use leverage appropriately. To do that we have to understand the domestic politics that are driving the Party and, importantly, the economic challenges facing China now and in future. That, in a nutshell, is the purpose of this book. Put differently, we need to consider the Red Flags, or economic warnings, which are both present today and also loom in Xi's China, and to assess how well equipped it is to deal with them. I will try to explain in this book why Xi's China is in jeopardy.

1

ECHOES

China experts all agree about one thing: you can't understand contemporary China without knowing something about its rich, long history. Chinese leaders speak to citizens about their country's glorious past, its imperial dynasties, and a time when its place in the world was assured and its demeanour confident. President Xi Jinping invoked the concept of the Chinese Dream when he took office in 2012, subsequently telling the nation that China must 'push forward the great cause of socialism with Chinese characteristics, and strive to achieve the Chinese Dream of great rejuvenation of the Chinese nation'.[1]

Much discussion has centred on what Xi means by this term. It conveys an important contemporary image based around facts, names, events and legends, but also some self-serving myths that go back in Chinese history for a thousand years or more. The Chinese Dream was coined to evoke that history and present China as a significant and strong nation that can take on the mantle of global leadership, and an alternative model of governance to the liberal democracy that has held sway for so long.

On becoming general secretary of the Communist Party in 2012, Xi Jinping reminded his audience that 'During the civilisation and development process of more than 5,000 years, the Chinese nation has made an indelible contribution to the civilisation and advancement of mankind.'[2] He likes to link China's history to its present and future. The old Silk Road is a classic example, now reborn as the Belt and Road Initiative, but it is by no means the only connection between China's past and modern times, as we shall see.

The purpose of this chapter, then, is to trace a little Chinese history, draw a line between the past and the present, and dig up a few roots and myths so as to help put contemporary China into a fuller perspective. It is helpful to appreciate what it was about China that the rest of the world so admired before many colonial countries went there in the nineteenth century for a piece of it. It is important to look at what the Chinese call their 'century of humiliation', lasting from the First Opium War to the founding of the People's Republic, which encompasses the damage wrought by foreign powers and the consequences of internal rebellions and weak institutions. It is interesting to see various connections or echoes of economic, social and institutional characteristics that have either always been present in China or left their mark on China's economic development.

We should remember that when people talk about the emergence of China into the global system in the last thirty years, what they really mean is 're-emergence', because China was once and for a long time the biggest part of the global economy. According to the Angus Maddison project at the Groningen Growth and Development Centre, China accounted for between 22 and 30 per cent of world GDP from AD 1 until the eighteenth century, peaking finally at about 33 per cent in 1820.[3] More recently, this widely accepted narrative has been challenged by analysis suggesting that China's dominance in the world started to fade much earlier, perhaps as long ago as the twelfth or thirteenth century.[4] If true, this would have a significant bearing on the historical debate about how and why China lost its relative economic position vis-à-vis Europe.

For the purpose of this book, though, the conflicting views of economic historians do not detract from the fact that China's economic star faded, first relative to a rising Europe, and then more dramatically in absolute terms. China's position in the world, measured by its share of world GDP, fell especially quickly during the nineteenth century and the first half of the twentieth century, not reaching a trough until the 1950s. Let us take a look back in time and map some of the contours which these measures describe.

Connections

Long ago, China was a pioneer. Its claim to economic fame included the use of farm cattle, horses and implements, the exploitation of crop rotation, irrigation, the production of iron and salt, textiles, the application of water-powered spinning machines, and the development of private ownership structures and, albeit for the gentry only, basic property rights. It adopted paper as a replacement for silk and bamboo as early as the second century, and invented movable type printing technology in the eleventh century, some four hundred years before Gutenberg introduced it to Europe. The bureaucracy used this technology to disseminate information about technological best practices to farmers and peasants.

Trade figured prominently in ancient China as it does in modern China. It is best known in older times because of the Silk Road trading routes and caravan trails that went west from the imperial capital of Xi'an via central and southern Asia and the Middle East to the Mediterranean. They took spices, silk and cotton out of China, while new crops and payments for trade in silver, and, importantly, ideas about culture, philosophy and religion, came in the opposite direction. China was the leading producer and exporter of porcelain, ceramics, silk, zinc, copper, gold, tea and cupronickel (used for coinage).

Apart from major trading networks, old China boasted huge libraries, flourishing iron, metallurgical and transportation industries, a prowess in mathematics, engineering and civil administration, and a legendary capacity for maritime and navigational achievements and the construction of short- and long-range vessels. Indeed, in the early 1270s, when Marco Polo is thought to have arrived in China, he would have been impressed by the wealth of its palaces, the ubiquitous water transportation systems for bringing food into cities, and the subtlety and diversity of its food.[5] Admiral Zheng He is revered today for his maritime exploits in the early fifteenth century, in which ships under his command sailed the Indian and Pacific Oceans many decades before the adventures and discoveries of more celebrated European explorers such as Christopher Columbus and Vasco da Gama. Starting in 1405, Zheng made seven journeys, taking in Southeast Asia, India, the Middle East and Africa, in fleets of up to 300 huge ships with nearly 30,000 sailors in total. There is little dispute about Zheng He's accomplishments, but not all historians concur with the Chinese narrative that his missions were entirely peaceful.

The connections that link the China of dynasties and emperors forward to the present are also rooted in China's geography. The cradle of Chinese civilisation, the North China Plain, which sits below Inner Mongolia and south of Manchuria and spans over 400,000 square kilometres in and around the Yellow River basin and down past the Yangtze River, has always been an important and populous part of the country.[6] The coastal provinces and regions have always been central to China's trade. The administration of so many people dispersed as far as Tibet and Xinjiang has been and remains complicated by geography and the need to maintain social harmony.

China's historical expertise in administration is well known, as indeed is its modern capacity for administration in a country of 1.3 billion people. It pioneered bureaucratic modes of governance that imposed social and political order in a large unitary state long before anyone else. Confucian bureaucracy and an emphasis on the role of order, stability and social conformity in society have endured and lie even today at the heart of rule by the Communist Party.

China's bureaucracy was an important agent of economic progress, and instrumental in generating the surplus of savings over consumption needed to finance investment. In earlier and more primitive times, the surplus was in agriculture. The bureaucracy accomplished this by raising money from taxes and levies and allocating the proceeds to investment. The bureaucracy also relocated agricultural workers as needed and moved them to areas and activities to generate higher productivity. It created a public granary system to mitigate and deal with famines, and contributed to innovation, for example by helping to introduce new crops. It created the logistics for feeding a large imperial capital, including by building the Grand Canal, which is still the longest in the world – now known as the Beijing-Hangzhou Grand Canal, a UNESCO World Heritage Site. It maintained the Great Wall of China over many centuries as a defensive and border control structure, and raised taxes to fund the imperial and military establishments.

Important as the bureaucracy was to China's development, it was not without weaknesses. Autocratic governance and administration fostered what we would call nowadays rent-seeking, or the manipulation of public policy or positions of power to influence or generate money or profit. Rent-seeking, often associated with corruption, is a recurring problem in China to this day. The bureaucracies of past dynasties provided continuity of administration and security, but they were also associated with the corrosive forces of patronage and corruption. The Ming dynasty (1368–1644), for example, was noted for its touring inspectors who brought to book those suspected of bribery, embezzlement and other illegal activities. It was unquestionably the antecedent of other anti-corruption campaigns, including notably that unleashed by Xi Jinping in 2012. Like others before it, Xi's campaign was extrajudicial, narrowly targeted as far as Communist Party membership goes, and designed, at least in part, to cleanse the Party of indiscipline and self-advancement.

From emperors to Communist Party general secretaries, the task of diffusing power to subnational administrations but also controlling them has been and remains a daunting challenge. The cultural heritage in which the good of a hierarchical society is prized far above the democratic rights of the individual, and the belief that the unitary nature of the state and economic progress are inseparable, runs through the veins of the Communist Party, much as it did for the imperial dynasties.

Further, in the Chinese bureaucratic tradition Confucian ideology and education were undoubtedly instrumental in fostering pragmatism and order, but in the end they were no match for the mathematics- and science-based approach to understanding and experimental method or the effectiveness of disruptive curiosity that developed in Europe.[7] This too resonates today when we think, for example, about innovation and technology. China's approach is to try and become a leader, following a formalised top-down industrial policy driven by quantitative targets and objectives. To Western minds, it is more about incentives and markets, disruptive change and private initiative, with state intervention important but limited to facilitation, sponsorship, regulation and guidance.

The 'century of humiliation'

In the late eighteenth century, the Scottish economist, philosopher and author Adam Smith, considered in the West at least as the founding father of economics, wrote prolifically about China. He deemed it to be 'one of the most fertile, best cultivated, most industrious, and most populous countries in the world', and noted that it was the only non-European modern society to have reached levels of civilisation and opulence that rivalled those of Europe.[8] In his famous book *An Inquiry into the Nature and Causes of the Wealth of Nations*, published in 1776, he said that 'Even those three countries, China, Egypt, and Indostan, the wealthiest, according to all accounts, that ever there were in the world, are chiefly renowned for their superiority in agriculture and manufactures . . . China is a much richer country than any part of Europe.'[9]

Not long after Smith's *Wealth of Nations* was published, a famous meeting occurred that captured much of the debate about China and the West that continues to the current time. In 1793, Lord George Macartney arrived in China with the objective of establishing the first official permanent mission in Peking and opening up Chinese ports and new markets to British trade. Other countries such as Portugal, Holland, Russia and France had arrived in China before and tried to open up trade, but to no avail. This expedition, though, turned out to be a major turning point in relations between the West and the East.

The intellectuals of the Enlightenment in Europe had until then presented an idealised image of China as a stick with which to beat their conservative opponents in Europe. This much was evident, even before Adam Smith, in the first two chapters of Voltaire's 'An Essay on Universal History, The Manners and Spirit of Nations', published in 1759. Many Europeans regarded China as a model in which the country's population and wealth, and the stability and continuity of its institutions, were perceived as clearly exceeding those of the West. From this, reason dictated that if Western Europeans were to become more advanced themselves, they needed to emulate the Chinese model, at the root of which was government by an 'enlightened' despot and bureaucracy.[10]

Yet Macartney's visit, and the manner in which he and Emperor Qianlong behaved to one another, presented an entirely different image and corroborated a sharp reversal in the way many European intellectuals had come to think about China. Several, including Adam Smith, offered inverted versions of their previous arguments, now emphasising that upheaval was preferable to stability, that the mandarinate was corrupt, and that the Chinese emperor was only despotic, not enlightened at all.[11] The meeting was famous for Macartney's refusal to pay tribute or 'kow-tow' to the emperor, but this was a symbol of a much deeper rift between the longest established and proudest of civilisations rooted in custom and order on the one hand, and the first country to embrace the disruption of modern industrial change on the other.

Macartney spent months dragging around presents from King George III in which the Chinese emperor showed little interest: they included a planetarium, globes, mathematical instruments, chronometers, a telescope, measuring and chemical instruments and copperware. The Chinese were not impressed, and the emperor is reported to have said 'there is nothing we lack'.[12] In the words of Henry Kissinger: 'The Macartney mission was the most notable, best conceived and least militaristic European effort to alter the prevailing format of Sino-Western relations and to achieve free trade and diplomatic representation on equal terms. It failed completely.'[13]

The British were undeterred and remained keen on opening China up to trade, and also on showing the Chinese that Britain was the new kid on the block. Unsurprisingly, Macartney's hosts thought the British arrogant, and treated him and his entourage as uninformed upstarts seeking special favours. Macartney was equally dismissive, opining that 'the Empire was like a drifting wreck ... The Empire of China is an old, crazy, first rate man-o-war ... She may not sink outright; she may drift some time as a wreck and will then be dashed to pieces on the shore.'[14]

The dismissive attitude of the British was reflected in their behaviour and actions, which certainly contributed to China becoming an economic wreck. They waged two wars against China, and participated with many other imperial and colonial nations in carving it up and exploiting its people and resources. The background was the politics and economics of trade.

The British paid with silver for their growing demand for tea and Chinese porcelain and silk, but the persistence and volume of silver outflows led to financial pressures, not least for the East India Company. As a consequence, the British shipped opium from Calcutta to China as an alternative means of payment. It brought the British buoyant tax receipts for the colonial government in India, and a handy means to pay for imports back home and in Europe. The Chinese emperor tried to stop the trade, and ban opium use in China, but this early war on drugs did not succeed.

The British eventually manufactured a war in defence of what they labelled free trade, the First Opium War, that lasted from 1839 to 1842. It resulted in defeat for China, which had to pay a large indemnity and submit to the humiliating Treaty of Nanking (Nanjing). This and subsequent treaties were labelled 'unequal treaties' because they forced China to legalise the sale of opium within China, accept an artificially low foreign trade tariff of 5 per cent, and grant foreigners 'extraterritorial rights' while they lived in the treaty port enclaves or 'concessions'. In other words, foreigners and foreign businesses had the right to exemption from Chinese taxes and from accountability to Chinese law while enjoying the protection, tax and legal arrangements of their own countries, plus the services for which local people's taxes paid. The treaties also bestowed 'most-favoured nation' status on Britain and others, so that China had the impossible task of gaining unanimous consent from all foreign powers in order to recover any sovereign right lost in treaties. China's loss of sovereignty in these respects would not be restored until 1943 in negotiated treaties.

Unequal treaties also stripped China of some of the economic mechanisms used by the British and others to underpin their own industrialisation. Apart from having to succumb to the will of foreign powers regarding the proliferation and legality of the opium trade, China was unable to choose its own import tariff levies that protected local industries and financed government spending, and was constrained in its power to use tax and regulatory measures to its own advantage.

The 1842 Treaty of Nanking also gave control in perpetuity over an area that British naval forces had seized, called Hong Kong, or Fragrant Harbour (Heung Gong in the original language, or Xianggang in Mandarin). The treaty also established other 'treaty ports', including Shanghai, Canton (Guangzhou), Amoy (Xiamen), Foochow (Fuzhou) and Ningpo (Ningbo). Hong Kong, world-renowned and one-time symbol of the British Empire and British reach overseas, was returned to China in 1997 in a 'handover', the twentieth anniversary of which was celebrated in China in 2017. Some of its brick and stone buildings still speak to its colonial past, as do the names of its streets, such as Connaught Street and Wellington Street, and of some companies, such as the Hong Kong and Shanghai Bank, the modern incarnations of the old Butterfield and Swire Group, and the subsidiaries of Jardine Matheson Holdings. British influence, not confined to Hong Kong, extended along the whole Yangtze valley from Shanghai to Chongqing.

Not all treaty ports were coastal, and not all were created by treaty, but a pattern was set that would determine China's commercial and trade interactions with other countries for a considerable period, as nineteen foreign countries would acquire so-called 'extraterritorial' rights and privileges. The British were not the only ones whose sphere of influence was bolstered by the treaty port system. France took control of Yunnan and Guangxi, Germany controlled Shandong, and Manchuria in north-eastern China succumbed to Japanese and Korean control. These and other areas still reveal physical evidence of what became the scramble for China. Shanghai's Bund area sports the remains of colonial architecture, but so do many other cities including Guangzhou, Xiamen, Qingdao (home to the Tsingtao brewery), Wuhan, Tianjin, and Dalian. By 1917, when China entered the First World War, hopeful – but ultimately frustrated – that an eventual peace treaty would drive foreign influence out of China, ninety-two treaty ports had been established.

Some fourteen years after the First Opium War, in 1856, the British went to war again after failing to win new concessions from China, including the legalisation of opium. China's defeat in the Second Opium War ended with the Treaty of Tientsin (Tianjin) in 1860, in which China was again obliged to pay an indemnity, and which created new treaty ports, added Kowloon and the New Territories to the territory of Hong Kong, threw Chinese ports and the Yangtze river network open to foreign ships, legalised the use and import of opium, and removed restrictions on Christianity and freedom of travel within China. Structures were established to monitor and enforce China's commitment to low tariff trade with the outside world.

A sequence of rebellions and other conflicts caused great harm to China's economy. The Taiping Rebellion of 1850–64, ostensibly a Chinese and religious Christian revolt, was rooted in growing unrest related to the new foreign presence in China's treaty ports in which the Chinese authorities were implicated. The uprising affected over a dozen of China's provinces including its most prosperous ones, and may have cost up to 20–30 million lives at a time when demographic change was a key driver of economic growth. It also had other indirect effects in lowering birth rates and increasing morbidity, for example as a result of the 1855 flooding of the Yellow River, and famines, because of neglect of irrigation infrastructure. Although population growth in the parts of China unaffected by the Taiping and other rebellions mostly compensated for the provinces worst hit, it is most likely, given the distribution of population in the provinces, that income per head and living standards fell between the 1850s and the 1880s.

Between 1858 and 1860, Russia acquired Chinese territory and deprived China of access to the Pacific coast of Manchuria. In 1894–95, Japan captured ports and territory on the Liaotung (Liaodong) peninsula in north-eastern China, won the right to receive an indemnity, open factories and manufacture in China, and obliged its host to acknowledge the loss of suzerainty over Korea and Taiwan.

At this time, China had next to no manufacturing and only skeleton railway facilities. Farming and fisheries accounted for about 69 per cent of GDP, handicrafts for about 8 per cent and traditional transportation and trade for about 13 per cent.[15] Although China's history paints foreigners as interfering powers that came to carve up and exploit China, it is also true that foreigners were catalysts for economic progress and growing contact with the outside world.

Most of China's cities, as measured by their population, changed little between the 1820s and the end of the century, but the treaty ports were, by comparison with the rest of China, islands of modernity and change. Foreigners brought new transport in the form of steamships that operated on the Yangtze and coastal routes, as well as railway construction, banking and commerce, and mining and industrial activities and know-how. Moreover, the treaty ports they acquired or demanded, notably Shanghai and Hong Kong, developed Western banking, shipping and modern technologies from which indigenous Chinese citizens learned skills and trades. They also benefited from remittances sent by family members and friends who had emigrated to other parts of Asia. Gradually, the Chinese government responded and adopted development initiatives, such as telegraphy, while the so-called 'self-strengthening' movement was associated in the last two to three decades of the nineteenth century with several government industrial undertakings such as arsenals at Shanghai and Nanking, a dockyard at Foochow, coal mines in Tientsin, several textile mills, and iron works. The self-strengthening movement petered out, though, after the Sino-Japanese war of 1895.

During the last quarter of the nineteenth century, the scramble for China intensified. Russia, Germany, Britain and France all took opportunities to press new claims for ports, railway building rights and recognition of 'spheres of influence'. At the same time, the expansion of treaty port facilities contributed to the growth of not just railways, but banking, commerce, industrial production and mining. British interests lay principally along the Yangtze; French interests were in the south; and Japanese and Russian interests were mainly in the north and in Manchuria.

Russia was granted rights over the city of Dalian for twenty-five years by treaty in 1898, while a fast developing Japan, both economically and militarily, began to intensify its long-standing interests in China, and press for influence in Korea and disputed neighbouring islands in the second half of the nineteenth century. In 1879, Japan annexed the Ryukyu Islands, an arc of islands that runs south west from Kyushu in southern Japan to Taiwan. In 1895, Japan went to war with China and captured Port Arthur (Lushun) on the southern tip of the Liaodong peninsula, nowadays about an hour and a half's flight east of Beijing. China was defeated, forced to make territorial and financial concessions, and humiliated by being beaten by a country it viewed as inferior and a spin-off of its own history and culture. Japan's presence would loom more ominously for China after the occupation of Manchuria in 1931, and then during the brutal war from 1937 to 1945.

Germany used the excuse of the murder of two missionaries to force China to give it a concession including a port at Tientsin and railways in the Shandong peninsula. For China, Shandong was as important as, for example, Alsace-Lorraine was for France vis-à-vis Germany. It was the birthplace of Confucius, and it gave those who controlled it geographic command over Peking, the Yellow River and the Grand Canal. Allowing it to fall under foreign control was like handing over 'a dagger pointed at the heart of China'.[16] This, of course, was precisely how Japan saw it too in a rather different and more aggressive context about twenty years later at the Treaty of Versailles, when it wanted to be the one holding the dagger, and duly was.

After three years of anti-foreigner protests, the Fists of Righteous Harmony movement, otherwise known as the Boxers, started a popular uprising in 1900. It began with attacks on Chinese Christians and foreign missionaries but it soon turned into a broader anti-foreigner movement. The uprising, however, was short-lived. After an eight-power force comprising France, Britain, the US, Japan, Russia, Germany, Austria-Hungary and Italy arrived in Peking to relieve their embassies and suppress the Boxers and imperial troops, the movement collapsed. The major foreign powers in China thought at this stage that the Chinese state was precarious, and feared that China, 'like an Asian Poland, would cease to exist as European predators and Japan carved away slices of the Chinese melon'.[17] If they had set out to be lenient, they nevertheless imposed another 'unequal treaty' demanding a cash indemnity, and further occupation rights.

The heavy indemnities paid in 1842, 1860, 1896 and 1900, and associated with the Opium Wars, the war with Japan and the Boxer Uprising, saddled China with substantial financial obligations. The treaties prevented it from being able to raise tariffs, and so China had to seek foreign loans and higher taxes, both of which retarded its development.[18] The loans were 'tied' to ownership and operating concessions in new industries. It is estimated that annual payments on the stock of debt after 1920 amounted to about 40 per cent of government income.[19]

The collapse of the Qing dynasty in 1912 led to the formation of a republic, of which China had no experience and little understanding, under the nationalist leader Sun Yat-sen. But after a mere six weeks, he deferred to the military leader Yuan Shikai. Yuan, who died in 1916, left a divided country with a weak and ineffectual government, but also a popular protest movement called the May Fourth Movement, which was formed in 1919 in the wake of China's failure to recover territory at the Treaty of Versailles. This movement was the embryo of what was to become the Communist Party of China in 1921. China had joined the First World War in 1917, mainly because it thought that the eventual peace treaty would be a means of ridding itself of foreign powers. It was irked, though, that the Western powers refused to end the extraterritoriality of the treaty ports, and concerned that the European powers allowed most of Germany's concessions to pass to Japan.

In the early years of the republic, local armies headed by their own generals and warlords proliferated, civil strife ensued, and power fractured between regional governors, military commanders and the new Chinese Communist Party. China's economy stagnated. A new nationalist party, the Kuomintang (KMT) or National People's Party of China, also emerged.

Originally founded by Sun Yat-sen, it was soon dissolved, but reformed under his premiership from 1919 until his death in 1925. Chiang Kai-shek rose to prominence in the KMT and, after fighting warlords and Japanese troops, set up the Kuomintang government in Nanking in 1928. As head of the KMT in China, he opposed Western democracy and Sun Yat-sen's nationalist socialist politics in favour of a conservative and authoritarian style of government.

For a while, China enjoyed relatively peaceful conditions and was able to form an institutional framework for economic development. In 1928, a central bank was created in Shanghai, with the finance minister as governor, after which a significant expansion of bank branches followed. China regained control over tariffs in 1929, so that higher duties provided welcome sources of government revenue. In 1930, it enacted a land law to promote owner occupation and limit rents, though historians have questioned its effectiveness. A year later, it abolished the likin, an internal tax on goods in transit that had distorted development because foreigners had purchased exemption from it. It was able to restructure and write down foreign debt. The government made significant extensions to the networks of both road and rail, more or less until the war with Japan in 1937.

While China's policies failed to make any material difference to the dominant agricultural sector, other things did start to change. Income per head inched up annually though at a snail's pace compared with the West. Significant changes occurred, moreover, in the structure of the economy. Statistical estimates of the time are not reliable, but they suggest the share of farming and fisheries in GDP fell to 64 per cent by 1933, and that of the modern sector (manufacturing, mining, electricity production, and modern transport and communications), quintupled to over 5 per cent of GDP compared to 1900.[20]

Before the war with Japan, about three-fifths of China's factory output was produced in Chinese-owned factories, about a fifth by foreign companies, and the rest by mostly Japanese-owned companies in Manchuria. Chinese entrepreneurs dominated the handicraft industry, but foreign-owned companies accounted for between a third and a half of output in textiles, coal and heavy industry. What passed as modern industry, though, was indeed a relatively small part of the economy, but expanding, and was reflected both in trade volumes and in the growing role of Tianjin, Guangzhou and, above all, Shanghai.

The Kuomintang, therefore, had some success in presiding over belated development in the Chinese economy, including the gradual development of a small but significant modern sector, and a modest expansion in income per head (albeit mainly for a small, even tiny minority proportion of the population). Yet, plagued by political and social fissures, it was unable to pacify, let alone defeat the Communist movement, which built up support in rural areas, and it could not resist the Japanese establishment of a puppet state in Manchuria in 1931 (Manchukuo), or the demand that China turn the area around Peking and Tianjin into a demilitarised zone.

In 1937, Japan moved to step up its attack on China proper, fighting a war that lasted until 1945. The significance and effects of this war on China are beyond the scope of this book. China may have lost between 15 and 20 million people, and had to cope with up to 100 million refugees.[21] War weakened the Nationalists and emboldened the Communists, and after Japan's defeat in the Second World War and the withdrawal of its forces from the mainland, the Nationalists and Communists continued to fight until 1949.

Legacies and myths

It is not surprising that dark memories of this period of colonial exploitation, war and civil war persist in China. They have shaped and influenced China and its attitudes ever since the People's Republic was declared. In looking for explanations for China's chronically weak economic performance in the century before 1949, the carve-up of China occupies pride of place.

On the twentieth anniversary of the handover of Hong Kong, President Xi Jinping visited the city and noted in one speech that in the early 1840s, the Qing government, with 800,000 troops, could not stop a 10,000-strong British expedition force, or avoid ceding territory and paying indemnities. Recounting the story of the British takeover of Kowloon and the New Territories after the Qing dynasty was defeated in the two Opium Wars, he said: 'The history of China at that time was filled with the nation's humiliation and its people's grief . . . Twenty years ago today, Hong Kong returned to the motherland's embrace, washing away the Chinese nation's hundred years of shame.'[22]

The Chinese founding narrative of shame and suffering at the hands of foreign powers is about loss and legitimacy. It is about the loss of territory, of which Taiwan is the only part yet to be returned to the motherland. It is about losses that are even more sensitive, namely of control over the domestic and external environment, and of dignity in the world. It is also about the fundamental legitimacy of the Chinese Communist Party, which is portrayed as the only political organisation that could stand up to foreign aggression, and must therefore be relied upon as a guarantor of China's security and pride.

On the occasion to mark the ninetieth anniversary of the founding of the People's Liberation Army at the Inner Mongolia training base of Zhurihe in July 2017, President Xi told thousands of soldiers on national TV that the military must 'unswervingly' back the Communist Party and that 'we have confidence to defeat all invasions'. It isn't clear to whom he might have been referring, but the historical and contemporary connections the leadership makes between foreigners, the military and the Party are not accidental.

Yet that narrative, while including historical truths and facts, is also incomplete.

The idea underlying the narrative that China was a non-aggressive, non-expansionist victim of foreign intervention does not sit well alongside the imperial and sometimes bellicose policies of the Qing Empire in what is now Myanmar, and in Vietnam in the eighteenth century, and it wasn't always blameless with regard to the French and the Japanese in China in the nineteenth century.

The part of the narrative that blames foreigners for China's humiliation is also in reality much more nuanced than is made out. The treaty ports and foreign influences did impose an economic straitjacket on the Chinese government's room for manoeuvre in policy-making, as discussed, and the loss of economic sovereignty was self-evidently a drag on China and a humiliation. At the same time, though, we should also note that China suffered grievous damage from major domestic rebellions, including the fourteen-year long Taiping Rebellion, the Boxer Rebellion, the national warlord anarchy for eleven years after the fall of the Qing Empire, a weak and largely reactionary Nationalist government after 1927, and civil war until 1949 either side of the war with Japan. According to the seasoned and insightful China author and analyst Jonathan Fenby, compared to the impact of foreigners (excluding Japan in the Second World War), China suffered from 'internal divisions that sapped imperial authority on a much bigger scale'.[23]

China also had internal weaknesses that compromised its ability to progress economically. These included corruption in the public sector, relatively inflexible social and political institutions, the family structure of many Chinese enterprises in a world where the large scale was prized, and a traditional preference for conformity and consensus where disruptive technical and scientific change was beneficial. These phenomena existed in China before 1839, but were certainly constraints during the century of humiliation. Some, being rather more endogenous, survive to this day.

Although the treaty ports were symbols of economic theft and the exploitation of Chinese sovereignty and resources, they also brought new technologies and provided outlets for Chinese exports of tea and silk that generated receipts which paid for industrial imports. Many of the treaty ports and surrounding areas eventually became a major focus for economic development as they evolved into SEZs. It is hard to imagine how the pattern of China's take-off would have happened as it did but for early patterns of trade and economic interaction with Hong Kong still under British rule, and with Taiwan after diplomatic relations were established in 1979.

China's tortured experiences in the 1930s and 1940s, moreover, had some economic consequences that helped to shape China's development later. Its infrastructure was destroyed by the war with Japan and needed to be rebuilt and redeveloped. Reconstituting the commanding heights of a new, industrial economy was essential for Mao Zedong's diplomatically and economically isolated China. The People's Republic was able to harness the legacy of Japan's Manchuria as an industrial heartland producing the bulk of its electric power, iron and cement. The region would go on to become the epicentre of China's heavy industry, a status which it retains, though now it is of diminishing importance.

Further, war pressured the Nationalists and Communists to develop new ideas about the role of the public sector and 'create a new social contract based on greater obligations between state and citizen'.[24] It also spawned a new approach to state intervention in the economy on to which the Communist Party would graft an entire social and economic development model. Indeed, the Chinese government in the late 1940s, strongly Leninist in its economic as well as political intent, had already accounted for a substantial proportion of both employment and assets owned by corporations, the bulk of iron and steel production, and most major banks and transportation companies.

One of the abiding legacies of the century of humiliation is China's ambivalence towards and distrust of foreigners. This attitude, never too far from the surface, has certainly shaped a more truculent approach to what China perceives as threats to Chinese interests from foreign powers and 'Western values'. In 2012, the government stirred up anti-Japanese demonstrations, for example, over disputed islands that the Chinese call the Diaoyu and Japan the Senkaku. In 2017, the government again stirred protests against South Korea, which had agreed to install a new US anti-missile system. In both cases, there were boycotts of and protests against Japanese and Korean businesses, respectively. The Chinese response to President Trump's trade and investment pushback that started in 2018 was predictably edgy and nationalistic, and played again to the negative narrative about foreigners in general, and 'unequal treaties' in particular.

The ambivalence about foreigners – which pre-dates the century of humiliation – is ironic because, as I have argued, engagement with foreigners wasn't all bad for China's economy, at least during the century of humiliation, and it would prove positive for China in due course.

Finally, it is worth noting that the war with Japan crushed what had grown to be a Japan-centric model of East Asian integration for a generation. Japan had been Asia's manufacturing and service sector hub, served by Manchuria as a key supplier of agricultural and industrial materials, by Taiwan and Korea as agricultural producers especially of food, and China as a source of markets and destination for future investment.[25] The destruction of this construct left a big hole in the Asian system.

In the aftermath of the war with Japan and the declaration of the People's Republic, China was in no state to fill the gap. In fact, it would not have the capacity to do so until after the Asian crisis of 1997–98, by which time it was in the throes of rapid economic growth and a couple of years away from joining the World Trade Organization. By the late 2000s, China started to exhibit signs that it was able and willing to take on the role, gradually laying the basis for Xi Jinping's articulation and more assertive expression of that role, wrapped in the Chinese Dream. Yet China's success has also brought into view new and considerable challenges to its economic development that are the focus of this book. This, though, is to jump the gun in our narrative, and we must turn first to the economy under Mao and his successors.

2

FROM MAO TO MODERNITY

Flanked by political and military leaders atop the Gate of Heavenly Peace, or Tiananmen Gate, Mao Zedong proclaimed the People's Republic of China on 1 October 1949. It was followed by a military parade and a huge procession, led by the Young Pioneers, workers, peasants, government employees and students holding pictures of their leaders, dancing and singing traditional folk songs, and chanting the slogans they held on their placards, such as Celebrate the Founding of the People's Republic of China, Long Live Chairman Mao, Develop Heavy Industry and Improve National Defence.

Mao Zedong was born in the mountainous, southern province of Hunan in 1893 during turbulent times. He arrived in Beijing in 1919, and later became one of fifty founding members of the Chinese Communist Party in 1921. Starting as a somewhat marginal peasant leader, he eventually harnessed the forces of discontent and nationalism to create an army and movement of millions, and fought both the Japanese and a civil war with Chinese nationalists before and afterwards. After the surrender of Peking in 1949, the Chinese People's Political Consultative Conference was summoned to Beijing, where Mao declared: 'Ours will no longer be a nation subject to insult and humiliation. We have stood up.'

Mao was in power until he died in 1976, and will always be remembered for his role in visiting upon China the disastrous Great Leap Forward and the Cultural Revolution. Yet relatively soon after he died, Deng Xiaoping came to power, initiating a process of economic and social reform which set China on a path to become what it is today. Deng's reforms in the 1980s were followed and amplified by those of his successor Jiang Zemin. His contribution to China's economic explosion segued into a period of social reform under Hu Jintao and of rapid and pervasive globalisation in the 2000s, from which China, now as a member of the World Trade Organization, benefited greatly.

Under Mao, the Communist Party established and maintained a grip on power that has endured in spite of occasionally significant economic and social challenges. After Mao, China adopted a more collective and rule-based leadership style in order to prevent the emergence of new dictators, at least until now. Whether or not Xi Jinping is another Mao is for political scientists to discern. Modern China bears no resemblance to the violence and suffering that prevailed under the Great Helmsman. Yet, the approach by Xi Jinping to governance and institutions has roots that resonate with that period, and embeds the same structural barriers to the development of civil society institutions.

The so-called Document 9, released in 2013, stigmatised 'political perils' that include constitutionalism, civil society, historical nihilism, universal values, and the promotion of the West's view of the media. It was followed by a harsh crackdown on human rights lawyers, media outlets, academics and other independent thinkers. This austerity of attitude, as it were, continues to this day, and as the book unfolds, we shall see how it might affect the challenges that China faces in years to come.

Mao's economy

The French diplomat and close confidant of Charles de Gaulle, Alain Peyrefitte, claimed to have led the first official Western mission to Mao Zedong's China in the wake of the Cultural Revolution in 1966. He wrote that one of the main things that struck him were the 'strange similarities between the Maoist state and the one Macartney had confronted'.[1] Among them, he listed the same cult of the emperor, the same concern for the rituals of protocol, based around respect for tradition and hierarchy, the same adherence to a common set of references framed and articulated by the highest authorities, the same intrigue and plotting away from public view, the same distrust of foreigners, the same frugality, and the same taste for tobacco.

Peyrefitte's anecdotes sought to illustrate how little China seemed to have changed in terms of politics, structure and culture. Continuities, to which I referred in the last chapter, are not hard to find today either.

Xi Jinping's anti-corruption campaign, preceded by his exhortation to Party school members to pay attention to 'Party purity', could have been taken straight out of Mao's anti-corruption campaign in the first three years of the People's Republic, in which 'Tiger-hunting' teams were put to work to root out better-off officials and citizens who had become complacent and had weakened the purity of the Party after the early expansion of the Party's power.[2]

In those early years of the People's Republic, China had a new elite, and a new mode of governance under which its leaders adopted a Soviet-style, socialist command economy. China was mostly isolated from the rest of the world except for close relations with the Soviet Union. These ties may have been based more on opportunism than on ideology, especially as the latter was the principal cause of the parting of ways in 1956, which lasted for a decade. Nevertheless, the USSR had provided military help and organisational support to the Kuomintang in the 1920s, and helped the Communists retake Manchuria from Japan. It offered economic, technical and financial assistance during and after the Korean War, and continued to lend money and provide aid, which was central to the First Five-Year Plan of 1953–57, until relations between the two nations deteriorated, with Mao criticising the Soviet Union for its 'revisionism'.

Mao's China was austere, and the early years of the People's Republic were violent, tyrannical, and characterised by fear and intimidation. Mao set out systematically to destroy the social structure of pre-revolutionary China, which was rich in civil society bodies, from secret societies and religious associations to business and clan associations, trade unions, welfare bodies and professional guilds.[3] Civil servants, the business community, merchants, traders, bankers, and academics and intellectuals were all targeted and attacked. All private enterprises were expropriated. Campaigns of 're-education' spread to government offices, factories, workshops and businesses, schools and universities, and the countryside. The Communist Party destroyed China's existing civil society and any social organisations that could challenge it, and reserved for itself the right to frame everything in society from economic and political discussion to most mundane matters of human existence.[4]

Economically, Mao's China made only halting progress. When the Communist Party came to power in 1949, income per head was just $450, according to Angus Maddison's calculations.[5] By the time Mao died in 1976, income per head had risen to about $850, but this was still a small fraction of incomes prevailing at the time in Japan and the four Asian

Tiger economies – South Korea, Taiwan, Singapore and Hong Kong. Between 1949 and 1978, China's proportion of world income, measured by GDP, rose only fractionally to 4.9 per cent, and its share of world trade hovered around 1 per cent. To all intents and purposes, it was economically irrelevant to the world economy.

The Korean War in 1950, and the trade boycott imposed by the West, certainly didn't help China kick on, but the far bigger problems it faced were home grown. These included early reforms, such as radical changes to the system of land distribution and property rights as the government sought to change China's direction, and, crucially, two massive shocks, the Great Leap Forward in 1958 and the Cultural Revolution in 1966, which caused political instability and great suffering.

With the Party maintaining internal order and a monopoly of power to mobilise resources for defence and economic development, China's goals were to change the socio-political order, improve China's geopolitical standing, and boost economic growth. The last of these would be accomplished by owning the 'means of production, distribution and exchange', including land, factories, transportation, enterprises, finance, communications, and foreign trade and tariff administration. Heavy industry and capital-intensive production would be priorities. Foreign trade became a state monopoly, the main objectives of which were self-sufficiency and an import structure tailored by the demand for essential producer goods.

Plans would replace prices as the means of deciding what would be produced, how resources would be allocated and what people would get paid. Industrial firms were largely vertically integrated enterprises, which controlled and managed employment strictly, and which, from about 1951, took on typical urban spending and cradle-to-grave care commitments, commonly known as the 'iron rice bowl'. Agriculture was organised on a collective basis, migration from the countryside was subject to rigidly applied regulations and controls, and there was no labour mobility.

There was a price system, used to dictate the terms of trade between the state enterprise sector, which benefited from high set prices, and the countryside, which had to endure low prices. This provided the government with profits and fiscal revenues, which bore no relation to operating efficiency, but by the mid-1950s, the government was raising more than a quarter of GDP in budgetary revenues, far higher than anything its predecessors had ever achieved.[6] These revenues were essential to pay for expanded administration, defence, and a higher rate of 'accumulation', or, in other words, the surplus value of production over consumption needed for future investment in industry. The popular image of China at the time, and for many years after, of a society characterised by frugal consumption, drab and conformist clothing and low-quality housing and other services remains a poignant reminder of how the state determined the structure of the economy and the allocation of resources.

The Chinese government quickly set out to change fundamentally the system of property rights, targeting landlords, the national bourgeoisie or middle class, and foreign interests, largely in Manchuria and in the treaty ports. In 1949–52, agricultural reform saw the confiscation of about 43 per cent of cultivated land, along with buildings, farm implements and live-stock, and their redistribution to tenants and landless farmers. In a second phase of reform, which marked the first step towards the collectivisation of agriculture, peasant households were encouraged to pool resources in periods of seasonal shortages.

In the mid-1950s, China pushed on more intensively towards the command economy. Concerned about the slow pace at which peasants were joining cooperatives, it eventually abolished private ownership alto-gether in 1958, though this proved to be temporary. It also used rural production experiments as the basis for forming advanced cooperatives, in which peasants were compelled to participate in Soviet-type collective enterprises. Similarly, the Soviet-type model of industrialisation was intro-duced into urban areas, by which the government took over most enter-prises. The biggest focus was on the heavy industries in the north east of the country, specifically Manchuria, and initially the government was buoyed by significant increases in industrial output and in the share of industrial investment in GDP.

The Great Leap Forward (1958–62) was designed to implement Mao's big ideas for industrial and agricultural development and present a devel-opment model that suited China's economic conditions, especially regarding its labour resources. Whatever remained of China's property rights and incentives for farmers were swept aside as hundreds of millions of people were dragooned into about 25,000 large communes with an average of about 5,000 households. A few had over 100,000 members. Personal possessions, food and labour were pooled and the communes were assigned the responsibility for managing local administration, tax collection, health-care, education and the supervision of production.[7] The government's strategy reduced agricultural land and supply, and directed 30 million workers into rural factories, including backyard steel mills, while erroneous ideas about the 1958 harvest led to a significant rise in the procurement of compulsory deliveries.[8] The famine engendered by the Great Leap Forward cost at least 30 million lives between 1959 and 1961, though the total could have been as high as 40–45 million.

Much of what the Great Leap Forward sought to do was reversed or modified in the following years, and by the mid-1960s the economy showed some signs of recovery, with new investment and construction in agriculture, and in industry in the coastal provinces. A new three-tier organisational framework was established, comprising communes, production brigades and production teams, the numbers of which increased significantly by 1970.

The Cultural Revolution, launched in 1966, brought a decade of ideological frenzy, and a bitter political and cross-generational conflict. It may have had less devastating economic consequences for the Chinese economy and its citizens, but it had, nonetheless, important macroeconomic effects on agricultural production and industrial output. It undermined Chinese institutions and had important economic and commercial consequences. Although the signature achievement of the period was the so-called Third Front Initiative, under which large-scale investment was authorised in sectors such as defence, technology and heavy industry, it retarded economic development and reform at a time when other Asian Tiger economies, for example, were developing increasingly rapidly and confidently. Deng Xiaoping would later argue that the Cultural Revolution nearly destroyed the Communist Party as an institution and wrecked its credibility.

As the 1970s started, China's economy was experiencing serious imbalances. There was a sharp contrast between sluggish agriculture and food production on the one hand, and rapid industrial growth on the other. Industrial output continued to grow at 8 per cent per annum in the 1970s, which was half the rate of the 1950s, but too fast relative to the capacity of the countryside to keep up and provide enough food for both rural residents and urban workers. These manifestations of dysfunction in the Chinese economy lasted several years, but two things happened that would bring China out of its economic doldrums. In 1972, President Richard Nixon's first ever visit of a US president to Communist China ushered in a period of rapprochement and engagement. Soon after, moreover, Mao rehabilitated a Chinese political official – a victim of the Cultural Revolution – called Deng Xiaoping. The latter's return to power was short-lived. He fell out of favour again in 1976, but his time was approaching.

Failure with few silver linings

Even though the Mao period is associated with chronic political and economic instability, and some of the worst manifestations of political dictatorship, it was also characterised by some positive economic and social changes. According to National Bureau of Statistics figures, real GDP rose by just over 6 per cent per year between 1952 and 1978, and the share of industry (excluding construction) in GDP rose from 17.6 to just over 44 per cent. The stock of capital, or the value of physical assets such as buildings, factories, infrastructure, and machinery and equipment, rose by over 7.5 per cent per year, significantly faster than the population.

Population growth dropped from 1.9 to 1.5 per cent during Mao's period in power, and the fertility rate halved to three children per woman of child-bearing age. There were material improvements in mortality rates, especially of children, and in educational attainment levels. Under-five mortality, for example, fell from 205 per 1,000 live births to 73 thanks to an expansion of primary healthcare services, widespread public health campaigns such as immunisation, improvements in water, sanitation and nutrition, and gains in educational attainment. Overall, the quality of human capital certainly did increase.

In 1949, around 80 per cent of China's population were illiterate. Large investments in education, however, raised the primary school enrolment rate by a factor of four to 80 per cent by 1958 and then to 97 per cent by 1975. The secondary school enrolment rate increased from 6 per cent to nearly 50 per cent. The average years of schooling among people aged twenty-five and over increased from 0.7 years in 1950 to 3.7 years in 1980. For women the rise was even more dramatic – from 0.5 to 5 years.[9]

Mao's China, though, could not overcome three very familiar and self-inflicted problems: a standard Malthusian problem of inadequate food production; a typical Keynesian problem of inadequate employment creation to drive sustainable demand; and, despite quite respectable GDP and industrial growth, a Soviet-style neglect of efficiency and incentives. There was no material growth in what economists call total factor productivity, an efficiency term that captures the growth generated by the smart deployment of capital and labour resources, and technical progress.[10]

While the labour force grew to close to 200 million people, less than two-fifths of the rise was absorbed into the modern sector. In an outcome that flies in the face of 'normal' economic development, the agricultural labour force was 70 per cent bigger in 1978 than it had been in 1952, and significantly worse off relative to urban dwellers.

Mao's China paid next to no attention to constructing the foundations for a more lively consumer sector, which is important because as household incomes rise, people tend to spend a diminishing proportion of additional income on food and necessities and more on consumer goods. China's single-minded focus on heavy industry and capital-intensive production meant that traditional manufacturing and service industries, which are usually large employers of labour, didn't expand as they could have done relative to population size. Between 1952 and 1978, for example, the number of people per employee in the retail sector rose from 81 to 214, and the number of people per restaurant rose from 676 to 8,189.[11] Normally, we would have expected to see rising living standards and consumption trends reflected in a larger increase in the size of the retail and services industries.

The greatest economic legacy of the Mao period for China may well have been its shortcomings and failures. These spawned a willingness on the part of new leaders to experiment, and to learn lessons from the rest of the world. Some fourteen years before Mao died, in 1962, Deng Xiaoping had first used a phrase praising better incentives for peasants that has become widely associated with him. He said: 'It doesn't matter if the cat is black or yellow, as long as it can catch mice, it is a good cat.'[12] This came to typify the monumental change that was about to start on Deng's watch as he sought to experiment in pursuit of an economy that was socialist but would bring a better life to citizens and modernity to China.

'Reform and Opening Up'

The significance of Deng for modern China is hard to exaggerate, and it isn't even so much because of the specific policies he initiated or any particular programmes that he set in motion. Others would claim credit in due course. Rather, it is because, as Henry Kissinger said, he fulfilled the ultimate task of a leader, which was to take his society from where it was to where it has never been. Societies, Kissinger added, 'progress through leaders with a vision of the necessary and the courage to undertake a course whose benefits at first reside largely in their vision'.[13]

The slogan 'Reform and Opening Up' was promulgated at the third plenum of the 11th Central Committee of the Chinese Communist Party in 1978, and became the hallmark of Deng's influence over China thereafter. The third of the five annual plenums that coincide with the five-year cycle of Party leadership meetings is often used to unveil major policy plans and priorities. Sometimes these meetings are ineffectual or get bogged down in esoteric matters. Occasionally they are of major significance. Some hail the third plenum of the 14th Party Congress in 1993 associated with Zhu Rongji's endorsement of a 'socialist market economy'. Yet the confirmation of Deng's leadership and 'Reform and Opening Up' probably make the third plenum in 1978 the most significant of all. Without Deng, and 'Reform and Opening Up', China's economic and political history would not have taken the course it did.

The impact that Deng had on the Chinese economy is best appreciated by comparing the rise in labour productivity in the twenty-five years before 1978 with that of the twenty-five years that followed. In agriculture, productivity growth rose from about 0.2 to almost 4 per cent per year. In industry and construction, it almost doubled from 3.7 to 6.7 per cent per year. In the tertiary, or services sector, it surged from 1.8 to 5.9 per cent per year. This shift explained almost all of the rise in GDP growth that occurred.[14] Labour and capital were more productive because China was able to exploit, mix and manage them better, and to do this it had to reform the way markets and institutions functioned. Reform in China was never going to be straightforward, but was facilitated by three hugely important developments.

First, although Hua Guofeng, premier from 1976 to 1980, hardly ranked as a major reformer or leading economic light, he acknowledged that China needed to look far afield for new ideas and approved the creation of the Chinese Academy of Social Sciences. This institution spawned a new generation of economic thinkers who were committed to the idea that economic knowledge and tests of experience would be more valuable to Chinese economic policy-making than political edicts and statements of priorities.[15]

Second, the gradual and then more intense engagement of Chinese economists with peers overseas proved to be a powerful catalyst for change and critical thinking in China, as explained by Julian Gewirtz in his book *Unlikely Partners*. For example, the establishment of SEZs in China in the 1980s flowed from the observations of a delegation of Chinese economists in Europe in 1978. Engagement with foreign economists and economic institutions also led to student exchanges with the US, and a new intellectual openness in which economic ideas were assessed without having to be set in a rigid political straitjacket. China studied and imported ideas observed in Yugoslavia and other eastern European countries, especially Hungary, and gained access to Japanese investment and trade.

China's willingness to look abroad and engage with economic experts at the end of the 1970s and start of the 1980s was unquestionably an important factor in the pattern and pace of reform. Among the most notable channels that China opened up were to those behind the Iron Curtain, in particular to the Hungarian economist János Kornai, an expert in the economics of socialist economies who emphasised the significance of hard versus soft budget constraints. While this might seem rather esoteric, it was of great interest to the Chinese. With hard budget constraints, companies compete for loans and capital and have to repay lenders or shareholders. They produce and sell in markets where prices are determined by supply and demand, and if they're not profitable, they go bankrupt or are taken over. Kornai, though, emphasised that soft budget constraints, such as those that had characterised the USSR and China's early years, meant that companies qualified for preferential access to credit, were given non-commercial objectives, especially regarding employment, and conducted business with administered prices and with no risk of being wound up.

China took Kornai's teaching on board, and recognised that what mattered wasn't so much ownership – since private companies could also be inefficient and ineffective – but hard budget constraints.[16] This has again become an issue of contemporary relevance, since some of the concerns about the debt build-up in Chinese state enterprises and local governments, and about the overstatement of China's GDP, are attributable to more permissive attitudes to soft budget constraints.

China's interest in economics and economic thinkers abroad in the early Deng years went further still and included exchanges with and visits by many other Western economists, including the famed US free-market economist Milton Friedman, as well as other well-known economists such as Sir Alec Cairncross and Professor Lord Nicholas Stern.

The third catalyst for reform in China was the emergence of Deng himself, who helped to institutionalise it. His commitment to the primacy of the Communist Party was total, and his resistance to the threat of grass-roots democratic movements was amply demonstrated by his hard-line approach to the Tiananmen Square protests in 1989. He was, though, the architect of the opening up of China to new ideas and the world, the liberalisation of the Chinese economy, and the establishment of political structures designed to prevent the concentration of power in a single, autocratic leader. He saw that the Party's political strength was dependent on the implementation of limited but liberal economic reforms.

Interestingly, Xi Jinping sees things differently. For him, the Party's political strength and purity are an end in itself, to which needed economic reforms are subordinate. The contradiction between the necessity of economic reform on the one hand, and the political context in which it happens on the other hand, has ebbed and flowed since Deng, but has never been resolved. It has attained a significance under President Xi Jinping that is of major consequence, as we shall see later.

First phase of reform 1978–88

One of the first things that China's leaders did for the countryside was to ease the procurement burden on farmers, pay them higher prices, and then allow them to sell any excess at much higher prices. Agricultural collectives were given permission to experiment with various payment and production systems, and gradually an overarching theme emerged, which was to contract to farmers the right to manage individual pieces of land. In effect, farming households, which even then constituted 82 per cent of the population, were given use-rights to collectively owned land under long-term leases, and also the right to sell their marginal product, or what they produced over and above what they consumed, on the open market. By 1983, these practices had become universal, and the collective system had almost entirely disappeared.

The emergence of town and village enterprises (TVE) after 1978–79, created out of commune and brigade industries, played a crucial role in giving the countryside a structure in which to develop low-value, light-manufacturing activities. For a considerable time, TVEs offered China the opportunity to generate labour-intensive production, to which heavy industry was poorly suited. In this way, China was able to exploit better its ample supply of labour relative to capital. Between 1978 and the mid-1990s, TVE employment grew from 28 to 135 million, and their value-added increased from 6 to 26 per cent of GDP. With their focus on abundant supplies of cheap labour, TVEs tended to specialise in products such as textiles, food processing, furniture, building materials, and simple machinery and metal processing.

TVEs fulfilled other important functions. They offered employment and income-earning opportunities, and helped to bridge at least some of the development discrepancies between rural and urban areas. Perversely, as publicly owned entities, they also acted as a lightning conductor for the transformation of the command economy into one in which market-oriented enterprises were allowed to flourish. Significantly, they also provided publicly owned enterprise competition to state enterprises, which slowly became engaged in pilot projects in which they were allowed to retain some of their profits and use them to re-invest or pay higher wages and salaries. Over time, most TVEs would gradually be restructured into privately owned firms or go out of business altogether.

The Chinese housing sector was very simple until 1978. Land owner-ship had been nationalised and the state was the monopoly landlord and developer. The state allocated public rental facilities to 'work units', which were not so much places of work as entities that provided a full array of housing services, and which in turn allocated housing to households. In other words, China had a housing welfare system, not a housing market. For several years, China's political leaders and institutions engaged in a discussion about the ideological fundamentals of a market-based housing system, introduced pilot projects to see how markets could be made to work, and gingerly allowed private agents to build and purchase their own housing, and charge for land use.

Then, in 1988, some six years after the first pilot project, the State Council took one of the most important steps in housing reform, giving its blessing to the commercialisation of housing as a target for housing reform.[17] Nothing further would happen, though, until after the Tiananmen crisis. In 1991, the State Council decided that the property rights of priva-tised housing would be officially recognised. This would pave the way for further market-based housing reform in the 1990s.

Second phase of reform 1992–2003

At the end of the 1980s, China ran into several problems that combined to produce a major social crisis. The dual-track system of prices, in which state-set prices coexisted with limited freedom for producers to sell above quota output at market prices, provided plenty of opportunities for graft and nepotism. The development of competition, of which Chinese leaders had limited experience, produced winners but also losers. Reforms that weren't always able to balance demand and supply responses smoothly gave rise to macroeconomic consequences including a burst of inflation from about 10 per cent at the end of 1988 to nearly 30 per cent in 1989.

On top of this, a cocktail of corruption, market instability, and political tensions at the top of the Party emerged. When a gathering wave of student protests about corruption, inflation, and academic, press and personal freedoms erupted, and was then joined by a democracy movement, the consequences ran out of control. They ended in 1989 in the horrific events at Tiananmen Square.

For the next two years, a major power struggle ensued between conservatives and those eager to advance Deng Xiaoping's agenda. Those in the Party who wanted to use the opportunity to back away from reform succeeded temporarily, but failed to do so in the end. In January 1992, with the economy stabilising and inflation dropping back sharply to below 5 per cent, Deng fought back, though he was now experiencing poor health. What he did was 'the last action of his life and one which would set a decisive stamp on the evolution of China into the twenty-first century'.[18] He embarked on what came to be known as his Southern Tour, visiting the SEZs of Shenzhen and Zhuhai, and also Shanghai, with the explicit goal of re-energising the drive for reform. It has also been called 'a crusade for reform on behalf of socialism with Chinese characteristics'.[19]

China went on to capitalise on what had been accomplished in and learned from earlier rural reform, and applied the lessons incrementally to the urban economy, to housing, to state-owned enterprises, and to its international economic interests. This second phase of reform was distinguished by an important development – the introduction of rules-based, institutional mechanisms and regulations as a substitute for political directives and planning by diktat. Perversely, precisely the reverse is happening in Xi Jinping's China, where the centralisation of power around Xi at the head of a strengthened Party is a substitute for the institutionalisation of rules and processes.

Yet, during the 1990s, political leaders could see that the new practices of land use-rights and production and income incentives in rural areas were delivering efficiency and productivity gains. They could also see that the first reform phase had provided useful institutional learning about economic arrangements and property rights based on contracts, which could be extended in the future to housing, and industry and commerce.

The steps taken to 'marketise' urban housing before Tiananmen were consolidated, and served as the basis for deepening the reform agenda and creating economic and affordable housing for the less well-off on the one hand, and a green light for what the Chinese called 'commodity' housing for the better-off, on the other. For much of the 1990s, China moved incrementally to establish a nation-wide housing market and in 1998, the State Council published the cumbersomely titled 'A Notification on Further Deepening the Reform of the Urban Housing System and Accelerating Housing Construction'.

Put simply, this initiative sounded the death-knell for China's housing welfare system, and the start of a new era for housing market development. In 2003, it specified for the first time the rights and responsibilities of all parties involved in the housing sector, and the steps to be taken to address legal disputes over property management.

With this, a housing boom was born, and the authorities turned their attention to shaping and regulating the market by passing laws affecting land administration and land-use, mortgages, and real estate prices, taxation and administration. A private housing market became embedded in the structure of China's economy, and was one of its key economic drivers during the 2000s and until about 2011, when residential investment accounted for about 14 per cent of GDP, three times as much as in 2003.

The creation of limited property rights in the countryside and TVE cottage enterprises served as a model for the spontaneous formation of individually owned businesses. The de facto recognition of a new enterprise structure eventually gave rise to constitutional amendments to protect the legal status of enterprises, though as complementary to and supportive of publicly owned businesses and public policy goals as determined by the Party.

State enterprises learned to operate a 'dual-track' system under which they had price and production obligations under the planning system, but also an opportunity to learn about market operations, and sell surplus production at a price above that decreed by the state. Surplus production transactions became a steadily more important part of their operations, subject to contracts set by China's state planners. Entry barriers were lowered, allowing greater competition, and managers were given more leeway to hire and fire middle-level staff, pay bonuses and establish direct links with suppliers.

New ownership

The first change of ownership of a state-owned enterprise (SOE) occurred in 1986, when three individuals put up 34,000 yuan as collateral to lease the Wuhan Motor Engine factory. In the same year, three Guangzhou-based SOEs introduced private shareholding by allowing employees to purchase 30 per cent of their companies' shares. In 1988, the State Council issued regulations on the leasing of small SOEs, providing formal legal grounds for the practice. These were the early steps towards a more institutionalised private ownership framework, which gathered pace and resulted in the opening of the Shenzhen and Shanghai stock exchanges in 1990 and 1991, respectively. With this, a limited number of SOEs were able to issue shares to the public.[20]

In the wake of Deng's Southern Tour, a new drive for ownership reform was born. There was not then, or since, any chance that the primacy of the state in the economy would be abandoned. New regulations were introduced, though, to allow the structure of inefficient industries to be overhauled, and a few enterprises to be leased or sold to the public or to employees.

Deng's inspiration to carry out reforms and to experiment, including with private-sector ownership, was carried forward by a new standard-bearer of what the 14th Party Congress in October 1992 endorsed as the 'socialist market economy'. He was Vice Premier Zhu Rongji, who went on to become premier in 1998 until he stepped down in 2003. The momentum behind reform now featured changes in market institutions and incentives that had not previously existed in China, and a shift from rule by discretion to rule by regulation and law.

Ownership reform got a boost in 1993 from a new Corporation Law, which provided for a slow transformation of the organisational structure of the public sector. The main purposes of the law were to restructure SOEs, address their myriad inefficiencies, encourage greater competition and productivity, and remove the influence of the government from day-to-day operations. Although there was no provision in the law for privatisation, it nonetheless sought to encourage the development of small private enterprises as a desired and complementary adjunct to the all-important state sector, and to help absorb labour.

This was a significant moment in the evolution of Chinese reforms. In the mid-1990s, under the slogan, 'Grasp the big, let go of the small', China transformed the large number of SOEs under state control. Small ones were privatised or closed, while larger ones were turned into more major corporations and merged into large industrial groups. The government decided to retain ownership of between 500 to 1,000 large SOEs and allow smaller SOEs to be leased or sold. In 1997, the 15th Party Congress approved plans to convert some SOEs into shareholding corporations, and in 2000, the Shanghai Stock Exchange issued China's first corporate governance guidance principles, later drafted into legal requirements by the China Securities Regulatory Commission.[21] By 2001, 86 per cent of all SOEs had been restructured and roughly 70 per cent had been fully or partially privatised.[22]

The employment consequences of SOE reforms were considerable, though the private sector absorbed a lot of the slack created. Between 1998 and 2007, the number of workers in SOEs dropped from about 90 million to 62 million, according to National Bureau of Statistics data, but a different sample of SOE changes suggests a fall from 70 to 26 million, while employment in private and foreign firms, for example, rose by 644 and 202 per cent, respectively.[23] The government required buyers of sold SOEs to sign a contract of intent to re-employ people, and established various government compensation, subsidy and re-employment funds to help finance re-employment. The public to private job shift was also helped by the dynamism of the growing private sector, the growth of private enterprises, and the structural changes underway in preparation for entry into the World Trade Organization.

Looking back at the downsizing of state enterprises in the late 1990s, the scale and speed of change were impressive. China actually went further than János Kornai might have expected by laying hard into the SOE sector, and clearing the way for the substantial expansion of private sector firms. In this way the economy, and for a while many major SOEs, became subject to important market disciplines, namely hard budget constraints and bankruptcy or failure. State firms were required to be more disciplined, and were certainly influenced by competition from a rising private sector.

Yet a little over a decade later, a more pervasive soft budget behaviour re-emerged in the state enterprise system and in an array of enterprises created by local and provincial governments in the wake of the major stimulus programme launched in 2008. Against a backdrop in which the underlying pace of economic growth was slowing down, and the pace of economic liberalisation had become incremental or was waning, soft budget constraints resulted in misallocated and excessive investment, and excessive reliance on bank and other financial credit for funding projects.

Fiscal, foreign trade and financial reforms

China has struggled periodically to determine the optimum relationship between Beijing and local governments when it comes to the responsibility for offering services and public goods, for example, and even more importantly, how to pay for them. Historically, though, the central government has played a relatively limited role in the economy. Local governments, whose officials have been incentivised to meet government targets, are the main agencies charged with delivering economic growth.

In 1994, important fiscal and tax reforms were introduced that returned a lot of financial control to the central government that had been farmed out to local governments in earlier reforms. The new reforms created a modern, simplified and unified tax system that divided fiscal authority between central and local government, and introduced revenue-sharing on the basis of rules rather than by discretion. The central government took over the prime responsibility for tax administration, and for controlling the nation's fiscal deficit via the issuance of bonds. The reforms were designed to increase operational efficiencies in the conduct of fiscal policy, and strengthen the government's revenues, which had tumbled from about 30 per cent of GDP in 1978 to about 10 per cent.

Yet, in spite of further fiscal changes after 1994, the centralisation of fiscal control which the reforms sought to implement did not really establish a viable, commercial or legal basis for the separation of authority between central and local governments. By 2016, local governments were still doing about 85 per cent of total fiscal spending, compared to Beijing's 15 per cent. This was not so different from the situation in 1994. Apart from the revenues they raised themselves, including from land sales which were and remain an important source, local governments relied heavily on transfers from Beijing, more so in the 1990s than now, but still significant. The manner in which Beijing allocates transfers to help local government finances is opaque. It is not set by election mandates, of course, or by notions of welfare and population distribution or devolution. Instead, it is a highly political process, designed to maintain the loyalty of the Party's supporters and promote economic growth in line with national objectives.[24]

The shortcomings of local government finance arrangements became more visible after the financial crisis in 2008, when the government implemented a major stimulus programme. Local governments were the principal channel for delivering that stimulus through spending on infrastructure and housing. While they have a monopoly over sales of land, they needed to find additional ways of raising revenues, and set about creating off-budget borrowing platforms known as local government financing vehicles. According to a 2013 nationwide audit, there were almost 7,200 such vehicles, but a more recent estimate by the China Securities Regulatory Commission in 2017 put the number at 11,728.[25] These and other local government borrowing platforms have made the local and provincial government sector one of the principal sources of China's debt accumulation over the last decade.

Mindful of the risks posed by local governments to China's financial stability, Premier Li Keqiang said in 2013 that the central government should consolidate its macroeconomic authority and ensure local government officials respected its orders and policies without hesitation. In this way, he explained, Beijing would assert its authority over fundamental economic goals, such as lower sustainable growth, environmentally friendly expansion, fiscal reform and lower income inequality. He wanted local governments to switch their focus from chasing growth and engaging in GDP growth statistics competition with other provinces to providing public goods and services.

Yet, Li famously said at the time that tackling vested political and Party interests at the local level was a task that was harder than 'stirring the soul'.[26] He was right. Since then, little has happened to alter the balance of power and function between central and local governments, even though Beijing has tried to define more closely some central and local government spending responsibilities and change the incentive arrangements that result in an excessive focus on economic growth and often low-quality growth statistics.

Foreign trade and finance reforms in the 1990s were coordinated with fiscal and tax reforms. China's original application to join the General Agreement on Trade and Tariffs, or the GATT, the forerunner of the WTO, was actually lodged in 1986. Around this time, a new embryonic openness to foreign trade, foreign investment and the import of foreign technology, albeit under close government regulation and oversight, began. Initially, reforms focused on decentralising trade rights to local governments, industrial ministries and producer enterprises. Reforms that had started in Guangdong and Fujian SEZs which were close to Hong Kong gradually evolved into a coastal development strategy, allowing all types of firms to engage in processing and assembly in more than a dozen SEZs. Stringent currency controls were relaxed, the Renminbi was devalued, and a dual exchange-rate system was set up in 1986 in which exporters could sell foreign currency earnings in a lightly regulated secondary market at more attractive levels.

In 1994, China unified what had previously been a dual exchange-rate system, by aligning the official exchange with the 'swap' or unofficial exchange rate, devaluing the former by 33 per cent to a US dollar equivalent of 8.7 yuan. It also set up the first interbank currency market in Shanghai, and the China Foreign Exchange Trade System to provide trading, information, benchmark and training facilities to the interbank lending, bond and foreign exchange markets. In 1996, China allowed the yuan to become fully convertible against other currencies for so-called 'current account' transactions, that is in the exchange of payment for goods, services and transfers such as remittances.

In 2001, China was admitted to the WTO, having already lowered tariff barriers and removed many import quotas. Fiscal policy innovations, such as the introduction of a VAT system, fitted into the WTO structure, which permits exporters to claim a rebate on VAT. China had also adapted its regulatory regime to meet WTO standards, particularly as regards currency management practices, and the opening up of its banking and financial sectors.

Although China has claimed to have an objective of liberalising capital account transactions since the mid-1990s, progress has been limited and fleeting. While some regulations have been removed or relaxed since the Asian Crisis in 1997–98, most initiatives have been about making it easier for foreign capital to come into China rather than the other way round.

During the Asian Crisis, a number of countries, including Thailand, South Korea, Indonesia and Malaysia, succumbed to extreme financial instability. The crisis itself was due to incompatible economic policies but was triggered by large capital outflows that overpowered the countries' ability to maintain exchange rates that were pegged to the US dollar. In the event, they experienced large devaluations, financial turbulence at home and deep recessions.

For China, which came through the crisis more or less unscathed, the lesson was to make sure capital movements were closely controlled. Removing restrictions on outward capital movements has always lagged behind, therefore, and there has always been an unresolvable tension between managing an open capital account in which Chinese citizens and companies have full access to foreign markets and assets, and the control which the Party has never wanted to cede. After some protracted financial turbulence in 2015–16, Chinese capital controls were again tightened significantly.

Financial reform

Over time, China has broadened and deepened its financial system from what was originally a rigid, unsophisticated and doctrinaire means of financial control. Broadening refers to the growth of financial assets as a share of GDP, as well as to a wider universe of financial institutions and financial products on offer. Deepening refers to a rise in the range and size of claims on a diverse universe of borrowers. According to the IMF, financial development along these lines helps to mobilise savings and improve information sharing, resource allocation and risk management. It also promotes financial stability to the extent that deep and liquid financial systems with diverse instruments help enhance countries' resilience to shocks.[27] On the other side, we have also learned from financial crises in recent decades, including the 2007–8 crisis, as well as from China's own experiences, that financial instability can and does arise in economic systems where banks and leverage are given free rein.

China's experience of financial liberalisation dates back only to the 1990s and has come a long way since, most notably in the last ten to twelve years. It was one of the least politically sensitive of all the major areas of reform, and championed by a strong enthusiast in Zhou Xiaochuan, governor of the People's Bank of China from 2002 to 2018. China's ultimate goals were to liberalise both lending and deposit interest rates so as to make the allocation of capital more efficient, and also to introduce a nation-wide deposit protection scheme so that households would be protected up to a point in a more market-oriented system. I have already referred to the opening of the Shenzhen and Shanghai stock exchanges at the beginning of the 1990s, and during the following decade several initiatives were taken to introduce new financial products, tools of monetary control, and flexibility in the setting of deposit and lending rates. New regulatory agencies were set up in the form of the China Securities Regulatory Commission in 1998 and the China Banking Regulatory Commission in 2003.

During the 2000s, a 'shadow finance' sector began to emerge in which market practices were able to evolve more quickly in a much less well regulated environment than in the formal banking sector, but progress was slow. By 2008, little more than 10 per cent of total credit in the economy originated in the 'shadows'. In the last decade, though, financial liberalisation and the growth of the shadow finance sector developed apace. The liberalisation of interest rates was in effect completed inside two years. In 2013, all restrictions on lending rates were abolished, except for mortgages, and, after the introduction of a deposit insurance system in 2015, the ceiling for interest rates on bank deposits was abolished too. The People's Bank of China no longer sets official benchmark interest rates, though banks continue to practise favourable discrimination in lending to SOEs. The principal interest rate targeted by the People's Bank nowadays to manage liquidity conditions and steer the overall monetary policy stance is the seven-day repurchase rate, which is used heavily to price money in the interbank market.

The financial system has been both the engine of vibrant economic growth in China and a source of rising angst. Financial deregulation and innovation are often urged as the agents of economic efficiency and growth, but there are circumstances in which they can also wreak havoc and threaten economic and political stability.

China's financial system played a central role in funding growth in the 1990s, for example, but it was eventually riddled with non-performing loans and instability. These originated from many years of imprudent lending to financially fragile or weak SOEs. It has been estimated that by the late 1990s, bad loans amounted to the equivalent of 40 per cent of total lending, and the authorities had to intervene.[28] They had to recapitalise the banks, encourage the banks to write off or down some of their non-performing loans, and set up 'asset management companies' to buy up bad debts from the banks and recover as much value from these loans over time as they could.

In 2008, as China's leaders watched the ripples of the Western financial crisis roll into the mainland in the form of lost exports, a steep downturn in growth and rising unemployment, they launched an economic stimulus package of $580 billion, or around 14 per cent of GDP. The bulk of this package was in the form of credit stimulus, but China's addiction to credit stimulus continued for several years. So began a dependency on and rising vulnerability to credit on a scale that is many times larger than the crisis encountered in the 1990s. I shall examine this and the measures being taken to counter these trends in Chapter 4.

Modernity

During the 1990s and 2000s, China embarked on a major change in the relationship of the state to markets and market institutions on the one hand, and in its relationship with the outside world on the other. The SOE system was transformed relatively quickly and radically, but without incurring large-scale permanent unemployment. The private sector expanded rapidly, the right to private home ownership was established, and China became progressively more integrated into the global economy under the auspices of global institutions such as the WTO, IMF and the World Bank.

China's experience demonstrates that successful economic development is not just about harnessing physical labour and capital, mixing them together and delivering high economic growth. It is also about delivering good outcomes that endure by changing attitudes and institutions, and adhering to fairly administered rules and regulations. By its own standards, China registered important successes in granting and protecting property rights, forging trust in the law, and introducing much greater transparency and accountability into the regulatory framework within which private enterprises and individuals could work and compete without threat or interference. Both flourished. Local government finance was reformed, though the effects were to prove temporary, while financial reforms affecting domestic financial markets, and the exchange rate and interest rate systems, were carried out at a rapid pace.

President Hu Jintao and Premier Wen Jiabao were in power for the decade to 2013, a period in which the Chinese economy erupted. With annual growth of 10 per cent, China went from being the world's sixth biggest economy to the second largest, and gained the status to demand a bigger seat at the global governance table. As income per head rose from $1,293 to $7,080, or in purchasing power parity terms, from $3,940 to $12,205, China could proudly justify its status as a middle-income country.

For urban citizens at least, the decade was also one to savour. Wages rose steadily, owner-occupied housing boomed, and urban car ownership rates soared; Chinese car sales were almost 25 million in 2017, accounting for about a third of global car sales. The construction of highways, airports and high-speed rail networks also surged, education spending doubled to 4 per cent of GDP, and health and pension coverage and benefits were broadened.

Yet, while modernity came to China with speed during the 2000s, there were also other, more untoward developments that were not always noticeable at the time and that formed the roots of some of China's contemporary problems. When Hu and Wen stepped down in 2013, their critics charged that, for all their rhetoric, they had been essentially inactive, ignored the central organising role of the Party, and had fallen victim to vested political interests.

President Obama's advisers were of the view that Hu was at the 'mercy of a diffuse ruling party in which generals, ministers and big corporate interests had more clout, and less deference, than they did in the days of Mao or Deng, who both commanded basically unquestioned authority'.[29] Jiang Zemin's influence and allies were everywhere, including on the Politburo Standing Committee, and it is fair to ask whether Hu and Wen ever had the kind of control that their predecessors enjoyed.

In some ways, they presided over a reversal of reform. Indebtedness and a rising dependency on credit to sustain high rates of economic growth became entrenched in public policy. Pollution and corruption became much bigger political and economic problems. When Premier Wen stepped down from office, he admitted that 'even among top officials, abuse of power, trading power for cash, and collusion between officialdom and commerce continue unabated'.[30] Income inequality between the countryside and the cities and within urban areas increased. The role and influence of SOEs expanded again, not just in the economy, but as powerful and well-heeled interest groups politically.

Social unrest became a more important problem, with the number of 'mass incidents' – many about low-level public sector corruption, construction and planning injustices, and pollution and environmental degradation – reportedly rising from about 50,000 a year in 2002 to about 180,000 a year by 2012. Those with money left China. It is estimated that about 27 per cent of Chinese with at least $15 million in assets emigrated, citing the quality of the educational system, the environment, healthcare, food safety and protection of assets as the drivers.[31]

Some have argued that Hu Jintao and Wen Jiabao's period in office was 'the lost decade', and that they failed to realise three major objectives: a sustainable economic growth and development model; greater economic and social equality; and a Communist Party that was trusted and respected by the citizens. In their defence, we could counter by saying that they were leaders during a time when China prospered enormously in the global economy. Perhaps, as is customary, the pressure and urgency to reform simply melted away in more favourable economic times. Moreover, Hu and Wen did preside over the introduction of welfare reforms designed to replace the so-called 'iron rice bowl' provision of cradle-to-grave care, formerly provided by state enterprises and institutions.

Just as I argued earlier that one of the legacies of the Mao era was new leaders who realised that China had to change, so perhaps one of the main legacies of the Hu and Wen era was the conviction, felt by Xi Jinping, at least, that the Party and China were in danger. Xi's principal focus was to strengthen the Party and ensure it regained its 'purity', a term with strong Leninist roots. Yet the economy, too, needed a makeover. It needed to become more balanced, more sustainable, more coordinated. It needed 'rebalancing'.

3

THE END OF EXTRAPOLATION
REBALANCING AND REFORM

Every now and again, you will hear or read about people talking about China as an export-led economy or otherwise implying that it relies on exports for its economic growth and success. Donald Trump accused China of 'raping' the US with its unfair trade policies when he was campaigning for the presidency in 2016, and while his administration has used more temperate language, it has persisted in emphasising an image of China as a global export predator that has stolen US jobs. Several years ago, this argument may have had relevance, but China is no longer an export-led economy. The real issue in China as far as imbalances are concerned is not in the trade account but at home.

From the beginning of the 2000s, China increasingly became an investment-led economy. After 2008, it became ever more reliant on credit expansion to drive growth. The expansion and liberalisation of the financial sector have proceeded far more quickly, and sometimes recklessly, compared to the rest of the economy. State-owned enterprises (SOEs) have continued to lag far behind private firms in terms of profitability and efficiency, but remain privileged and important in the economy. Income inequality between urban and rural areas and among the urban population has risen significantly. Migrant workers have fared much less well in Chinese cities than city dwellers with residence permits. Too little attention was paid to the energy, carbon emission and pollution consequences of high-growth economic and industrial strategies, creating deep and dangerous environmental imbalances.

In short, China has reached a point we can call the end of extrapolation. It simply cannot continue to develop on the basis of the economic model that has existed until now. More credit-fuelled investment will risk economic and financial instability, possibly leading to an abrupt and painful growth crunch. In the medium to longer term, rising income inequalities and environmental degradation risk both significantly slower growth and major social dysfunction. Consequently, China needs to develop a more sustainable growth path and development model. This much, at least, is recognised well by the Chinese leadership. The question is how to construct and deliver it while keeping the Party in total control.

External rebalancing done and dusted

The easiest part of the rebalancing story seems to be the external side of the economy, which is done and dusted, at least for the time being. For twenty years until China joined the WTO in 2001, China's external balance, or the current account, oscillated between −2 and +2 per cent of GDP. It was in deficit for five of those years and in modest surplus for the rest. To all intents and purposes, it was a non-issue. But for several years after 2002, in the wake of WTO membership, and with an undervalued exchange rate and the extraordinarily benign global trade circumstances of the time, China's external surplus exploded. By 2007, it had reached 10 per cent of GDP, and it was for good reason that the prevailing debate in international economics in the first part of the 2000s was about large global payments imbalances and the destabilising role that these played in the world economic system. China, as the biggest surplus country, was a particular focus of this debate, as was the US, the biggest deficit country.

Since then, though, China's external surplus has tumbled, averaging just 2.3 per cent of GDP between 2012 and 2015, and falling to 1.4 per cent of GDP in 2017. It is simply not an issue from China's standpoint, or from that of the rest of the world. For comparison's sake, South Korea ran a surplus of 5.6 per cent of GDP in 2017 and Germany ran a surplus of 7.8 per cent of GDP.

It is an issue, though, because the fall in the external surplus is misleading. China's seemingly hollowed out current account surplus is made up of a manufactured goods surplus that is still over 10 per cent of GDP, but offset by other factors including high commodity imports and a surge in tourism. This matters politically, with respect to the US for example, but from a simple imbalances perspective, it is easier to bypass. China's surplus fell back partly because of the overall weakness of global demand since the financial crisis, but there were important made-in-China factors too. Wage rates rose a lot in China, tripling in US dollar terms between 2005 and 2016, outpacing almost every other country in Latin America and many in Asia, and converging quickly on the weaker Eurozone countries.[1] The steady if sometimes erratic appreciation of the Renminbi until 2015 certainly contributed to a loss of competitiveness, while much of China's low value-added manufacturing, for example textiles, footwear and apparel, has moved to countries such as Vietnam, Cambodia, Laos, Myanmar and Bangladesh.

Fundamentally, however, the reason China's external surplus collapsed has to be seen in the context of the imbalance between savings and investment in the economy. In simple national income accounting, an excess of savings over investment is reflected in an external surplus, while a deficiency shows up as a deficit. The main reason for the fall in China's current account surplus, therefore, was the surge in domestic investment that started in 2007 and 2008, coinciding with the Western financial crisis.

Strictly speaking, if China succeeds in rebalancing the economy away from investment and towards consumption, China's external imbalance will remain modest, and could even transform into a flow of deficits. However, this also presupposes there will be a significant decline in the savings behaviour of Chinese households and companies, and this is going to require vigorous action by the government to boost social welfare, for example, and increase the economic security for farmers and wage earners that persuades them to save less. Failing this, or in a cyclical downturn, China could end up with much bigger external surpluses again if the investment rate drops while the savings rate doesn't. This could then manifest itself as a new bone of contention vis-à-vis the US and other major trade partners.

Why rebalancing is necessary

There is little question that China's political leaders themselves know that rebalancing is necessary.[2] Awareness has been evident since the 2010s and was reflected in the 13th Five-Year Plan (FYP) 2016–2020, which set out to address China's 'unbalanced, uncoordinated and unsustainable' growth.[3] The principal goal is to rebalance the economy away from increasingly inefficient investment-led growth towards a model that emphasises the contributions of consumption, innovation, social welfare and environmental protection. Care for the environment accounts for ten of the twenty-five targets set in the FYP.

The reason China has to act with some urgency to rebalance is because the surge in investment as a share of the economy in the last ten to fifteen years has become associated with higher levels of inefficiency. China's investment rate, which peaked at 48 per cent of GDP in 2011, is still about 45 per cent of GDP. The slippage, though, is still more noise than substance and remains unusually high both historically and compared with other emerging countries when they, like China now, were experiencing peak investment rates. Economic growth in the Asian Tiger economies, Japan, Brazil and Russia all peaked with investment at significantly lower levels as a share of GDP. The only country that came close to China's investment metrics was South Korea, which had an investment share of 41 per cent in 1991.

High investment rates reflect high savings rates, and the Chinese save a great deal. Household savings rose from about 5 per cent of disposable income in the late 1970s to about 38 per cent in 2016, or just over 25 per cent of GDP. Savings by companies are also elevated, amounting to about 17 per cent of GDP in 2016.

High household savings reflect China's demographics, the rise in the working-age population, and the continuing weaknesses in the social security system. An inadequate level of social welfare is a problem specifically for China's 150 million or so internal migrants without 'hukou', or urban registration. They are denied access to a wide range of public housing, education and social services and benefits. The social security system as a whole is becoming broader in terms of coverage, but benefit levels remain relatively low, and Chinese people still have to pay a lot towards healthcare. Ultimately, if China's investment rate is to fall in a smooth and orderly way, Chinese savings have to come down too, and that means supporting those who have to spend a high proportion of their income on basics and essentials.

The counterpart to a high investment rate is, of course, a low consumption rate, which was 39 per cent of GDP in 2017. This was 4 percentage points higher than in 2010, but still far away from the rates of 50–60 per cent or more associated with advanced economies and most major emerging countries. Although there is some controversy about the measurement of China's low consumption rate, the fact that it is low, regardless, does not mean Chinese consumers have been suffering.

In fact, household spending, adjusted for the change in inflation, has risen at a compound rate of 9.7 per cent per annum since 2005, living standards have surged by any benchmark, and consumption contributed nearly 64 per cent to total economic growth in 2017. Chinese consumers, then, are not spending slouches, but if the consumption share of GDP is low, as various measures show, it is unrealistic to imagine that households can spend even more quickly than they have been doing. It follows that rebalancing must mean a shift down in the investment rate, and up in the consumption rate in the context of slower economic growth overall.

The reason the investment rate has to fall is because the more China relies on it, the more inefficient that investment will become. Economists measure this by estimating what they call the incremental capital–output ratio, or the change in investment relative to the change in output. While this ratio has typically fluctuated between values of 2 and 4, the National Bureau of Statistics estimated it reached 9 in 2014. It has almost certainly slipped since then, perhaps to around 7, but that remains absolutely and historically very high. Moreover, the financing of that investment has relied increasingly on credit creation.

Evidence about the inefficiency of investment is supported by a decline in the return on investment (return on assets) among enterprises. Private enterprises have consistently fared better than SOEs over the last twenty years, but even their return on assets peaked at 11 per cent in 2011, and slid down to 8–9 per cent in 2017. SOEs, which caught up with private firms about a decade or more ago, realised their peak return on assets at 6 per cent in 2007, but this halved over the following decade.

We also know that China has had to invest more and borrow more to get the same amount of GDP, or, that the investment and credit intensity of GDP has been rising. Between 1978 and 2006, for example, China spent between 2 to 4 yuan of investment to get 1 additional yuan of GDP. Since then, the amount has risen steadily to reach about 9 yuan in 2015, corresponding to a marked fall in investment efficiency.[4] Similarly, the financial system has been allocating more and more resources to finance that investment, as evidenced by the constant worries about China's rising debt level. Higher credit dependency, suggested by the rise in the amount of credit needed to generate a single unit of extra GDP, is known as the credit intensity of GDP. According to the IMF, the credit intensity of GDP has quintupled since the late 2000s to over 5, meaning that it now takes five times as much credit to produce one unit of GDP. In 2007–8, about RMB (Renminbi) 6.5 trillion ($1 trillion) of new credit was needed to raise nominal GDP by about RMB 5 trillion per year ($769 billion). In 2015–16, it took more than RMB 20 trillion ($3 trillion) in new credit for the same nominal GDP growth.[5]

Much of China's investment surge has been and remains in infrastructure, which accounts regularly for between a quarter and a third of fixed asset investment. As any visitor to China knows by looking around, China commits a lot of resources to roads, railways, airports, bridges, tunnels and other projects that contribute to urbanisation and modern living. For example, by 2017, China had built over 124,000 kilometres of railway lines, of which about a fifth comprised high-speed track, or roughly 60 per cent of the world's total.

The 13th Five-Year Plan provides for a 50 per cent rise in the construction of high-speed track, as part of a RMB 15 trillion transportation infrastructure expansion covering rail, roads, civil aviation and water transportation. China also plans to expand the number of airports in the country from 206 to 272 by 2020, half as many again as existed in 2011. Beijing's second international airport is expected to open in June 2019, complete with seven runways and the capacity to process 72 million passengers a year.

Just 50 kilometres south of Beijing, moreover, in a backwater of Hebei province, there are plans to build a new megacity, called Xiong'an New Area, which is supposed to rival Shanghai and Shenzhen one day. It is thought that the project could attract 3–6 million people over the next decade, along with RMB 1–2 trillion of investment, making it the biggest single infrastructure project in the history of modern China.[6]

Yet, for all these and similar statistics, there is also a litany of stories about ghost towns with empty apartment blocs and few residents, lonely and underused airports in impoverished counties of China, empty roads, the chronic overcapacity of multiple transportation projects to the same access point, and industrial zones that are barely occupied, and to which foreign companies rarely go.[7]

It is all very well to argue that, in the long run, more people living in more cities will gradually chip away at the overcapacity in infrastructure. They might, but it matters if that infrastructure is uncommercial. Meanwhile, Chinese infrastructure keeps getting built, and debt keeps being issued to finance it. One report found that cost over-runs in Chinese infrastructure construction were equivalent to about a third of the country's outstanding debt, or about $8–9 trillion. The report's authors looked into ninety-five road and rail projects undertaken between 1984 and 2008, and confirmed that while China can hardly be beaten when it comes to speed of decision-making on infrastructure, it lags well behind others when it comes to the quality, safety and environmental effects of projects, and many only receive paltry levels of traffic.[8]

These examples of investment inefficiency and misallocation of capital suggest that, sooner or later, the investment rate is going to come down, either in a managed fashion or otherwise. The last time that China experienced a double-digit decline in the share of investment in GDP was between 1993 and 2000 when it dropped from over 43 to around 34 per cent. During this period, economic growth fell back from almost 14 per cent to about 8.5 per cent. If the government rebalances China successfully, we should expect growth to slow significantly.

Managing a growth slowdown in the next decade or so is likely to prove a challenging task for China's political leaders. There will be no export boom from WTO membership as there was in the 1990s. The 45 per cent starting point for the investment share of GDP is higher now. The growth rate is lower than then, and the debt to GDP ratio of around 300 per cent is nearly three times as big as it was in 1993.

It is helpful that the share of service producing industries in GDP is rising, as is the contribution of service sector growth to GDP, which is gaining slowly at the expense of industry and construction. Between 2000 and 2016, for example, the share of services in GDP rose from nearly 40 to over 51 per cent in nominal or money terms, while the share of industry and construction dropped from over 45 to about 40 per cent. The differences are much less pronounced when adjusting for changes in prices in both services and industry but it is clear that China is changing, and the official goal is to boost the services share of the economy to 60 per cent by 2025.

Service industries are more labour-intensive and help to tilt the economy more to consumption. Services are also less energy-intensive, and this helps public policy on the environment and pollution. On the other hand, China's service industries are dominated by 'old' services such as wholesaling, transportation, and finance and real estate. The last two have reached a high plateau, and are in the front line for retrenchment as the government tries to tame property markets and risk-taking in financial services. China needs to deregulate and open and develop new service capacity and participants in the information, communications and professional sectors, as well as in health and education.

Paving the way for reform

Anti-corruption doesn't normally figure as one of the leading edges of economic reform, but in China's case it has been important, not so much to purge political opponents, which it undoubtedly has, but as a major weapon of governance. Designed to bolster the power, discipline and legitimacy of the Communist Party, and underpin the centralisation of authority, Xi's campaign has tried to enforce compliance and obedience all the way from the top, and down through lower levels of government and administration.

The campaign actually started before Xi came to power. At the Party school in Beijing in March 2012, Vice-President Xi spoke at length on the very familiar Leninist topic of 'party purity', which is about the integrity, reputation and effectiveness of Party members at all levels. Cadres were told to take their Marxism seriously and to carry out the programmes, regulations and policies of the Party, and shun all interest in personal gain and influence. Xi insisted that party purity was essential if China was to succeed in building a prosperous society, implementing reform and changing the development model. Put into practice by the extra-legal Central Commission for Discipline Inspection, the anti-corruption campaign subsequently targeted over 200,000 'tigers and flies', that is high- and lower-level officials in the Party, People's Liberation Army (PLA) and state enterprise system.

Some notable victims of the campaign include Bo Xilai, former governor of Chongqing, who was at one stage seen as a rival to Xi Jinping, and Zhou Yongkang, former Minister of Public Security and member of the Politburo Standing Committee. Other senior victims have included a former general in the PLA and other officers, top officials in SOEs, and high-ranking local and provincial government officials.

Yet serious questions have been raised about the effectiveness of the campaign and whether, in the absence of transparency and formal and independent judicial oversight, it is just papering over some, but by no means all, of the cracks of official corruption. In one study, for example, it was revealed that between 2012 and 2015, fewer than 36,000 Party members, or 0.5 per cent of officials working during those years, were referred to the courts for prosecution, and that of the 750,000 people disciplined by the Party, just 35,000 were arrested or prosecuted.[9] Nevertheless, there is little question that the anti-corruption campaign has changed behaviour and influenced governance. The question is, how?

Optimists argue that the campaign will ultimately have positive effects on economic growth because it should lead to better and more efficient public servants, managers and business enterprises, and to more compliant officials and better implementation of economic reforms. Yet, this may be more political rhetoric than judgement. The centralisation of power around the person of President Xi Jinping and around the Party has contributed to indecision and inertia lower down the hierarchy, and may have stifled, rather than stimulated, reform by creating a risky environment for officials to take initiatives or actions for which they might later be blamed or punished.

Under Xi, the Communist Party has, in effect, usurped the machinery of government as far as the process and implementation of reform is concerned. Leading Small Groups (LSG), which are certainly not small and the most important of which are chaired by President Xi, are the main (Party) agents of economic decision-making nowadays. The LSG processes, however, become highly political and are obfuscated by multiple participants and committees. It is often unclear who actually makes final decisions, and there is little transparency about the criteria for evaluating policy choices. The outcomes of economic policy-making have often led to policies that are 'not effectively specified or implemented, and a pattern of erratic and inconsistent policy commitments'.[10] The implications of the politicisation of governance, as I shall explain further in discussing governance issues related to the middle-income trap in Chapter 7, are of great significance.

Third plenum ambitions

In November 2013, the third plenum of the 18th Congress of the Central Committee issued a report entitled 'The Decision on Major Issues Concerning Comprehensively Deepening Reforms'. It laid out 60 broad points, broken down into 338 initiatives, designed to lead to, among other things, better resource allocation, a 'decisive' role for markets, public sector efficiency gains, and a more robust private sector. There was, though, and there remains a major contradiction, between a 'decisive role for markets' and the continuing parallel objective of a 'dominant role for the state'. Since then, the depth of that contradiction has, if anything, sharpened, with the result that reforms have had a mixed impact, at best.

The Party's ambition to make material headway in environmental policies with a view to lowering pollution, and to promote Chinese innovation rather than taking items off the global shelf, has had some success. Less than two years after the third plenum, China launched Made in China 2025, an industrial policy strategy that sets the country on a path to speed up and realise major changes in modern and advanced manufacturing with a strong emphasis on Chinese prowess and origination.[11] We will look at Chinese industrial policy a little more in Chapter 7 when considering options to avoid the middle-income trap.

The goal of financial liberalisation has been pursued by and large, though with some setbacks since 2015. Yet in other areas, reform progress has been disappointing, or actually gone into reverse. These include SOE reform, land reform, hukou reform, social security reform and a slew of proposals to change policies affecting investment, competition and the central–local government division of fiscal responsibilities and new forms of raising revenue. Water scarcity, which is increasingly pressing, is hardly aired as a matter of urgency. Some of these issues are examined below.

One reform that was announced with great fanfare and which was fairly simple to implement was the decision to formally abandon the one-child policy, introduced in 1979. It was formalised in 2015. There had always been some exceptions to the policy, and the most intrusive acts by the state into the lives of citizens faded away many years ago. Nevertheless, the policy had been a hallmark of China's population control policy, and its removal was long overdue. As explained in the previous chapter, China's fertility rate fell even before the one-child policy was introduced. The policy, though, did have a significant effect on gender imbalance. The ratio of male to female births for first children rose to 121 boys per 100 girls in 2004 before starting to decline slowly to about 113 boys in 2016.

With the change of policy, births rose. In 2016, 45 per cent of couples who already had a child had a second one, compared with 30 per cent in 2013.[12] Roughly 1.8 million more babies were born in 2016 than in 2015, a rise of more than 8 per cent. Yet the mini baby boom was short-lived, as the number of newborns dropped in 2017 back to levels that had prevailed in prior years. As we shall see in Chapter 6, it is hard to lift the fertility rate in China, as it is elsewhere. Two-child or other fertility-friendly policies are up against a very powerful form of contraception, called rising income per head.

Financial reforms advanced

Financial reforms have generally been pursued without much political opposition, and consistently with the support of the People's Bank of China, whose head Zhou Xiaochuan stepped down in 2018. Interest rate liberalisation was completed in 2015, along with the introduction of a deposit insurance system. In terms of the domestic finance sector, however, we should also note that the authorities have not totally abandoned what is called 'window guidance' to banks to boost or lower lending, and banks have not abandoned discriminatory lending terms and arrangements for state enterprises. Nevertheless, in general the liberalisation of China's financial markets has helped to spawn innovation, greater inter-connectedness between institutions, and more sophisticated financial products. These changes are widely viewed as a positive to the extent that they lower transaction and financing costs, enhance the flow of credit, and strengthen the process of intermediation, or transference of deposits into productive use.

On the other hand, we also know that financial innovation has often been the harbinger of instability, and of complex challenges for the regulatory authorities. China is witnessing both the positive and negative aspects of such innovation. Between 2015 and 2017, the central bank and regulatory authorities had to deal with a stock-market crash, exchange-rate instability, currency-reserve depletion and capital flight, and then they had to backtrack on many of the liberalisation initiatives as they proceeded to implement a regulatory crackdown in 2017.

Liberalisation of the exchange rate over the years has proceeded in fits and starts, culminating in the adoption in 2014 of trading bands that were 2 percentage points either side of a daily central rate, the admission in 2015 of the Renminbi to the IMF's Special Drawing Rights and, in the same year, the announcement that the Renminbi would be managed not only against the US dollar, but also against a new basket of currencies. China's long-standing intention to have a fully convertible currency, and to have a flexible currency, however, does not necessarily mean that the authorities are getting any closer to having a floating exchange rate. Indeed, if anything, the activities of the People's Bank suggest that a free float is not on the agenda anytime soon.

Liberalisation of the capital account has a mixed scorecard. Inward and outward flows are controlled by the Qualified Foreign Institutional Investors, and Renminbi Qualified Institutional Investors quotas, and the Qualified Domestic Institutional Investors ceiling, respectively. The government's approach to inward capital movements is much more relaxed than it is to outward movements. To support the former, China established the Shanghai Free Trade Zone (FTZ) in 2013, and this was joined by other FTZs in Tianjin, Guangdong and Fujian. The Shanghai–Hong Kong Stock Connect scheme was launched in November 2014 to facilitate greater equity market inflows from global investors with accounts in Hong Kong. The Shanghai market is dominated by banks and industrial and state-owned enterprises. Following this, a Shenzhen–Hong Kong Connect scheme started up at the end of 2016, giving global investors access to the more private sector-oriented and technology and other emerging-sector stocks listed on that exchange. Both schemes allow investors to buy up to a certain quota via their brokerage accounts in Hong Kong without prior approval. While both schemes kicked off with an enthusiastic response from investors, interest soon fell away with investors using only a small fraction of the permitted quotas.

Another attempt to lure foreign capital into China was launched in June 2017 with the China–Hong Kong Bond Connect scheme. This allows global investors to access China's $11 trillion (and growing) bond market, the world's third largest after the US and Japan. It is a market dominated by banks and policy development banks, and also by central and local government. Corporations accounted for about a fifth of bonds outstanding at the launch. Although the Chinese bond market may prove more interesting to foreigners in the future, it is not very effective in pricing credit. The vast majority of issues have some kind of government backing, the incidence of default is still quite low though more are being permitted, and local credit rating agencies tend to assign top ratings to most issues. These and other shortcomings are highlighted in Chapter 5.

When it comes to capital outflows, on the other hand, China has always been more vigilant. Capital outflow restrictions have always been an integral part of the overall financial system and, notwithstanding the official rhetoric over twenty-five years about liberalisation, the authorities are still very cagey about allowing Chinese residents free rein to move money overseas, and that goes as much for companies as for individuals.

In spite of this more restrictive environment, Chinese companies and citizens have found ways to get money out of China into Hong Kong and Macau, and much further afield into property markets and luxury goods vendors in the Western world. Capital flight from China became a serious problem in 2015–16, prompting the authorities to tighten supervision of capital transactions and regulations governing the flow of foreign currency outside China. The array of measures taken at that time to stabilise financial markets, currency reserves, capital flows and the Renminbi were a clear demonstration of China's limited tolerance for markets to work freely. This was seen again in 2017 when the financial authorities tightened the controls on the ability of people and companies to send money and capital overseas, restricted banks from providing foreign exchange to companies looking to finance activities overseas, and started scrutinising the activities of companies looking to make foreign acquisitions much more closely, or stopped them altogether.

SOE reforms stalled

Officially, and according to some China-watchers, SOEs now account for just a fifth of output and a tenth of employment. The presumption, though, that the rest of the economy is in private hands, as we understand it in the West, is incorrect. Many private firms have large or majority state owners, who exercise significant control over senior appointments and corporate strategy, and state ownership is often disguised by multiple layers of investment companies ultimately owned by a state entity. Allowing for these opaque adjustments, the purely private part of the enterprise sector may actually be little higher than 20–30 per cent. It is important to bear this in mind while recognising that SOEs still retain a prominence which distinguishes them from their peers, say, in other emerging countries, such as India, Brazil, Russia and South Africa.

Some SOEs, mostly those in coal and steel, are under pressure now to cut capacity, merge and become more efficient. Yet others are being urged to become even more engaged in the economy as national champions in technology and as agents of investment and employment creation. SOE reform, as we saw in the last chapter, was undertaken with commitment and resolve in the 1990s, and many enterprises were privatised. No such commitment was adopted at the third plenum in 2013, though the intention to reform SOEs to make them more efficient and perhaps more significant was spelled out very clearly.

The lack of meaningful progress, however, does call into question what the government may actually want to achieve. It has been pointed out, for example, that the political command of an urban elite with a strong commitment to state control long ago changed China, leading to a strong SOE-centric economic structure, which was always going to have a number of key characteristics: the state would always retain the 'commanding heights'; the lines between private and state companies would become increasingly blurred; and foreign companies would be welcomed either for their technology or their venture-capital expertise.[13] And this pretty much describes China's industrial structure today.

SOEs remain at the heart of this structure, even though they officially account for about 10–15 per cent of total employment, and represent just 15–20 per cent of the total number of enterprises, excluding sole proprietorships. They account for 9 of the top 10 firms, and for about 40 per cent of enterprise assets. Indeed, while their numbers have been shrinking, the assets they represent have risen sixfold since 2000, from about RMB

20 trillion ($3 trillion) to roughly RMB 120 trillion ($18.5 trillion) in 2015. They are financially less efficient, more leveraged, and less profitable. Their sales revenue amounts to 35 per cent of GDP, but they account for only 3 per cent of enterprise profits, and half of all bank credit.[14]

About a fifth of SOEs are in key sectors such as electricity, oil and coal, communications, aviation and shipping, and a quarter are industrial with interests in machinery, automobiles, electronics, construction, metals and chemicals. Most of the remainder are in social services, education and health, sports, real estate and other sectors.[15] China is becoming increasingly active in fortifying the role that SOEs play in advanced manufacturing and the new industries in which it hopes to develop global leadership.

The 2013 SOE reform proposals nourished hopes that the raison d'être for state ownership would become more transparent, and that they would mandate a marked improvement in corporate governance. Yet, very little of substance really emerged from the four agencies supposed to be responsible for SOE reform, perhaps partly because their agendas were full of contradictions.

The State-owned Assets Supervision and Administration Commission of the State Council (SASAC), which manages around a hundred SOEs under the supervision of the central government (as opposed to the many more under the supervision of local governments), wanted to build globally competitive SOEs. The Finance Ministry wanted bigger dividend pay-outs from SOEs, and state asset management firms to run SOEs. The National Development and Reform Commission's interest was in mixed ownership. The Ministry of Human Resources and Social Security was concerned about compensation and pay differentials.[16]

Another modernising initiative, mixed ownership, didn't really plant roots. It sought to introduce private shareholders, and initiatives to expose SOE oligopolies to more competition, but has proven to be limited, disappointing or has effectively been discarded. Instead, policy became more focused on consolidations and mergers, designed to avoid awkward restructuring decisions and to bolster SOEs as national champions. In any event, President Xi Jinping favours bigger, stronger and better SOEs, evidenced, for example, by his backing of a former head of Chinalco, China's major aluminium company, Xiao Yaqing, as chairman of SASAC.[17]

The investment companies that were gradually supposed to take over supervisory functions for SOEs had extremely broad, ill-defined and interventionist mandates, and the guidelines backtracked on the third plenum's call for 'marketisation'. A number of confusing and conflicting objectives were adopted instead. For example, it was proposed that state capital be injected into important industries, but also to prioritise several key areas where SOEs had no track record or special expertise, such as national security, people's livelihoods, innovation-driven development, and advanced manufacturing.

With the adoption of the 2015 'Guiding Opinions of the Central Committee of the Communist Party of China and the State Council on Deepening State-Owned Enterprise Reform' document, the hopes for SOE reform expressed at the third plenum were effectively shelved. The fault-lines were unsurprising: it wasn't possible to gloss over the differences between 'market forces' and a 'dominant role' for SOEs, and the nitty-gritty details of SOE reform were allocated to too many institutions that sought to preserve the status quo.

Initiatives to reform SOEs, inaugurated in 2017, were built around four main themes, but in all cases they were more about continuing existing practice than new ways of making SOEs profitable or market-oriented. The four themes were: adopting corporate structures such as limited liability or joint stock structures for the 10 per cent of SOEs that had not yet been restructured; mergers; mixed ownership; and the creation of state capital investment and operation companies, or SCIOs.

Mergers, which were intended to reduce the number of central SOEs from 101 to fewer than 80, have been ongoing for many years, but it is worth noting that the total number of SOEs has risen sharply since 2010 from just short of 120,000 to about 170,000, largely due to local government entities, notably local government financing vehicles.[18] Some of the major mergers include China's two largest train builders, CNR and CSR, which formed the largest rolling stock company in the world; China Power Investment Corporation and State Nuclear Technology Corporation; China Ocean Shipping Group and China Shipping Group; China International Travel Service Group and China National Travel Service (HK) Group; China Metallurgical Group and China Minmetals Group; Baosteel and Wuhan Iron and Steel; and ChinaChem and Sinochem, which will form the world's largest chemicals company.

SCIOs looked at one stage as though they might be the most promising initiative, copying the very successful model represented by Temasek in Singapore, a state holding company that manages state companies, for example Singapore Airlines, mandating them to make profits and deliver good returns to their most important shareholder, the government of Singapore. Yet the Chinese government's plans for SCIOs are quite dissimilar. Loaded with cheap capital and functioning like state-directed private equity firms, they are supposed to identify and fund companies or industries of which their political bosses approve, especially in modern technology sectors, but without concern for commercial viability or profit. Analysts worry that the state is on a new mission that will crowd out private investors, 'hogging capital and allocating it poorly'.[19]

Fu Chengyu, a former chief of Sinopec, China's major petrochemicals company, reflecting on the state of play regarding SOE reform, said that the government was too focused on reforming the supervision of state assets and enterprises rather than on the SOEs themselves, including their management and operating systems. Moreover, the idea of mixed owner-ship and the introduction of market mechanisms hadn't really got off the ground, and innovation could not be 'ordered' from the top down. Fu went on to identify a crucial agency problem, in which the government is owner and manager. He said this has created a discordant situation that is frus-trating reform: what the government wants to change is very difficult to change, while what enterprises want to change they dare not change.[20]

Residual hopes for governance reform were certainly dealt a major blow when SASAC published an article in *Qiushi*, a Party magazine, in which it argued that the diminishing role of the Communist Party in SOEs should be reversed, and that it should have real power in key decisions, manage-ment appointments, and matters of political and corporate culture. It also said that 'party construction' in SOEs should be a key performance indi-cator for managers, and that all key SOE decisions should be reviewed and approved by Party committees before being submitted to the Board of Directors.[21]

It seems, therefore, that in Xi's China, technocrats, who were previously at the helm of SOE policy and management, are increasingly giving way to political apparatchiks and officials. This does not bode well for the future of SOE reform, and suggests that they will become bigger and more focused on political strategy than on commercial efficiency.

Land and Hukou

Rural land reform has been an ongoing feature of Chinese economic devel-opment going back to Mao but its significance continues to rise in a country where urbanisation is growing quickly. Although the rural population amounts to just 44 per cent of the total, compared with 64 per cent in 2000, and 82 per cent in 1978, over 600 million people are still classified as comprising the rural population. Their significance in Chinese society and in the economy remains considerable.

Land reform is not only about efficiency in the countryside on farms and in rural enterprises, but is an essential component of China's urbanisation strategy. In recent years, land reform and urbanisation strategies have been rolled out slowly and in pilot form. The cities of Chengdu and Chongqing were selected several years ago, for example, and have generally won favourable plaudits from the Chinese government and the World Bank for more efficient land use, enterprise start-ups, and controlled sales of land-usage by farmers.[22] Yet, the widening out of these pilot projects has not been extensive or purposeful.

Part of the problem is that everyone wants cheap land over which the government has monopoly ownership: property developers, industries including SOEs, and local and provincial governments, which rely on land sales for about a third of their annual revenues. These vested interests will not willingly part with their privileges or wealth. It has been estimated, for example, that local governments expropriated rural land between 1990 and 2010 at a cost of RMB 2 trillion (roughly $300 billion) below market value. Had this compensation generated returns similar to economic growth, famers would have been RMB 5 trillion better off.[23] Offering farmers and their families the chance of better financial security, land ownership rights, and the right to migrate and then return to family plots and so on would help to make for more successful rural development and urbanisation, but these measures would conflict with so much current practice that these vested interests will be reluctant to contemplate change.

There have also been mixed outcomes in reform initiatives involving China's system of household registration or 'hukou', affecting China's 277.5 million migrants. Having urban hukou allows migrants in cities to access public services such as education, health, housing and pensions. It follows that not having urban hukou breaks up families, caps social mobility, and, from a macroeconomic standpoint, limits significantly the scope for expanding aggregate consumption in the economy. Given that migrants constitute 36 per cent of the workforce, marginalising them is a major economic shortcoming.

Introduced in 1958 to restrict the flow of rural migrants to China's cities, the hukou system remains very much in place. Changes occurred following the tragic death in 2003 of a migrant, Sun Zhigang, who had been detained by police in Guangzhou.[24] Until then, migrants caught without hukou permits could be and often were evicted, but following the incident involving Sun, this practice was abolished and migrants no longer needed a permit per se to work and live in cities legally. Nevertheless, migrants still needed a permit to have access to social services and welfare.

A new policy, adopted in 2014, set up a single national resident registration for both rural and urban citizens, and attempted to steer rural migrants away from larger cities towards small- and medium-sized conurbations. The larger the city, the more scope the local authorities have to set stricter settlement criteria, and the largest cities are actually urged to control population inflows very tightly. The strict link between hukou status and welfare entitlement isn't as strict as it was, but the goal of allowing access to services for long-term residents still leaves the ball in the court of local authorities in so far as fulfilling the criteria for long-term residents is concerned, and these authorities are in any case constrained by both political will and resources.

The 2014 change was certainly a step towards making significant strides in land and hukou reform. Yet much more needs to be done. The authorities need to provide for the security, land and ownership rights of rural migrants as the next stages of urbanisation proceed. Moreover, while it is a positive that migrants will find it easier to settle in smaller towns, the fact is that they are attracted mostly by the life and employment opportunities of the larger cities that are tend to be less willing to take them. Around 60 per cent of China's migrant workers are located in the eastern provinces.

The State Council's new regulations leave cities considerable 'wiggle room' in setting income, tax and residency standards that few migrants meet. Local governments and cities focusing on immediate costs, rather than medium-term paybacks, don't want to shoulder the financial burden of expanding benefits to migrants, while those urban residents with hukou are resistant to the idea of having to share their privileges and possibly the costs with a wider universe of recipients. Somehow, though, China has to find a way of changing the status quo, and that is going to cost money that Beijing, or a broad property tax system, will have to provide.

Energy and water

Energy, or specifically China's commitment to a cleaner environment, is a key goal that has top billing by Xi and the Party. Water, or rather water scarcity, doesn't, and yet in important ways, it is as, if not more, significant. Both are important in the rebalancing and reform agenda, not least because of the threats to growth and to China's development that they may pose if unaddressed.

Xi Jinping has expressed the government's intention to address two key problems in China: environmental degradation and pollution. In his long speech to the 19th Congress, he opened his remarks on the topic by saying that any harm 'we inflict on nature will eventually return to haunt us'. For the time being, grainy images of Beijing or Shanghai will continue to circulate around the world on bad smog days, but China certainly seems to want to be seen as a leader on climate-friendly policies. It has committed to greenhouse gas and clean energy development targets that require a fall in the energy intensity of economic growth of 40–45 per cent below 2005 levels by 2020, and 60–65 per cent by 2030.

Slower economic growth, successful rebalancing and emission reductions that have already been achieved suggest that China could continue to make progress in combatting not only global warming but, as importantly, the pollution of land, soil and water that has blighted China's economy and society in the past dash for growth.

The proof of the pudding will lie partly in China's investment in clean energy, and the rigorous implementation of regulatory and administrative measures affecting the environment. At the same time, China will also have to demonstrate a willingness to embrace continuous coal production capacity and usage cutbacks, markets in carbon trading, and measures to relieve water scarcity and improve the distribution and efficiency of water allocation.

China's attempts to improve its carbon footprint and turn its back on pollution-oriented growth are mixed. It has cancelled numerous new coal-fired power plants and shut down capacity, but announced cutbacks in capacity often fall short of actual shut-downs. There have been several examples of over-ambitious or ill-thought-out plans to cut coal-fired power or switch to natural gas that have either had to be reversed or postponed because of disruption, inadequate heating supplies, or a failure to allow for the development of alternative energy infrastructure. In a further example of good plans that haven't quite lived up to expectations, China invested over $78 billion in renewable energy in 2016 (more than either the US or the EU), but a considerable amount of its wind and solar power capacity lies idle.

Although water distribution and usage systems are being improved, the structural problem of water scarcity, in the north of China especially, remains acute. Indeed, over the next decade or two, water scarcity could develop to become one of the most significant constraints on China's economic development.[25] In 2016, each Beijing resident had access to just 178 cubic metres of water (nationally, 438 cubic metres), compared to a United Nations benchmark of 'water stress' of 1,700 cubic metres.

The major problem in China is not water availability in aggregate but the distribution, with four-fifths of the water in the south, and twelve northern provinces suffering various degrees of water scarcity. The Beijing, Tianjin and Hebei region, with over 120 million people, has less water per head than Saudi Arabia. China's water-intensive coal industry and big agricultural centres are predominantly in areas of high water scarcity. Falling groundwater levels, diminishing supplies from lakes and major northern rivers, collapsing aquifers and pollution are slowly but surely aggravating China's looming water crisis. Nearly 60 per cent of underground water is believed to be polluted.[26]

Yet water figures almost nowhere in the policy and political rhetoric of Chinese leaders. There is a huge policy agenda which the government should be articulating and implementing to conserve water, improve water infrastructure, distribution and quality and, ultimately, bolster availability. Water may lack the perceived relevance of debt and finance as growth and development constraints, but in the end countries can survive the kind of crises these cause and move on. With water, and its connections to agriculture, food supply and prices, power generation and economic activity, such assurances are much more questionable.

What now for reform?

In May 2016, the *People's Daily* front-page interview with an 'authoritative person' represented a strong pitch that China should stick with reforms and shift away from a debt-oriented economic model.[27] The commitment to supply-side structural reforms was repeatedly confirmed both before and after the Party's 19th Congress, but it is important to note that what China means by supply-side reforms is quite different from what this means in Western parlance.

In the West, we take supply-side reforms to mean deregulation, greater competition, and other policies designed to release labour market and enterprise initiatives which boost growth and productivity. Chinese supply-side reforms don't mean this at all. They are sometimes aimed at boosting small- and medium-size enterprises, but in the main, they comprise policies affecting bureaucracy, administration and regulation that have the objectives of strengthening SOEs, reducing capacity in industries such as coal and steel, which have undermined SOE profitability and efficiency, and, more recently, improving the quality of the environment and bolstering state-driven policies to propel China's industrial policies forward in new and advanced industries. In this sense, therefore, we can say that China has achieved some successes with supply-side reforms. Nothing, however, has been done or will be done to rebalance the Party's control and the dominance of state enterprises towards liberal, market-oriented reforms.

In the next few years, successful economic rebalancing will have to entail a willingness to accept four important things: markedly slower economic growth; an active and sustained campaign to reduce leverage in the economy and the financial system; a focus on reducing income inequality and strengthening the social safety net; and the adoption of economic incentives and regulations to move the economy's balance away from investment and towards consumption and new service-producing industries.

Support for the consumer sector could be strengthened by creating new jobs in services and building up the social security and healthcare coverage safety nets. Such policies would most likely help to lower household savings, accelerating a change that will probably happen anyway over time as China ages. The working-age population is now in decline, and the old-age dependency ratio is predicted to double between 2017 and 2030. Social benefits should rise and be extended to all working people and their families. The growth in services should be actively encouraged, both in megacities such as Beijing or Shanghai, which are already well served, but also and importantly in other cities, especially those inland, which are not.[28] Modern service industries, which remain relatively closed, could be deregulated and opened up, for example in a wide range of communication, professional, business, entertainment and information services.

Income inequality should be lowered across both income groups and regions. China has a relatively high Gini coefficient (a measure of income inequality between 0 and 1, where, theoretically, a reading of 0 means that income is equally shared by all, and a reading of 1 means income accrues to just 1 person). The latest data from official sources in China revealed a Gini coefficient of 0.47 in 2015, compared with 0.3 in the 1980s. Gini coefficients around 0.3–0.4 are generally thought to be high. Another measure of income inequality shows that 1 per cent of Chinese households own a third of the country's wealth, while just 1 per cent of wealth is owned by the bottom 25 per cent.[29]

Rebalancing is complex and Xi's China will be unwilling to adopt many of the reform proposals and suggestions that Western thinking normally urges. The irony is that many of China's prominent leaders understand fully the dynamic role that private sector and more liberal markets play. Yet there is no chance that they will, given the prevailing political environment, be deployed to rebalance the role and function of the state vis-à-vis the private sector or sanction the transfer of wealth from the state to the private sector.

In Xi's China, the private sector is going to succumb to much greater intrusion by the Party. Since 2015, the Party has been extending its organisational and ideological reach formally into the operational management of not just SOEs but also private and foreign firms, which are expected to align with the Party-state's industrial planning objectives. There will be more capital intrusion as the state 'puts equity to work' in private companies. There will be more direct intrusion as the government intervenes in what they may do overseas, for example, or, as in the case of Anbang Insurance, takes it over 'temporarily'.

For the time being, though, the major focus is going to remain on financial stability. The government should take a strong, proactive role by encouraging the deleveraging of the corporate and local government sectors, and ensuring that credit growth is lowered to levels below the rate of GDP growth in money terms. Stabilising the rise in debt, and then managing the economy through the deleveraging, are going to be of the utmost significance. The manner in which this happens, and the length of time it takes, are liable to determine whether China faces a necessary but manageable economic slowdown, or a riskier outcome that might entail a recession, or even systemic financial risk. It is the debt trap.

4

DEBT TRAP

In 1999, after many years in which banks had extended loans aggressively to weak state-owned enterprises (SOEs), and following the large-scale restructuring and closure of many SOEs, the Chinese government had to deal with a serious problem. The major banks were riddled with bad loans, or so-called 'non-performing' loans, which amounted to roughly 40 per cent of their total lending. The government set up four asset management companies, or what are colloquially called 'bad banks', to buy up many of these bad loans.

In the event, about half the bad loans were transferred to these new institutions in 1999–2000, amounting to about a hefty 18 per cent of GDP at the time.[1] Additional loans were transferred in subsequent years. China's bank rescue programme helped to unclog the balance sheets of the big banks, but what really happened was a sort of financial pass-the-parcel, with bad loans simply being moved around the state financial system. Although China's bad banks were based on the successful Swedish banking sector rescue introduced in the early 1990s, they never worked as well. They were supposed to dispose of the bad loans over ten years but they still own a significant proportion of them to this day.

It is important to keep this in mind as we consider China's current debt issues, for five reasons. First, the scale of the excessive lending and debt accumulation is far larger than in the 1990s. Second, the big four banks account for about a quarter of total financial assets today, compared with over three-fifths in the earlier crisis. The risks, in other words, are more diffuse today. Third, there are now about thirty-five bad banks, or asset management companies, including local and provincial government-backed firms, and while no one really knows how large the bad loan problem is nowadays, it is bound to get worse when the economy slows down more significantly. Fourth, China's credit expansion cycle has been going on without serious interruption for an unprecedented fifteen years. When the credit cycle ends, the consequences could be far-reaching. Fifth, China's economy has become increasingly credit-dependent. Economic growth might have been about 25 per cent lower than officially recorded between 2012 and 2017 but for the contribution made by credit expansion.

This chapter, then, takes a deep dive into the weeds of finance with a focus on China's debt and debtors, banks and so-called shadow banks, different types of banking sector fragility, and what the government has been trying to do since 2017 with Xi Jinping's personal authority to keep systemic risk at bay. The issue that many are inclined to forget is that, sooner or later, someone always has to pay for bad debt and banking sector problems. It's just a question of when and how the costs are allocated among consumers, companies, the government and, sometimes, foreign creditors. It all ends up as lower economic growth, one way or another.

Accumulation of debt

China's debt problem started to get worse in 2008 when China's attention was elsewhere, including a terrible earthquake in Sichuan province in May, which claimed the lives of 90,000 people, and the coming Beijing Olympics. By the time the Games started, however, with Beijing skies clear and blue following the temporary shutdown of coal-fired power stations and other smokestack industries, another ominous crisis was brewing.

By late summer, tens of thousands of factories in the export-focused coastal provinces had closed because of flagging demand. Hundreds of thousands of workers were laid off, several million migrant workers went back to the countryside, and up to a quarter of China's 6 million new graduates were unable to find a job.[2] In early November, the State Council urgently put together an economic stimulus package, valued at Renminbi (RMB) 4 trillion, or $586 billion – the equivalent of 14 per cent of GDP. The government's plan was a two-year boost to spending on affordable housing, infrastructure, public health and education, the environment and innovation. Regulatory measures affecting the property market were relaxed to stimulate demand. The bulk of new spending was financed not by government borrowing, but by a surge in bank lending.

The cyclical boost worked. The economy bottomed out at a growth rate of a little over 4 per cent, and by 2011 double-digit growth returned, albeit briefly. Between 2008 and 2012, the state sector increased borrowing so that debt as a share of GDP rose by 35 percentage points to reach 170 per cent of GDP. If that had been the end of the story, China's subsequent economic and financial history would have been quite different.

China's addiction to debt, though, had only just begun. By the middle of 2016, just four years later, the ratio of debt to GDP had risen to 255 per cent of GDP, and by the end of 2017, it was over 300 per cent of GDP. A recent audit and analysis of China's debt has estimated the stock of debt then stood at 329 per cent of GDP.[3] In fact, the surge in China's debt was so big that it accounted for the bulk of the build-up in global debt, which, according to the Institute for International Finance, rose from about $150 trillion in 2007 to $233 trillion in late 2017. China accounted for about a half of all new credit created worldwide between 2005 and 2016.[4]

The size of China's debt and the speed with which it has accumulated make China a prime candidate for future instability in the eyes of many independent observers and institutions. The IMF and Bank for International Settlements have pointed to the sharp rise in what they call the 'credit gap', a measure of how far credit as a share of GDP is deviating from its long-run trend line. They say that a sustained and significant increase in the credit gap tends to forewarn of financial crises. Out of forty-three countries studied since the 1960s, the IMF found that where the credit gap rose to 30 per cent or more in a five-year period, all but five of the sample countries went on to experience a financial crisis, a sharp slowdown in growth, or both. China's credit gap reached 30 per cent in 2016, about the same, for example, as Japan in the 1980s, Thailand in the 1990s and Spain in the 2000s.[5] By the middle of 2017, the credit gap had fallen back to 18 per cent, lessening the risk of systemic instability slightly, but the gap was still almost twice as high as the threshold deemed to represent overheating.[6]

Apart from the speed of debt accumulation, it is worth noting also that China's debt ratio is far in excess of other countries with the same level of income per head. Yet, so far, China has muddled through, dampening down the concerns that many analysts have expressed in recent years that it was courting a financial crisis of some description. There was a period of acute financial instability in 2015–16 but this was related more to the equity market, the currency and capital movements, than to debt. There has been no sign of a systemic breakdown. With Xi Jinping now in power for the foreseeable future, does this mean that he and his colleagues will get a handle on the debt problem, show assorted Cassandras the errors of their ways, and prove that finance works differently in a state-owned financial system? Or is it simply that the build-up to and working-out of China's debt denouement are on a longer and more complex fuse than many people anticipated?

China's debtors

Chinese households have not typically been major borrowers by global standards, but they are becoming more important. Household debt has risen from about 40 per cent of disposable income in 2008 to 106 per cent in 2017, about the same as it is in the US. Much of the rise in the last several years has come not from conventional banks but from newer and less regulated financing companies. Debt has risen from about 20 to 43 per cent of GDP. The level was appreciably lower than in, say, the US or the UK, but higher than in Turkey, Mexico, India and Indonesia. China's middle class and urban population are turning increasingly to mortgages to fund real-estate ownership. Outstanding mortgage loans more than doubled between 2011 and 2016, with a significant acceleration after 2014, and again during 2017.[7] Household borrowing, defined more broadly than just simple mortgages, may already have reached about 60 per cent of GDP, and on current trends, it could be on course to reach US-type levels of around 90 per cent of GDP by 2020.[8]

For now, then, China is not a classic example of overextended borrowers to whom banks have lent too much for the acquisition of property. There is no cause for complacency, however, because the boom in housing construction has permeated the economy. Investment in real estate in China has risen to about 15 per cent of GDP, compared with 6 per cent in the US in 2007. Many people worry that the Chinese real-estate market embeds distortions that make it vulnerable to an economic slowdown or other disruptions to house prices and orderly financial flows.

Local governments have a monopoly over land supply and have a vested interest in high prices to finance about a third of their spending. Households see real estate as the major alternative to bank deposits as a form of savings and wealth formation. If real-estate prices were to drop back significantly one day, the consequences would be far-reaching, not least because China has never experienced a significant fall in national real-estate prices. Banks would be hit by a rise in non-performing loans, lower profits and weaker capital protection. The value of real-estate collateral in transactions that encompass both property and non-property deals would fall. Highly leveraged, smaller real estate developers, as well as joint stock and city commercial banks would be especially exposed to losses. Lower real-estate prices would have ripple effects on the real economy and asset quality, and back again.

So far, the Chinese authorities have been diligent, keeping the market from overheating in general. Some major cities such as Shanghai, Guangzhou, Beijing and Shenzhen have recorded large price rises and, by early 2017, prices were on average 80 per cent higher than in the middle of 2010. Yet these four cities are China's equivalent of London or Manhattan. They are not representative of the country, and only account for about 10 per cent or so of real-estate-sector market activity. In any event, real estate prices in these cities weakened significantly towards the end of 2017 and in the first months of 2018.

Other cities, which are mainly provincial capitals and towns, account for the bulk of real-estate investment and home sales and completions. Prices in these places, labelled as Tier 2, 3, or 4 cities, have experienced lower price appreciation, but bore the brunt of the housing market slowdown in 2014–15, in which inventories of unsold homes soared to between twenty and forty months of supply. Gradually the oversupply was worked off, and prices started to rise again in 2017. Home-buyers are frequently hit by regulations affecting downpayments, some purchase restrictions, and mortgage rates, all designed to dampen down real-estate market activity and prices.

The bulk of China's non-financial-sector debt is owed by corporate and government entities. According to the IMF's annual economic survey of China, the so-called Article IV report, the central government is not, strictly speaking, a major borrower, with debt standing at just over 15 per cent of GDP at the end of 2016, but the accounting is opaque. Measured more broadly, it may be about three times as big. Most of the rest of the debt is owed by companies, some private, but largely SOEs, and local and provincial government administrations and borrowing platforms, which together amount to about 200 per cent of GDP.

Local governments have attracted a lot of interest, largely because they have been the agents, directly or otherwise, of a significant rise in debt, principally through local government financing vehicles (LGFVs). Several thousand were created in 2008–9 to implement the infrastructure and construction parts of the stimulus programme, partly because local governments have limited sources of tax revenues, tend to rely to a significant extent on land sales, and were restricted until 2014 from issuing bonds. More and more LGFVs have run into financial difficulties and debt-service problems as a result of the sheer weight of debt, slowing growth and diminishing asset returns from investment, but they continue to borrow in spite of Beijing's insistence that they should not.

Under significant budget reforms introduced in 2014, the debt owed by LGFVs was reconfigured as explicit government debt, and the central government authorised a bond swap programme to allow local governments to trade bank loans for somewhat cheaper and longer-term bonds. By the end of 2017, about RMB 11 trillion ($1.7 trillion), or roughly 66 per cent of formal local government liabilities, had been swapped.

What the central government trumpeted as an initiative to clean up and cheapen the outstanding LGFV debt problem, it discretely used, in effect, to allow new debt creation. The reforms authorised LGFVs to borrow on strict commercial criteria but they have continued to borrow, often in a new guise, for example as special or designated investment or construction platforms, or in so-called public–private partnerships where the private partners were SOEs or other state entities. According to the World Bank, LGFV liabilities rose by over 20 per cent per year between 2014 and 2016, even though they were supposed to be scaling back their debt.[9]

Bad debts

It is hard to get a reliable picture of how much bad debt the banks are sitting on, but some listed Chinese companies and local government entities are experiencing debt-service problems, that is, they are experiencing difficulties meeting their interest payment obligations and/or debt repayments. Officially, there is no obvious reason to worry about bad debts. The acknowledged ratio of non-performing loans in major Chinese banks is around 1.7 per cent of total assets, double what it was at the recent trough in 2011, but still quite low. Banks have even started attracting private equity funds, looking to buy distressed assets cheap. However, many analysts believe privately that these numbers understate the real scale of the problem.

For the sake of comparison, the share of non-performing loans in total loans in the US peaked at 6 per cent during the financial crisis, while in Europe it was comparable at the time, but then rose subsequently to reach around 8–9 per cent, though this included over 40 per cent in Greece, and 15–20 per cent in countries such as Italy, Portugal and Ireland.[10] In China, some private analysts have estimated that a realistic non-performing loan ratio estimate is around 22 per cent.[11] The IMF has estimated that risky corporate bank loans amount to about 15 per cent of all lending, confronting banks with potential losses of $756 billion, or 7 per cent of GDP.[12] The IMF also calculated in banking sector stress tests in 2017 that in extreme circumstances, the non-performing loan ratio at thirty-three banks would jump to 9 per cent, and they would have to raise a lot more capital.

It would certainly seem that Chinese banks, under the watchful eye of their regulators, are making hay while the sun shines – writing down or trying to dispose of bad debts and raising new capital while the economy is in good shape. Since 2017, moreover, the authorities have impressed on banks their concerns about risky loans and exposures held off-balance-sheet and in other places where capital adequacy regulations are lighter or don't apply. That makes sense.

Non-performing loans alone, though, are not necessarily robust leading indicators of financial stress. Governments and regulatory authorities can get banks to change their behaviour, especially if they are state-owned. Bad loans can be rolled forward, or 'ever-greened'. Banks still keep many of their trading and investment transactions off-balance-sheet. Regulatory and accounting practices may not encourage and can even complicate the recognition of bad loans in the first place, so that reported non-performing loans do not give an accurate picture of the incidence of bad debt. Yet, it is worthwhile to keep an eye on what analysts are saying. Bad loans convey useful information about the health of the banking system, and they correlate negatively with both economic growth and the robustness of banking systems in the face of shocks.

Banks and shadow banks

We have been reminded by the financial crisis that banks and financial institutions exist in a political context, and getting them to change their behaviour requires more than just a policy tweak. For example, in their book *Fragile by Design*, Charles Calomiris and Stephen Haber argue that the political institutions of a society structure the incentives of politicians, banks, bank shareholders, depositors, debtors and taxpayers to form coalitions in order to shape laws, policies and regulations in their interests, and against the interests of those not in the coalition. To quote them, 'a country doesn't choose its banking system, it gets a banking system consistent with the institutions that govern the distribution of political power'.[13]

This concept fits China. Politicians, most banks and their most important shareholders, and SOE and local government debtors, are all agents of the Party or the state. Depositors and taxpayers are, for the most part, citizens. The Chinese banking system exists to further the interests of the former, and it is impossible to imagine that regulatory or supervisory changes in the Chinese financial system will alter that. Anything else would require a major transformation of ownership of the financial system and of the fundamental principles that determine the allocation of credit in the economy. It is as well to bear the political context in mind as we consider closely the contours and nature of the financial system.

During the last decade or so, everyone has learned that banking systems form a vitally important platform on which our societies and economies are built. When the banking system fails, the veneer of stability cracks quickly, exposing economic and political fault-lines from which it takes a long time to recover. The essential lesson, though, is that financial crises happen because financial institutions create leverage, which, over time, is liable to become excessive and end up with what I called in 2007 a Minsky Moment. Named after the economist Hyman Minsky, this is the point where the highest state of leverage – when lenders are providing funds to borrowers in order to service and repay debt – leads to systemic financial instability.[14]

We know that the growth of domestic credit facilitated by banks and other financial institutions is central to financial crises. Indeed, in a seminal work on this topic covering 17 countries over 140 years, domestic loan growth was found to be the best single predictor of financial crises. These ensnared both balance of payments surplus and deficit countries and there were no mitigating circumstances from prior trends in real interest rates or inflation.[15] If you're looking for a template for a financial crisis, then on the surface, at least, China fits it well.

China's banks include the world's four largest, scaled by assets: Industrial and Commercial Bank of China ($3.47 trillion), China Construction Bank ($3.02 trillion), Agricultural Bank of China ($2.82 trillion), and Bank of China ($2.6 trillion).[16] Sometimes this is a plaudit that is not always welcome. In 1989, just before Japan's financial crisis erupted and ushered in two lost economic decades, it was able to boast that it was home to the world's largest ten banks. In 2007, the world's largest three banks were American. We shall soon see if China's position at the top of this tree is a curse or not.

China's 140 banks, comprising the big four, other large banks, and small- to medium-sized city commercial banks and joint stock banks (which have private shareholders but in which the government has majority ownership), rural credit cooperatives and the three major 'policy banks' (China Development Bank, Export–Import Bank of China and Agricultural Development Bank of China), command assets worth around $33 trillion. All told, China's bank assets equate to about three times the country's GDP but these numbers don't take account of the whole of the financial sector. If we do that, then total financial assets amounted to 472 per cent of GDP in 2017, which is around RMB 360 trillion, or $53 trillion.

Financial assets had been 248 per cent of GDP in 2008. Because GDP more than doubled over the period 2008–17, the money value of financial assets increased 4.5 times. The principal drivers of this expansion in assets and liabilities were not China's big four banks, but other banks, especially city commercial and joint stock banks. The big four accounted for a slightly higher share of assets (109 per cent of the 472 per cent), but the others almost doubled their share to 192 per cent. The assets of trust banks, asset management companies, wealth management products (WMPs), securities, pension and insurance companies all rose significantly.[17] WMPs are essentially financial products that pay higher returns than bank deposits, but as we shall see later, they are riskier and can be used in a variety of ways by financial institutions.

To understand China's financial system, we also have to look at the shadow banking sector.[18] Shadow banks are non-bank financial institutions that exist outside the formal banking system. They include the finance arms of large corporations, trust companies, finance and leasing companies, asset management and insurance companies, credit funds, and financial brokers. They accept deposits and make loans, often in much less conventional ways than banks, and they have traditionally been less well or less tightly regulated than conventional banks. They and regular banks engage in transactions in the shadow banking markets which are often 'off-balance-sheet', that is, they are not recorded on the formal statement of assets and liabilities, where they would be subject to conventional capital adequacy and liquidity regulations, and they can be hidden away from the eyes of regulatory agencies. While it is certainly true that shadow banking can be an agent of financial innovation and economic growth, our experience of the financial crisis has taught us to fear its other capacity, which is as an agent of systemic instability and financial and economic crisis.

The biggest shadow banks are trust banks, which were once local investment funds set up by provincial governments, and which became very active after the stimulus programme was announced in 2008. The shadow finance system, though, is a 'market' in which all banks, asset managers, hedge funds and insurance companies come together to lend and borrow in cash, derivatives and complex financial products, along with companies specialising in securities, interbank and market trading, broking, financial leasing, microfinance, and pawn shops, peer-to-peer and underground lenders. Widely traded WMPs were introduced originally to get round the ceiling on normal deposit rates. In essence, they are a substitute for deposits, issued mainly but not only by banks and trust banks, and may comprise simply cash or more sophisticated and structured credit designed to pay higher rates of interest. Many of the latter are opaque and not well understood by investors, as we shall see later.

China's shadow banking system, however, is somewhat different from others in the West. It exists, literally, in the shadow of the banks, because the mainstream banks are so dominant in the economy.[19] Unlike the US and other Western countries, there are relatively few independent non-bank institutions, and securitised assets and market-based financial instruments play a quite limited role. The $9 trillion bond market is closely linked to funding from WMPs. An important feature of China's system, moreover, is the pervasiveness of perceived and actual guarantees, which shield investors from loss and incubate moral hazard. The Chinese regulatory authorities have stepped up so-called macro-prudential regulation considerably since 2017. They have instructed banks to refrain from certain types of investment and from issuing forms of financial support for some investment products. These measures are designed to remove or weaken bank guarantees from certain asset management products by 2019, which would be a positive development, but we must wait to see if this happens.

China's shadow banking system is young and only began to take off in the 2000s. In 2002, for example, the shadow system was estimated to be just $80 billion. When the banking system was required to go into overdrive after 2008, banks wanted to keep their balance sheets free to make new good loans, and so developed new financial products, instruments and source of deposits 'in the shadows' to finance projects that often had weak or negative returns. The shadow sector expanded to $700 billion by 2008.[20] According to the credit rating agency Moody's, China's shadow finance sector amounted to almost $10 trillion in 2016, equivalent to about 29 per cent of banking system assets and 87 per cent of GDP.[21]

The rapid growth in shadow banking, especially after 2009, was partly facilitated by China's regulatory agencies themselves, as all the agencies of the state competed to deliver on China's response to the financial crisis.

Gradually, though, non-bank institutions became more and more involved. The China Insurance Regulatory Commission, for example, allowed insurance companies to invest in much riskier assets than is customary for this normally conservative sector, and to sell policies – the most contentious were called 'universal' insurance policies – that were not so much insurance policies, as 'guaranteed return' investment products. More broadly, financial companies competed to raise money from investors and depositors and put the money to use in an array of dubious financial schemes, egged on by new forms of finance such as online payments and savings schemes, peer-to-peer lending, and a permissive regulatory attitude towards the use (and abuse) of leverage.

Banking crisis more likely than a debt crisis

During the financial crisis in 2007–9, as the destruction of balance sheets tore through the financial system, some people used to say wryly that 'there's nothing right on the left side of the balance sheet, and nothing left on the right'. In other words, the assets held, typically on the left side of the accounts, were flawed, and the liabilities that funded them, on the right, had disappeared or been withdrawn. The point about this little anecdote is to emphasise that in finance, it's not just the assets or lending that matter.

There's no doubt that they both do, and concern has been expressed about the 'collateral damage' lurking in the Chinese banking system, in a chilling reminder of the 2008 financial crisis. Collateral, which is the security pledged against a loan, is vulnerable if the asset prices underlying it, say, real-estate prices, fall. The recipients of the collateral, the lenders, are also vulnerable in the event that the collateral is fraudulent – that is, it doesn't really exist, it is easily sold by the borrower to raise cash, or it has been pledged multiple times to different lenders. The anecdotal evidence for widespread fraudulent collateral in China in the form of buildings, private apartments and commodities is 'haunting loans across a wide swath of business and industry'.[22]

Yet the liabilities or the funding of the loans are absolutely key. In fact in important respects, they matter more. Few banks fail because they are insolvent, in the sense that their assets are worth less than their liabilities. But they can and do fail when they become illiquid, and can't raise deposits or borrow funds in the financial markets any more. This is precisely what happened to the British bank Northern Rock in 2007, which was one of the first financial institutions to fail in the build-up to the financial crisis.

Other bigger institutions, such as Bear Stearns and Lehman Brothers, would later fail in the same way.

The liabilities of the financial sector, then, are what we really need to focus on because banks are always vulnerable to so-called 'funding shocks', since their business revolves around mismatches in the maturities of their assets and liabilities. Typically, they lend over long periods, and borrow over much shorter periods, but when the liabilities are being rolled or renewed every day, week or month, banks are especially vulnerable.

In China, a substantial proportion of the growth in total lending has been carried out by smaller and medium-sized banks which have had to look beyond the familiar and stable deposits originating from households, to less stable and short-term sources of funding in the shadows, so to speak, by, for example, using the interbank market for deposits and by issuing WMPs. Household deposits used to account for between 60 and 70 per cent of the banking system's total liabilities about a decade ago, but as recently as 2017, they accounted for about 45 per cent. If we broaden the banking system to include all financial institutions, then the share of household deposits is even lower.

One senior banker, Yi Huiman, the chairman of the Industrial and Commercial Bank of China, speaking at the annual China Development Forum event in 2017, made specific reference to the spread of banking activities into the 'shadows', noting that shadow banking 'is not subject to full regulation, or any regulation at all. We have to focus. If not, the real economy will suffer.'[23] He was right. China's political leaders had allowed financial reform and liberalisation to run far faster than reform and liberalisation in the rest of the economy. Until 2017, at least, the authorities paid insufficient attention to the balkanisation of the financial system, the spread of unregulated or weakly regulated financial institutions, or the funding that became increasingly dependent on riskier and more leveraged instruments and products. This spawned 'regulatory arbitrage' on an industrial scale, or, put another way, the exploitation of loopholes in financial regulation leading to increasingly risky behaviour by financial companies and market participants, poor regulation and risks to financial stability.

Repo markets and wealth management products

Repo, or repurchase, markets came to play a central role in the build-up of financial leverage in the Western world in the 2000s, and were instrumental in transmitting the shocks of the financial crisis. Similarly, in China, repo markets have grown to play a key role in China's money and shadow financial markets and are an important part of the leveraging of the financial system.

Repo agreements are essentially loans, secured by collateral in the form, mostly, of bonds of one type or another. A repo buyer will lend cash, and take securities from the borrower as collateral for the loan, while the repo seller borrows the cash, and offers the securities. The contract between them provides for the terms, including the date and price, for the securities transaction to be reversed. Over 95 per cent of transactions in China's repo market are done at overnight or seven-day maturities.

The amount of net borrowing in the repo market in 2015 stood at RMB 20 trillion, or almost $3 trillion.[24] According to the People's Bank of China, about 10 per cent was owed by insurance companies and foreign banks, 20 per cent by securities companies, 30 per cent by small- and medium-sized banks, and 40 per cent by 'other' entities, comprising credit cooperatives, financial leasing and trust companies, asset managers, money market funds, and off-balance-sheet vehicles such as wealth management products (WMPs).

Institutions use the repo market because it offers access to low-cost and voluminous funding, which they can leverage and increase the effective returns. In other words, they can borrow cash (and give securities) and use it to buy more bonds, while others can take on securities (as collateral for lending cash), which they can, in turn, sell in a new transaction. And so on. This merry-go-round exposes the contracting parties to continuous and multiple roll-overs of transactions every day or week, and to complex risks. If interest rates rise, the value of the bonds, which comprise the collateral, will decline. There have been cases where this has caused financial stress which the central bank has had to relieve by providing liquidity. If non-bank contracting parties, which do not have access to 'lender-of-last-resort' liquidity lines from the People's Bank of China, get into trouble or need cash urgently, they could become forced sellers of assets, and spread contagion throughout the market.

When things are going well, and confidence is solid, these markets work with few hitches. It is when financial conditions tighten that they start to freeze, triggering stress or panic among counterparts that can be transmitted rapidly in a self-feeding spiral. It is important to monitor financial conditions in China in case – or when – the People's Bank and the regulatory authorities choose to tighten policy, as they did for example between the end of 2016 and May 2017. Alternatively, financial conditions may tighten simply as investors lose confidence because of faltering economic growth, a fall in asset prices, or excessive leverage. As a rule, most people think that if liquidity were ever at risk in Chinese financial markets, the People's Bank of China would step in and alleviate any shortage to prevent financial stress. Normally, the central bank is pretty good at doing this. But does the central bank know enough – or more than Western central banks did in 2007 – about the complex inter-connectedness of financial institutions and products to forestall a crisis?

WMPs warrant some additional explanation because they have constituted an important and, some say, risky, part of the shadow banking sector. They have certainly been in the crosshairs of regulators for some time. In March 2017, for example, China Minsheng Bank, the biggest joint stock bank, was fined by the China Banking Regulatory Commission (CBRC) for breaching internal controls regarding the sale of WMPs to high-net-worth individuals. The RMB 3 billion that the bank raised was allegedly used to make good a credit note which had been fraudulently drawn up to cover losses on a loan to a subsidiary of the state-owned China Railway Group. This particular incident served as a reminder of the vulnerability of investors to, and the abuse by financial institutions of, this part of the product family.

Between 2009 and 2016, WMPs increased from about 2 per cent to roughly 12 per cent of total deposits, or the equivalent of almost two-fifths of GDP. In 2017, the China Banking Regulatory Commission estimated the outstanding stock of WMPs at RMB 29 trillion or $4.5 trillion. About three-quarters sit off banks' balance sheets. However, there are many other types of wealth management products, and altogether they totalled about 2.5 times as much, as of March 2017.[25]

As suggested earlier, WMPs are popular with investors because they offer higher yields than bank deposits. Most of them are relatively safe, and are invested in bond and money market assets, cash and equities. About 16 per cent are invested in 'non-standard' debt instruments, which are riskier. So are those that are invested in non-performing loans, and other WMPs, or used in other forms of leverage. According to a Bloomberg report, leveraged varieties of products have grown by a factor of eight to over RMB 4 trillion since 2014.[26]

The regulatory authorities are now paying much more attention to WMPs, including not just riskier forms of products, but also where banks hold them, that is on or off the balance sheet. Banks have held them largely off-balance-sheet to bypass or minimise regulations, including capital adequacy. Regulators have been concerned about the ways in which WMPs are used to leverage up capital returns by using securities companies and markets, and to repackage loans or tranches of loans, which are vulnerable to loss from higher interest rates, lack of market confidence, or investors wanting their money back. When you consider that the average maturity of WMPs is very short, typically three to four months, and that the assets on which the WMPs are based are loans with long maturities, it is easy to see why. The IMF noted that in 2015, 61 per cent of WMP assets had maturities of less than three months, and 13 per cent had maturities of less than a month.[27] This means that investors have to renew their subscriptions all the time and roll over their investments continuously. If they didn't, and new investors couldn't be found, banks might have to sell the assets to pay depositors, perhaps at a loss, and lose a crucial source of funding.

The IMF has expressed its concerns about WMPs and other short-term funding instruments that make the Chinese financial system vulnerable to a loss of liquidity, or to an event that hits confidence, causing asset market prices to decline. Land or property, for example, is the collateral behind about 40 per cent of all loan transactions, and weakness in this sector could be both the cause and the effect of liquidity drying up in short-term markets. According to the IMF, short maturity wholesale funding for banks rose from a 10 per cent share of total funding in 2010 to 30 per cent more recently. For joint stock and city commercial banks, and many regional banks, interbank funding, for example, has grown to account for a significant proportion of assets. Joint stock banks rely most heavily on interbank financing and WMP liabilities (45 per cent of total funding), followed by regional banks (34 per cent), and the big five banks (20 per cent).[28]

As a result of more stringent regulation, net issuance of WMPs and the usage of interbank repo markets stabilised in 2017. These developments were in line with the stated goal of trying to de-risk the financial system and curb the dependency of riskier investment products on short-term funding in the financial system. Yet we should remain alert because of the opaque connections between products and funding in the system and the vulnerability of smaller banks especially to liquidity shocks and limited capital buffers.

Regulators react

At the start of 2017, a serious event took place that wasn't appreciated at the time for what it meant. Xiao Jianhua, founder of the Beijing-based

Tomorrow Group, an investment company reported to be worth nearly $6 billion, was abducted by Chinese police officers from the Four Seasons Hotel in Hong Kong on the eve of Chinese New Year and taken into custody in the mainland. Under interrogation, he admitted to helping the rich and well-to-do move money out of China.

Remember that prior to this, China took action to plug at least some of the holes through which capital was fleeing China, and soon after the abduction, the People's Bank of China placed severe restrictions on the ability of banks to finance foreign acquisitions by Chinese companies. Xiao fell foul of the government, not only because of what he did, but also because he was alleged to have had ties to former President Jiang Zemin and associates, including the high-ranking security chief Zhou Yongkang, who was a prominent victim of Xi Jinping's anti-corruption campaign.

Xiao's abduction was one of the opening salvos in a national financial security campaign, embraced by President Xi, approved by the Politburo, and executed by the People's Bank of China and the Banking, Securities and Insurance Regulatory Commissions.[29] For the first time, Xi Jinping talked about financial security in the same way that he addressed national security, giving it high significance: the finance sector, in which many of the progeny of the Politburo work, and the financial activities of Chinese companies, came under the watchful eyes of those seeking to consolidate power around the president and within the Party.

The appointment of Guo Shuqing as head of the CBRC in February 2017 was welcomed by many who had been worried by excesses in China's financial system. Guo, who had been one of former Premier Zhu Rongji's young protégés, was an outspoken proponent of financial reform and had served as deputy governor of the People's Bank of China, chairman of China Construction Bank, and head of the China Securities Regulatory Commission. Soon after being confirmed at the CBRC, he vowed 'to clean up the chaos' in the banking system and began to issue a number of edicts aimed at speculators, excessive risk-taking, and lax or corrupt management. He asked banks to provide information about the overseas loans made to four of the biggest foreign deal-makers in corporate China: Anbang, the insurance company; Dalian Wanda, a property company with other diverse interests; HNA, a conglomerate; and Fosun International, a conglomerate and investment group.

Soon after Guo's appointment, the head of the China Insurance Regulatory Commission, Xiang Junbo, was named by the Central Commission for Discipline Inspection as being under investigation for serious violations of Party discipline, and fired. The new management lost precious little time in getting to work on what was probably one of the principal catalysts for the 2017 regulatory firestorm, the hostile takeover in 2016 of Vanke Real Estate Corporation, a large real estate development company, by the Baoneng Group, a construction and financial conglomerate. The move was eventually blocked, amid allegations that Baoneng's chairman, Yao Zhenhua, had exploited regulations, clients and leverage in various illicit or illegal dealings. Yao was later banned from the industry for ten years after it was claimed that Baoneng's life insurance unit, Forsea Life Insurance, also chaired by Yao, had provided false data and used insurance funds in contravention of regulations.

A number of insurance companies were reprimanded as the insurance regulators tried to rein in risky business practices, including flamboyant business acquisitions abroad, which, to be fair, the authorities had either encouraged or tolerated. A particular target was Anbang Insurance Group, which was unknown in 2015 but built up a 10 per cent market share in life insurance, and Forsea Life Insurance, both of which were banned temporarily from issuing fashionable, universal insurance products. Anbang and its chairman, Wu Xiaohui, also came under suspicion for overseas acquisitions, market manipulation, broader shadow lending activities and other 'economic crimes'. Wu was eventually convicted of fraud and abuse of power in a Shanghai court in 2018, and sentenced to eighteen years in prison.

Earlier in the year, the government and regulators seized control of Anbang, initially for a year, as its funding and solvency caused the government serious concerns. Anbang provides a useful example of government meddling gone wrong. It encouraged the company, among others, to build up an overseas presence and then became worried when the company turned out to have been unstable and over-extended. The bulk of its products were life insurance products that customers could opt out of after two years, but still enjoy high returns. Anbang was basically borrowing money from customers to fund a reckless overseas expansion programme. The government stepped in to stop its collapse and the possibly ominous implications for financial stability of maturing products, customer withdrawals and a wider contagion.

Official concern about shadow banking activities, including WMPs, prompted the People's Bank of China and the Banking, Insurance and Securities Commissions to issue a spate of new rules and draft guidelines, designed to show they were acting in unison to clamp down on the use of leverage, restrain universal life insurance policies and peer-to-peer lending, and discourage short-term fund-raising. The authorities were especially concerned to dampen down the growth of WMPs, to subject them to tighter regulation and scrutiny, and to ban certain practices in which WMPs were used to boost leverage but also raise financial risks.

It is noteworthy that President Xi took a personal interest in the campaign to act against the risk of financial instability. Debt or leverage cycles in which financial and corporate balance sheets get blown up – literally in the end – can result in serious damage to the economy and to medium-term growth prospects. We have seen this many times in the last decades, and China must be careful that it does not succumb, as it did in the early 1990s.

Xi led the five-yearly National Financial Work Conference in July 2017, at the end of which he said that 'China must strengthen the leadership of the Communist Party of China over financial work'.[30] The conference set up a new body, the State Council Financial Stability and Development Committee, to coordinate the work and activities of the regulatory agencies with the People's Bank of China at the heart. It also agreed that priorities would henceforth be to make finance serve the real economy, pay close attention to financial stability risks, and promote 'direct financing' (meaning a greater role for equity and fixed income markets).

Pressing issues for the committee will be to dampen down leverage and arbitrage in the $15 trillion asset management industry, and to try and end the ubiquitous practice of guaranteeing capital and interest payments to investors, which speak to a low level of confidence in the security or value of contracts. Draft rules, which have a mid-2019 target for implementation, would force banks to move many assets back on to their balance sheets, where they would be more transparent and subject to established capital adequacy, liquidity and risk rules. Ending the guarantees, while justified from a moral hazard point of view, might nevertheless run into stiff opposition from both banks and investors, and even other regulators if this involved sudden and large losses. Banks are worried about their income and liquidity if regulators succeed in introducing measures that end up curtailing their access to short-term deposits.

In March 2018, at the National People's Congress, the merger of the Banking and Insurance Regulatory Commissions under the State Council was announced as part of a sweeping restructuring of government ministries and agencies. This move was designed to streamline financial regulation and curb the opportunities for regulatory arbitrage, leaving the merged commissions with operational responsibilities, and referring the power to initiate laws and regulations, as well as macro-prudential oversight, to the People's Bank of China. Yi Gang, the deputy to Governor Zhou Xiaochuan, was promoted to governor, and Guo Shuqing, the CBRC head, was also made Party secretary of the People's Bank, and Yi's boss. Guo's boss, in turn, is Vice Premier Liu He, whose portfolio spans all the nooks and crannies of economic and financial affairs.

These changes amounted to a sea-change in the organisation of financial control and management, with almost a direct line now from the president down through Liu He and Guo Shuqing to the immediate and outer reaches of monetary policy, financial stability and regulation. From an organisational standpoint, there would not now seem to be any obvious reason for a repeat of past financial excesses and abuses. Any mistakes or failures in future will be down to the decisions made by the holders of high office.

Is there systemic risk?

It is sometimes suggested that China might have a 'quiet' debt crisis, if it has one at all. Some say it could grow its way out of debt, as economic growth and inflation combine to drive the money value of GDP higher. Provided debt grows more slowly than money GDP, the debt ratio must fall. In theory, this looks neat, but the idea actually conflates debt and growth incorrectly. It treats them as distinct items, whereas in fact, in China's case, they are closely related: it is higher debt creation that drives higher growth in the first place. This dog, as they say, won't hunt. If China is to leave its debt problem behind, it will have to do something else.

Other people argue that China's high savings rate – close to about 50 per cent of GDP – is a special factor that both determines a high level of debt, and protects against the risk of a debt crisis. The argument is that Chinese households hold the bulk of their savings in the form of cash deposits in banks (as well as property), which banks then lend. There is little borrowing from overseas, and little foreign debt. It is, in effect, a fully funded domestic currency system, shielded also by capital controls, and underpinned by both the state in the form of its budgetary capacity, and the People's Bank of China in the form of lender of last resort liquidity.

Much of this is correct, and yet the argument misses the point. Chinese households have had high savings for a long time, and excessive bank lending hasn't been a persistent problem. What is new is the scale and speed with which debt has risen over the last ten years, the credit-oriented drivers of investment and economic growth, the significant increase in banks' loan-to-deposit ratios – a typical warning sign of trouble – and the increasing riskiness of deposits originating in more volatile financial markets.

The risk in China, then, is certainly not an Asian-crisis-type risk related to excessive borrowing from abroad in foreign currencies, but a predominantly domestic set of circumstances, based around the banking system's Renminbi assets and liabilities. Domestic banking crises are fortunately not frequent, but they happen. The 2008 financial crisis is still fresh in our minds, but they have happened regularly, including in the US in the 1930s and Japan in the 1990s. High savings did not keep the US out of trouble in the former period, or Japan in the latter.

By way of a reminder, note that China's financial assets and liabilities have exploded in recent years to more than five times its GDP, that a substantial part of this has happened away from the main Chinese banks, and that much has occurred in the lightly or weakly regulated shadow banking system. Consider also that China is no stranger to financial instability. It happened in the 1990s, and the asset management companies set up then and subsequently to deal with bad debts are still doing so. Since 2015–16, China has experienced a stock market rout, a mini currency crisis, corruption and risk management scandals in the financial sector, a new round of rising non-performing loans, and the exposure of excessive leverage in the finance sector and among SOEs and local governments. All in all, these events add up to a serious problem not just of weak regulation, which is now being partially addressed, but also of weak corporate governance and operational management which are not only being inadequately addressed but are being exacerbated because of new political interference.

As I have suggested here, China could become embroiled in a debt crisis arising from the increase in the burden of debt and the decline in capacity to shoulder it, but this does not seem a likely outcome. It is much more likely that debt will loom over the economy, manifesting itself as lower economic growth than as a crisis per se.

On the other side of the balance sheet, though, the liabilities and their funding structure do pose more a risk. We can draw some comfort from the fact that the risk of systemic shock in the financial system from a sudden 'drying up' of interbank and short-term funding is mitigated by two important features. First, the People's Bank of China, like any central bank, is a lender of last resort and should be expected to play that role unflinchingly in a largely state-owned banking system. Second, the big four banks are not as reliant on volatile funding sources as their smaller brethren.

This, though, is comforting only to the point where opaque connectivity comes into play. Smaller banks, especially, are thought to be particularly vulnerable. They have relatively flimsy capital buffers to absorb losses and are much more exposed than their bigger brethren to liquidity risks. The IMF thinks they have wholesale liabilities that are more than twice their liquidity buffers. Moreover, they are connected in a myriad of other ways, such as cross-holdings of bonds, swapped loans and other obligations, and complex asset management products, including so-called 'directional asset management plans', which are really camouflaged loans from a bank to a company, using securities firms or asset managers as intermediaries. These loans are now the biggest item on the balance sheets of many banks.[31] These and other forms of interconnectedness mean that funding shocks in opaque parts of the financial system could spread with speed.

The increased riskiness in the funding structure of banking sector liabilities has three important implications. First, borrowers in the repo market have big and frequent purchasing needs, even daily, to roll over their liabilities. This exposes them to both interest-rate and illiquidity risk.

Second, a high proportion of wholesale repo funding originates with non-bank financial intermediaries and other institutions, and is tied to financial products that could be withdrawn or disappear quickly in the event of elevated credit risk, for example in the event of slower economic growth.

Third, while the authorities have clamped down sharply on interbank borrowing, banks have proven adept at making good shortfalls by issuing high yield 'structured deposits', and negotiable certificates of deposit as substitutes. The more than 1.5 trillion yuan rise in the latter in 2017, for example, just exceeded the decline in interbank borrowing. Important as the process of deleveraging is, it is still at an early stage and not immune from reversal if economic conditions should worsen.

The financial clampdown that has been going on since 2017 is a step in the right direction in attempts to lower the economy's susceptibility to systemic risk. Yet there is a long and uncertain road ahead. There has been some, but not great, financial or liquidity stress, and no market panic. Interest rate levels and volatility have risen only slightly, especially judged against past tightening cycles. Nearly all borrowers and lenders are fully funded, and liquidity is plentiful. Some measures of credit expansion have shown a slowdown, broader measures continue to show growth at uncomfortably high levels.

It is hard to imagine how the government can avoid the key challenge of the debt trap, other than by accommodating a proper and sustained deleveraging. Appropriately executed, this must entail an extended growth hiatus. And this at a time when the government's other priorities – including capacity cutbacks, lowering inequality, improving the environment, subjecting all enterprises to Party influence, and rising trade friction – will all be reinforcing such an outcome.

The authorities will have to choose, sooner or later, either to persevere and risk a significant growth slowdown, or tread again on the credit pedal, deferring the debt denouement to a later, and perhaps more troublesome time. The bottom line is that China cannot have high rates of economic growth on the one hand, and on the other hand simultaneously reduce the risk of financial instability, and get banks, companies and local governments to run pristine balance sheets. That choice now looms with growing urgency, and the rest of the world will need to watch with patience and concern.

Eventually, the debt trap will have to be inflated or deflated away. The good news might be that Xi Jinping can now take a long view: he doesn't have to get things to come right by 2022 or even 2027 for that matter. The bad news is that neither outcome is likely to sit comfortably in a country with major income and wealth inequality, and a questionable level of social cohesion if economic stress were to rise significantly. Under such circumstances, capital flight is likely to resume, exposing the Renminbi to a sharp decline. It is to the currency that we now turn.

5

RENMINBI TRAP

Financial markets refer to the Chinese currency as the Renminbi just as they do to the UK currency as Sterling. In shops, people spend yuan in China, as they do pounds in the UK. In the last few years, finance people have taken the slang term for the US dollar, 'greenback', and applied it to China's 'redback'. They are all the same thing, but the currency of a country is much more than a name, what you spend, how you get paid, or what you exchange at a bank or money counter. It is, as the Chinese translation of Renminbi says literally, the 'people's money', and it is as significant to China as the US dollar is to America, or Sterling is to the British, or the Deutschmark once was to Germans before the advent of the Euro, to which most EU citizens now also feel tied.

The case was put best by the Austrian-born US economist Joseph Schumpeter, who wrote a tract in 1930 in which he reflected on the passionate interest people have in monetary systems and the value of money. In his view, the reason was that 'the monetary system of a people reflects all that the people wants, does, endures, is, and that simultaneously the monetary system of a people exercises a significant influence upon its economic activity and its destiny in general'.[1]

For many years, China has been driven to maintain the stability of its currency, partly for economic purposes, but also to anchor expectations at home about the management of money and finance, and to build trust abroad in the Renminbi itself, and in the Chinese foreign exchange rate regime. It is, in effect, a form of soft power.

During the Asian crisis in 1997–98, the IMF and other bodies urged China to devalue, but China resisted the path followed by several Asian governments, whose currency pegs had proven unsustainable. It is true that China was different from its Asian neighbours. The Renminbi was not freely convertible, and China neither experienced significant capital flows from overseas, nor allowed capital to leave China freely. Nevertheless, China's concern was to build trust in its reputation as a stabilising force, to be a leader in east and Southeast Asia, and ultimately to develop a Renminbi bloc with other Asian countries, albeit to the chagrin of Japan, South Korea and Taiwan.

China still places a high priority on currency stability, it still wants and needs to build trust in Asia and beyond in its economic leadership, and it still maintains strict controls over the outward movement of capital. On the other hand, the Renminbi is fully convertible for current account transactions, that is for goods and services, and the exchange rate regime has been liberalised. The currency has been the subject of an active campaign in and outside China to internationalise its usage in denominating trade and investment transactions, and as a reserve asset held by other central banks. It is one of the constituent units of the IMF's Special Drawing Rights, and a lot of people believe that it is on course to become a more significant reserve currency, perhaps one day rivalling the US dollar.

This chapter is going to argue two things. First, that it is not enough to want currency stability – delivering it, if domestic money and credit policies are not compatible, is impossible. Second, that China cannot have a truly global currency when current account surpluses and capital controls restrict the accumulation of Renminbi by foreigners. In these ways, China faces a Renminbi trap.

The rise and stall of the Renminbi

The Renminbi plays a far more important role for China nowadays, compared with a decade or two ago when China was taking the world by storm as a low-cost producer of low-end manufactured products such as toys, textiles and shoes. It may have served China well in those days to keep the Renminbi cheap, but time has moved on.

Low-end exports have migrated to Vietnam, Cambodia and Bangladesh – clothing and footwear and other labour-intensive goods accounted for just 16.5 per cent of Chinese exports in 2016 – and companies have moved up the so-called value chain. Two-fifths of exports comprised mechanical and electrical products, and one-fifth were made up of high technology products, including computers. When Chinese companies like Huawei and ZTE Corporation compete worldwide with Ericsson, Cisco and Nokia in telecommunications, Lenovo outsells Hewlett Packard and Bell in computers, and seven out of the top ten global firms selling mobile handsets are Chinese, low prices and exchange rates are no longer enough. Competitive edge is more about financing, commercial selling and marketing arrangements, and trust in one's currency and financial system.

During the 2000s, the Renminbi was the most important currency in the world as the new kid on the block. It was a period when China's balance of payments surplus surged in the wake of WTO membership, and when China's role in the world economy changed rapidly. It made steady progress to become a top five trading partner of all major countries. The Americans were especially exercised by what they regarded as China's 'manipulation' of the value of the Renminbi, that is, keeping it undervalued, and Congress held regular hearings on whether to take action against China.

In 2005, partly as a response to threats in the US to impose significant tariffs on Chinese goods, China ended the peg against the US dollar that had been in situ for ten years, devalued the Renminbi by 2.1 per cent, and announced that it would henceforth be allowed to fluctuate against a basket of currencies, though the constituents were never announced. The Renminbi appreciated slowly but persistently, though with a short hiatus during the financial crisis of 2008–9. The Obama administration rarely made an issue about the currency, and the Trump administration has focused instead on what it regards as China's unfair trade practices. Peak Renminbi, measured against the US dollar, was reached in January 2016 at RMB 6.05.

Greater attention has also been paid to the ways in which China is trying to establish close links with countries in Asia, and other continents, by encouraging them to use and hold its own currency or, put another way, by creating a sort of Renminbi zone, in much the same way as the US previously established US dollar zones. In 2009, Governor Zhou Xiaochuan of the People's Bank of China wrote an essay on the bank's website that railed against America's hegemony in the global financial system, and argued that the flaws laid bare in the US by the Western financial crisis constituted a step towards the inevitable decline and eclipse of the Western system in the world order.[2]

He persuaded reluctant Party colleagues that China would gain enormous international prestige if the Renminbi were included in the IMF's Special Drawing Rights (SDR) – a basket of currencies which serves as an accounting unit as well as an international asset in which central banks hold a small proportion of their reserves. When the Renminbi came under pressure in global markets in January 2016, the *People's Daily* offered a sharp riposte to the financier George Soros – who had said he was 'going short' of Asian currencies – warning that it would be a mistake to declare war on China's currency.[3] Such are the passions aroused by currency markets and politicians from time to time.

Governor Zhou and like-minded officials were always enthusiastic about internationalisation of the Renminbi, not least because they believed that an internationalised currency would be an agent of domestic financial liberalisation by bringing competitive pressures to bear from outside China.

For a decade before 2015, China was active on a number of fronts in liberalising the currency regime. It introduced and subsequently broadened two major quota schemes for permitting foreign investors to convert foreign currencies into Renminbi and to invest the proceeds in Chinese equities and other Renminbi-denominated instruments. These were the Qualified Foreign Institutional, and Renminbi Qualified Institutional Investor Schemes. A Qualified Domestic Institutional Investor Scheme was introduced and later broadened to allow domestic financial entities to invest in portfolio securities, such as stocks and bonds, abroad.

To encourage two-way flows of capital, China established the Shanghai Free Trade Zone in 2013, followed by similar arrangements in 2015 in Guangdong, Tianjin and Fujian. There are, however, restrictions on foreign investment, and generally, few foreign firms have taken the opportunity to set up in these zones. The establishment of the Shanghai–Hong Kong Stock Connect and Shenzhen–Hong Kong Connect schemes in 2014 and 2016, respectively, was designed to stimulate two-way flows in stocks, subject to quotas. The Mutual Fund Connect, launched in 2015, allows a quota of eligible mainland and Hong Kong funds to be distributed in each other's markets. And the Shanghai–Hong Kong Bond Connect programme, launched in July 2017, was designed to give global investors access to China's $11-trillion bond market.

The Renminbi has made limited progress in the settlement of global trade transactions and financial flows. The currency is the sixth biggest for global payments, though its share of global payments was only 1.6 per cent in 2017, according to SWIFT (Society for Worldwide Interbank Financial Telecommunication). Renminbi-denominated bonds issued in both Hong Kong and London, known as dim sum bonds, were very popular at first, but interest has waned as China's domestic bond market developed, and because of capital controls. Even though issuance revived a little in early 2018, the outstanding stock of instruments is not much more than $50 billion.

Selected banks are allowed to offer offshore Renminbi deposit accounts, with clearing centres in London, Frankfurt and Paris. The People's Bank of China has also established a number of bilateral currency-swap arrangements, permitting an expansion in the use of Renminbi, with roughly three dozen central banks. As of 2014, thirty-eight central banks held small amounts of Renminbi in their reserves. These include Austria, Australia, Chile, Malaysia, Nigeria, Pakistan, South Africa, Switzerland, Tanzania, Russia and the UK.[4] More central banks have joined this group, which includes the European Central Bank, the Bundesbank and many other European central banks as of 2018, though Renminbi holdings remain a small proportion of total reserves. Globally the proportion is 1 per cent.

Yet, while it is undeniable that China has succeeded in propelling the Renminbi on to the global financial stage, aided and abetted by the self-interest of the international banking and consulting communities, there are four global currency boxes that China has not been able to check yet, and it isn't clear when, or even if, it will.

First, and foremost, there is only one way to have a significant global currency, which is to allow foreigners to acquire and accumulate claims on you. In other words, just as the US has allowed foreigners to build up holdings of US bonds and other US assets (which are America's liabilities), so China would have to as well. There are, though, only two ways this can happen. One is by running current account deficits, so that foreigners receive more of your currency than they pay for goods and services. The other is by having an open capital account, so that capital flows freely abroad.

China runs a current account surplus, smaller than it used to be, but structurally entrenched for the time being. To balance this surplus, capital has to flow out but it is subject to controls that keep it locked up at home. The likelihood of China running current account deficits or allowing a meaningful liberalisation of capital account transactions any time soon is negligible. If anything, the surplus is likely to increase again as growth slows in the future. Consequently, the Renminbi is strongly handicapped when it comes to becoming a more serious global reserve currency. It is still possible for businesses and commercial organisations to use the Renminbi more for transactions in the future but that is quite different from becoming a more important global reserve currency.

Second, for all the fanfare about the Renminbi's inclusion in the Special Drawing Rights, it isn't clear that this has much practical purpose other than to confer modest status. The SDR is not going to dethrone the US dollar, and there haven't really been any significant initiatives to issue substantial quantities of SDR bonds or enhance its global usage. It is an accounting unit, and not much more.

In fact, once you get passed the political rhetoric, China's exchange rate and financial policies, far from threatening the role of the US dollar in the global system and boosting that of the Renminbi, are doing precisely the opposite.[5] By running trade surpluses, and restricting capital flows abroad, China is a willing party to the status quo. If it really wanted to challenge US hegemony, or lead the world to a multi-currency reserve system, it should boost Chinese aggregate demand, lower savings, and do the rest of the world a favour by running trade deficits; or, it could remove restrictions on capital outflows. Realistically, the former is by far the preferred option. The world needs China's trade deficits far more than it needs its capital, but no one is holding their breath that this is going to happen any time soon.

Third, while the gradual rise in Renminbi reserve holdings at other central banks certainly counts as progress towards a global currency goal, the Renminbi's share of global reserves is still very small. According to the IMF, global reserves stood at $11.3 trillion at September 2017, of which $9.6 billion were 'allocated reserves' – that is, their currency composition was identified, while the rest were 'unallocated'. The Renminbi share of allocated reserves was 1 per cent. The plausible assumption that unallocated reserves were largely US dollar assets owned by China suggests that the Renminbi share of all reserves was even a bit lower. Renminbi reserves are about a quarter of the size of those accounted for by both the Japanese yen and Sterling.

Fourth, the process of financial reform deserves the plaudits often given, but there are several barriers to China's making material progress, at least for the foreseeable future. It is fair to point out that important measures have been taken over time to liberalise the currency regime, the latest being in 2015 when the Renminbi regime officially shifted from being a US dollar peg to a trade-weighted basket, with weights and values published on the People's Bank of China website. Strictly speaking, this means that the risk of overvaluation against any single currency, notably the US dollar, should be lower in future. That said, the currency is still closely watched and managed against the US dollar, especially when volatility and uncertainty increase or when the US dollar rises or falls significantly against major currencies.

Beyond the currency regime itself, a global currency requires broad, deep, trusted and liquid bond and other capital markets. China has made progress in this regard, and the onshore bond market is the third largest in the world, but serious reservations persist about governance, openness and structure.

The development of China's bond market is being retarded by, for example, the existence of outward capital controls, inconsistent regulatory standards applied to its fragmented parts, the absence of the rule of law, and an unreliable credit rating system which tends to bunch ratings at the high end of the spectrum. Market discipline is weak when it comes to defaults and pricing systems, and liquidity tends to be low. With most financial participants expecting more significant deleveraging in the future, and financial repression keeping bond yields low, there is a cocktail of factors that explains why China's bond market attracts less domestic capital than it should, and relatively few global investors. In spite of schemes to attract foreign investors, the foreign ownership share in March 2018 was a lowly 1.6 per cent. Japan, with the world's second biggest bond market, is routinely put down as one where foreigners own a small share – roughly 11 per cent.

Fundamentally, the Party's inherent mistrust of markets and its penchant for control sit uncomfortably with the trust it seeks for itself and the Renminbi financial regime. This was exemplified in the summer of 2015, first when China's stock market crashed, and then soon after, by the mishandling of a small and seemingly innocuous 1.9 per cent devaluation of the Renminbi that led to a further small official devaluation and then a more sustained depreciation.

The stock market in China is not that important in or to the economy, but it is instructive to reflect on how the authorities encouraged a stock market boom and then attempted to stop it from collapsing, which it did anyway. The Renminbi experience is more important as it has a greater impact on Chinese citizens and on the rest of the world. When the authorities devalued it in August 2015 by a modest amount, but without explanation, it sent shock waves around global markets. These developments revealed the tension between the rhetoric of more room for market forces and the fundamental interventionism of the state. It is a difficulty in physical markets for, say, food and commodities, but in financial markets the contradiction is impossible to mask. The experience of 2015–16 testified to this in a spectacular fashion.

The stock market collapse

It all began in 2014, with the anti-corruption campaign in full swing. In China's real-estate market, sales and prices were dropping and inventories of unsold apartments were rising, along with market interest rates. With the real-estate market off-colour, investors and households started to pour money into the stock market, aided and abetted by the central bank which lowered policy interest rates at the end of the year, and state media, which encouraged people to buy equities, even suggesting it was their patriotic duty. The government was very happy to allow the stock market to rise, because higher valuations for equities would offset to an extent the rise in debt and make the balance sheets of state enterprises look stronger.

Xinhua News and the *People's Daily* published daily commentaries encouraging the world's largest population to buy more stocks. In an August 2014 article, *Xinhua* said that 'economic and social development will bring precious confidence and strong support into the stock market.'[6] The government also tried to draw foreign investors into the Shanghai stock market via brokers in Hong Kong. From that summer to the peak in June 2015, the Shanghai Composite Index rose 150 per cent, with a third of the rise occurring in the last few months.

Money flowed quickly into brokerage accounts on a scale far exceeding any previous rise, and the use of margin financing – the business of acquiring stocks by borrowing a small percentage of the total cost – proliferated. By early July 2015, margin credit stood at RMB 2.3 trillion ($354 billion), five times as much as a year earlier, and unregulated borrowing on margin was estimated at around one-fifth to two-fifths as much again.[7] Turnover on the Shanghai Stock Exchange quintupled between November 2014 and April 2015. Most of the new investors, according to the China Household Finance Survey, had educational attainment levels of high school or lower, and little in the way of financial literacy.[8]

Yet they were sucked into a speculative frenzy, and after a couple of weeks of great volatility in the market in early June 2015, the stock market crashed following an announcement by the China Securities Regulatory Commission placing restrictions on margin arrangements. After a peak of 5,178 on the 12 June, the Shanghai index tumbled to around 2,850 in September, after which it stabilised just above 3,000 for a while, before falling again during the financial turbulence in January 2016, when it bottomed out at 2,737.

It was extraordinary at the time, and it still is curious to consider just how far the authorities went to prop up the market and to stop it from falling. In late June 2015, the People's Bank of China cut interest rates for the fourth time since November 2014, but in this instance it was as an emergency measure. It did so again in August, but the easing of monetary policy at this point was merely a palliative. The first direct intervention occurred at the end of June, when local government pension funds were allowed to buy equities, and the main civil servants pension fund was authorised to lift its equity holdings from 30 to 40 per cent of total assets.

In early July, panic set in, and a state-led bail-out of the market began. The China Securities Regulatory Commission gave permission to investors to buy shares against the security of their homes, and injected RMB 260 billion ($40 billion) into the China Securities Finance Corporation to lend to twenty-one brokerage firms. The latter had already been requested to set up a share-purchasing fund of RMB 120 billion ($18 billion). Initial Public Offerings or IPOs were suspended for four months.

After a week, the Securities Regulatory Commission prevented shareholders with stakes above 5 per cent from selling for a period of six months, and ordered executives and board members of companies who had sold shares in the prior six months to buy them back. The China Insurance Regulatory Commission announced that insurance companies would be allowed to increase the proportion of stocks in their assets from 30 to 40 per cent. An investment arm of China Investment Corporation, China's sovereign wealth fund, announced it would buy exchange-traded funds, and the China Securities Finance Corporation injected RMB 200 billion ($31 billion) into five mutual funds so as to be able to buy more shares.

Even after this tsunami of regulatory interventions, the market did not really calm down until after over a third of Shanghai-listed firms, accounting for a half of all Chinese shares on all exchanges, halted trading. At one stage, 1,331 companies' shares, or about 40 per cent of the Shanghai market's capitalisation, had been suspended.

It is hard to guess how much this state-orchestrated campaign cost, but it has been estimated at around $144 billion.[9] The authorities were clearly shaken by what had happened. We don't really know why. They might have been anxious about the damage to their reputation as competent managers. They could have been worried about a political backlash. The government may have thought that by allowing corporate asset values to rise on the back of a booming stock market, corporate debt burdens would look less problematic, and programmes for state-owned enterprises (SOEs) to swap debt-for-equity would become more popular. Perhaps they were fixated on stabilising the market to demonstrate a new source of economic optimism and growth as the economy and real-estate market were slowing down.

In any event, in early 2016, after things had settled down again, the head of the China Securities Regulatory Commission, Xiao Gang, was dismissed amid stories that senior people in the organisation had leaked information about the stock market bail-out in order to profit from subsequent reactions. The government anti-corruption campaign's first forays into the financial sector started at around this time. What the stock market experience revealed was the deep contradiction that existed – and still exists – between wanting a 'decisive' role for markets and prices in resource allocation, and insisting on a dominant role for the state sector. This same dichotomy was also much in evidence in the crisis over the Renminbi.

Renminbi 'devaluation'

On 11 August 2015, while the stock market was still unstable, the People's Bank of China lowered, without warning or commentary, the daily fix of the Renminbi rate against the US dollar by 1.9 per cent. The change in the fix by the People's Bank prompted the biggest sell-off since the much larger devaluation in 1994, which occurred in a very different context of exchange-rate system reform. Officially, this new move and the technical change in the way the central bank proposed to announce the daily fix were designed to boost flexibility and facilitate the admission of the Renminbi into the SDR later in the year.

Yet, whatever the authorities were thinking at the time – Yi Gang, the newly installed head of the People's Bank, who was the deputy at the time and took the flak – they were forced to spend hundreds of billions of US dollars to stabilise the Renminbi. It worked briefly before a new decline took the currency to almost RMB 7 against the dollar at the end of 2016. Between August 2015 and the middle of 2016, it is estimated that China burned its way through almost $500 billion of its currency reserves to support the Renminbi.[10] The currency didn't really settle down until the authorities strengthened and introduced new controls over the outflow of capital, and the economy stabilised.

China's currency reserves surged in the 2000s, rising from $400 billion in 2003 to peak at just over $4 trillion in 2014. By January 2017 they had fallen to about $3 trillion, with most of the fall occurring between June 2014 and June 2016. The rise in reserves had happened because of balance of payments surpluses, which brought US dollars into China, which the central bank bought from banks in exchange for Renminbi, and subsequently invested in foreign, mostly US, bond markets.

After 2014, the opposite happened. The People's Bank had to sell US dollar assets to support the exchange rate, not because of any big change in the current account, but because of a sharp rise in capital outflows to the rest of the world, comprising foreign direct investment, portfolio investments, trade credits, currency and deposit flows, and other financial transactions. Some of these outflows were what is colloquially called 'hot money', more commonly known as capital flight.

Some of the reasons for higher capital outflows were perfectly normal. The US dollar was rising with changing expectations about rising US interest rates, and Chinese companies looked to repay US dollar loans they had previously taken out. In any event, China was changing over time from being a net importer of foreign direct investment to a net exporter, with many Chinese companies investing more overseas, sometimes in non-essential areas such as property, gambling and entertainment, and sometimes in energy, industry and technology. Direct investment abroad rose from $123 billion in 2014 to $217 billion in 2016.

Yet China's experience in 2015–16 revealed something more. Confidence in the stability of the Renminbi rate against the US dollar – which is the only currency pair that matters – was low. People and companies found a myriad of ways to get money out of China, including over-invoicing of imports from, and under-invoicing of exports to, Hong Kong, purchases of insurance policies from Hong Kong providers, casino operations in Macau, money laundering, property purchases in cities such as London, New York and San Francisco, and even underground money smuggling operations.[11]

It is never easy to estimate capital flight but the item in the formal balance of payments documentation known as 'net errors and omissions' gives us an idea. This item is essentially unrecorded current and capital account transactions, which typically reflect money leaving the country illegally or at least unofficially. According to data from the State Administration for Foreign Exchange (SAFE), net errors and omissions indicate capital outflows averaging around $70 billion a year between 2012 and 2014, rising to $223 billion in 2016.

In order to stem the haemorrhage of reserves and stabilise the Renminbi, China finally reverted to stricter capital controls. Previous attempts to clamp down on some of the methods referred to earlier to get capital out of China proved to be inadequate, and so the government tightened controls in other ways. Foreign exchange transactions were subjected to tighter document verification, and banks had to place larger reserves against currency transactions conducted in forward markets, that is for future settlement. Domestic companies were restrained from lending Renminbi to offshore entities. All foreign exchange purchases or overseas transfers exceeding $5 million had to be accompanied by 'proper' documentation to SAFE. Any overseas investment deal worth more than $10 billion or any deal unrelated to a company's onshore core business that exceeded $1 billion was subject to control by the State Council. SOEs, moreover, were severely restricted in their investments in overseas property projects exceeding $1 billion. Among other announcements to help keep capital at home, the $50,000 personal limit on currency purchases was left intact, but individuals faced tighter checks on requests for foreign exchange, and banks were asked to report large or questionable transactions to SAFE.

Capital controls were also reinforced by the 2017 financial crackdown with President Xi Jinping's blessing, under the guise of national security, with stringent measures designed to slow down or stop companies with substantial debt from investing overseas. Ostensibly, the government's concerns were about the risky and frivolous behaviour of companies that might not be able to generate the earnings necessary to repay loans. Behind this, though, it is highly likely that it was also anxious about the commercial ambitions and conditions of private companies it once exhorted to 'Go West', but which it now regards as both risky and having hostile political connections.

Dalian Wanda Group, which had acquired a large portfolio of companies, including Legendary Entertainment, the UK yacht maker Sunseeker and a variety of other companies in media, entertainment and property, was the particular focus of a government ban on bank financing for the purpose of foreign acquisitions. HNA Group, the airline-to-finance conglomerate, which owned stakes in a variety of enterprises including Hilton Hotels, Deutsche Bank and Swissport, has become embroiled in a debt and political maelstrom. It has the equivalent of $120 billion of credit lines to Chinese banks, $20 billion of US dollar bonds due for repayment in 2018 and 2019, and many of its subsidiaries have cash-flow problems. Fosun International, which owns Club Med, Cirque du Soleil and other brands, and Anbang Insurance, which owned the Waldorf Astoria in Manhattan, for example, were also under the government's spotlight. Anbang is now under government ownership, at least for the present. These four companies alone had spent $55 billion on foreign acquisitions between 2015 and the middle of 2017, or roughly 18 per cent of the total spent by Chinese companies overseas.[12]

Calmer times returned during and after 2017. The authorities stemmed the tide of capital outflows, especially those it regards as risky and unnecessary. The reserves stabilised at around $3.1–3.2 billion, and although capital is still leaving China, the amounts pale in comparison to those that were recorded in 2015–16. All quiet on the Eastern front, then, but we should wonder for how long.

Can the Renminbi's stability last?

The government certainly has tools available to manage the Renminbi and keep the market orderly, but as we have seen in the not too distant past, these are not fool-proof. In any event, they may not always be so readily usable in future. Currency intervention is possible but limited to the extent that China's foreign exchange reserves are not infinite, and it would be imprudent to allow them to fall below some sensible level. Higher interest rates may at some point be incompatible with the government's objectives for economic growth and financial stability. Capital controls have steadied the ship in 2016–17, but people find ways around them sooner or later.

It is always possible that disturbances could arise from outside China. Lurking in the wings is the strong likelihood that the external environment for China may well become less benign. The US dollar is likely to appreciate again if the Federal Reserve tightens US monetary conditions sufficiently, which well it might in view of Washington's tax cuts and fiscal stimulus programme enacted in 2018 in a more or less full employment economy. Alternatively, investors may flee riskier assets when the global economy turns down again. Sino–US relations look set to remain tense, as the US administration steps up the pressure on trade and investment relations with China. For the most part, though, these factors should not test the Chinese foreign exchange regime to the core, unless there is a serious breakdown in political relations.

More importantly, the Renminbi could be tested much more easily by developments inside China. The factors, as we examined in the previous chapter, are likely to be how the economy performs and what happens to the underlying pace of credit creation. If China wants to manage its exchange rate within certain limits, there has to be a stable relationship between the growth of domestic Renminbi assets due to credit creation and the level of foreign exchange reserves needed to 'back' the asset base of the financial system and keep the currency stable. Countries with floating exchange rates don't have this problem, because the currency can fall without there being any reserves constraint.

Consider China's situation in the light of the experience of many countries during the Asian crisis just over two decades ago. In the run-up to that crisis, many Asian economies pegged their exchange rates to the US dollar, wanted to run their own monetary policy, and opened their capital accounts to large inflows of financial and physical capital. The result in the 1990s was a financial and economic boom, but it all ended in tears.

As it did, the world was reminded of the teachings in the 1960s of a Canadian economist, Robert Mundell, who reasoned that you cannot have a pegged exchange rate, an independent monetary policy and an open capital account all at the same time. Known as the impossible trinity, it allowed Mundell to warn that monetary policy becomes ineffective when there is full capital mobility and a fixed exchange rate, and that you can only ever run two of these three policies. Since few countries choose to give up sovereignty over their monetary policy, it follows that one of the other goals has to go. Either the pegged exchange rate has to be abandoned, or else capital restrictions have to be introduced.

How does China fit this script? China will never give up control over its monetary policy, and wants to manage its exchange rate, even if not as rigidly as Asian countries in the 1990s, and restrict outflows of capital. The impossible trinity for China is slightly less impossible because the Renminbi isn't pegged as such. Nevertheless, despite that element of flexibility, or what we could call a kind of 'soft peg', China can't escape the impossible trinity altogether.

China has a totally independent monetary policy, and an exchange rate with controlled and limited flexibility, and therefore it has to have a largely closed capital account as far as outward movements of capital are concerned. Yet, because of the exchange rate system, China has to keep adequate reserves. If Renminbi assets at home grow substantially faster than US dollar reserves, excess liquidity in the home market could leak overseas unless the capital controls are watertight. In that event, the currency could only remain stable by intervention, which means running down the reserves. This process cannot continue for long because eventually the reserves might be run down to levels considered inadequate, or imprudent. If that happened, the Renminbi would either have to be allowed to float, or be devalued.

Something similar happened in 2015–16. The central problem was that Renminbi assets grew very quickly between 2014 and 2017, almost doubling from about $16 to about $33 trillion, while foreign exchange reserves fell from $4 trillion to $3 trillion. Renminbi assets, then, rose from four times the reserve cover to eleven times. Alternatively, currency reserves as a proportion of Renminbi assets, therefore, fell from about 25 per cent to about 9 per cent. If Renminbi assets carried on expanding at double-digit rates, and reserves were more or less stable, or fell, confidence in the exchange rate could come unhinged quite easily. There isn't a cast-iron level of currency reserves that is guaranteed to be safe or unsafe, and $3 trillion provides a decent cushion of security. However, there is no cause for complacency either, and even a modestly lower level of reserves for whatever reason might not suffice to keep the Renminbi stable if domestic assets keep expanding at a high rate fuelled by excessive lending.[13]

It is hard to predict, as I pointed out in the last chapter, the precise circumstances under which China will embrace a real economy-wide deleveraging leading to significantly slower economic growth. I suggested that China's wealth distribution and social fabric were not ideally structured to cushion such an outcome, and that one response might be for companies and households to attempt to get money out of China. The new repression in China and the actions being taken to put the Party into places where private companies previously had no concerns could be another catalyst. It is by no means inconceivable under those circumstances that the Renminbi could fall by between 25 and 35 per cent. In extreme circumstances, it could be floated, but this would require the government to cede control over the currency to the global foreign exchange market, and a government for which 'control' is a lodestone seems very unlikely to do that.

For now, China can sustain its monetary autonomy and its exchange rate system but only, of course, by maintaining the regime of tighter controls over capital leaving the country. Capital controls, though, can become quite porous when the confidence to keep capital at home dissipates and drives people to take it out of the country. Even though the capital flight of 2015–16 was stemmed, the steady trickle of money leaving China and of people queuing up for visas at the embassies of foreign countries are reminders that the better-off in China feel insecure. In any event, capital controls run counter to broader ambitions for the Renminbi to play a bigger role as a global currency and for its use in Belt and Road financing and funding.

In the years ahead, it will not be possible for China to sustain a stable exchange rate and stable reserves, if banking system assets continue to grow significantly faster than reserves and GDP. The Renminbi's fortunes, then, are inextricably linked to the manner in which China eventually resolves its debt and deleveraging problems.

6

DEMOGRAPHIC (AGEING) TRAP

If your holidays have ever taken you to Italian hilltop towns and villages, the Japanese island of Okinawa, Christchurch on the south coast of England, or any number of towns in Florida, but especially Punta Gorda on the western coast above Fort Meyers, you've visited some of the oldest places on earth, defined by the age structure of their populations. You'll have been aware of ramp access to buildings, and retirement homes and health clinics where there used to be maternity hospitals and playgroup centres. These capture the essence of places where about a third of the population is aged over sixty-five. If you thought that this phenomenon was restricted to advanced economies in the West, though, you would be mistaken. Russia, the whole of eastern Europe, Singapore, Hong Kong, Taiwan and South Korea are also ageing rapidly, and so is China, which by some important measures is the fastest ageing country on the planet.

Rudong County is representative of Chinese places with the highest proportion of older citizens. Just a two-hour drive north of Shanghai, Rudong had a registered population of 1.04 million in 2014, of whom half were over sixty years of age. It is not uncommon to find shops selling funeral shrouds and electric mobility scooters. There is no nightlife, and even on a Saturday night, people are seldom seen on the streets after 8 o'clock. In the past decade or so, almost 60,000 students from Rudong went to colleges across China, but when they had completed their studies, two-thirds chose to stay away and find work. Schools have closed or merged, to be replaced by nursing homes and places of third-age learning.[1] Rudong is a taste of what lies ahead for large swathes of ageing China.

China's ageing population trap is different from the debt and Renminbi traps. It's not about the instability of balance sheets or financial shocks that could bring growth screeching to a halt along with unfavourable economic and political consequences. It is more about a glacial but cumulative phenomenon. At some point, it will suddenly be recognised as critical. The good news is that China still has some time to address the consequences of ageing. Demographics are not destiny, and there are coping mechanisms available to deal with the consequences.

The bad news, though, is that the time that is available is passing by rapidly. Consider that in advanced countries, the cohort of those aged over sixty roughly doubled to about 24 per cent of the population between 1950 and 2015. At that point, per capita income was about $41,000. In China, this process is going to take just twenty years, less than a third of the time it took in richer countries. Those aged over sixty-five as a share of the population will double to 25 per cent by 2030. As I write, that is only twelve years away. If recent trends persist, income per head in 2025 would still be only a third of the level in advanced economies in 2015. Thereafter, China will age faster still. This is what is meant by 'getting old before you get rich'. It is a huge challenge.

The essence of ageing

To most people, ageing is about two things. First, it is a celebration of living longer. Second, it's about 'who's going to look after grandma, or grandpa?' In other words, it's about the care issues we confront in our families and for ourselves as longer life expectancy gives rise to a greater susceptibility to non-communicable diseases and disability. Yet the significance of ageing for whole societies and countries, as opposed to us as individuals, is fundamentally about macroeconomics. It arises because of the unique combination in human history of weak or falling fertility and rising life expectancy. In fact, while rising life expectancy is self-evidently something we do both celebrate and worry about when it comes to care, it isn't actually the core issue in ageing. Rather, it is low fertility.

Low fertility means we don't produce enough children to become workers to fully replace those reaching retirement. As a result, the size and the growth rate of the working-age population (WAP), typically defined as those aged fifteen to sixty-four, are going to stagnate or decline. Low or falling fertility is pretty much a global issue. In Denmark, France, Russia, Singapore, South Korea and Spain, cash or other incentives have been tried to get women to have more children. In Mexico, there was once a programme to hand out free viagra to older men. None of these programmes or gimmicks has worked. In China, the coming dearth of younger people and glut of older aged workers with low skill levels are going to sit uncomfortably with ambitious economic plans, present a serious social welfare challenge, and validate concerns felt elsewhere about the major economic consequences triggered by ageing.

Although economic growth is influenced by a broad array of cyclical factors at home and abroad, trend or potential growth in the longer term rises or falls in line with the change in the WAP. As the age structure of the population rises, consumption patterns will change. Households save less, principally because older, retired citizens receive less income and have to live off or draw down their savings. Lower household savings mean that unless companies or the government save more, the rate of investment will come down. Lower investment and a stagnant or falling WAP drag down trend growth.

This is going to be especially relevant to China. Because of lower trend growth, ageing societies could be places where lower inflation and interest rates plant stronger roots. Or there could be acute skill and labour shortages which push wages and inflation higher. We don't know for sure because there is no template, but we have to be vigilant about both outcomes. There is a new school of thought that argues that inflation might not pick up because labour shortages won't happen thanks to the arrival of robots and artificial intelligence that could drive millions of people out of work, contributing to chronic technological unemployment. As a result, we will end up in a low-wage economy in which poverty and income inequality will become widespread.

We have never had sustained and large technological unemployment before, though it is hard to be sure about new technologies, which are about the substitution of both brawn and brain. There will undoubtedly be difficult years ahead but I lean towards a less dystopian outcome in which modern technologies will create new jobs and demand for new goods and services, which are no easier for us to identify today than they were for previous generations confronted with their technological challenges. Perhaps countries like China, which have benefited enormously from outsourcing and inflows of foreign investment and technology, will be at risk. It will become simpler and cheaper for companies to produce goods and services locally, and China itself is fast heading towards automation and advance with a labour force that is still geared more to labour-intensive manufacturing and agriculture.

In any event, as the WAP stagnates or contracts, tax revenues become less buoyant at a time when the larger, older population becomes entitled to pensions and demands more healthcare and residential care. This places enormous strains on personal finances and on the resources of national health and care systems. We are starting to experience these phenomena already, and I examined these macroeconomic and other consequences in detail in a book a few years ago.[2] It is helpful to recapitulate the main findings as we think about an ageing China.

There is a recurring fertility pattern in economic development. As people become better off, and as women especially become more literate, better educated, and urbanise, they tend to have fewer children. This trend is reinforced as, and if, they benefit from state-provided social insurance and income support systems.

Lower fertility rates mean that child dependency, measured by the number of children aged 0–14 as a share of the WAP, declines. It falls all the faster as the WAP itself expands as a result of previously higher birth rates. For a while then, lower fertility, and a more rapidly growing WAP, bring a sort of 'sweet spot' to the economy. Incomes, consumption, savings and investment all grow more strongly, and these trends continue for some time before old-age dependency, measured by the number of those aged 15–64 as a share of the WAP, increases. This phase is known as the 'demographic dividend'. It is open to all countries to exploit, but not all do. China, for example, is the poster country for successful exploitation. Yet, if you cast your mind back to the Arab Spring in 2010, for example, you will recall political and social troubles in countries with favourable demographics. The key to successful exploitation is employment. A booming WAP is unequivocally positive for the economy but only if people are productively employed, and fairly paid.

Eventually, though, the older members of the WAP reach the retirement or pensionable age, and spearhead a substantial withdrawal of ageing workers from the labour force. Some may be able to leave the labour force gradually in a phased retirement, but others may have to leave on a cliff-edge basis, that is from Friday to Monday. The old-age dependency ratio rises.

In most advanced countries, the fertility rate has receded below the 'magic number' of 2.07 children, which is the replacement rate at which the population size is stable. The WAP is growing only slowly, or is falling. Old-age dependency is going up. The demographic dividend is banked. With the passage of years, we will have progressively fewer working-age people to support each older citizen, and the adverse economic and financial consequences referred to earlier start to manifest themselves.

The shift in the age structure of the population is going to place substantial strains on public spending, especially as regards pensions, healthcare and long-term residential care. We don't know yet precisely how these costs will be financed and paid for, but the scale of expenditure looking ahead over the next three to four decades necessitates a thorough rethink – whether you are in Beijing or Berlin – about the entitlement rights and obligations of citizens and of the state. At an individual level too, most people do not have enough savings or pension or other assets to finance twenty or thirty years in retirement, especially when expensive residential care is needed. The personal finance implications of ageing, therefore, including the need for recourse to help from the state, also become highly significant for ageing societies. If you think these are problematic in advanced economies, think how much more challenging they are in China, in general, and in China's more economically backward rural areas in particular.

Coping mechanisms

What can we do to deal with the macroeconomic effects of rapid ageing? There are really only three main ways to address the macroeconomics of ageing. Think of them as the 3 Ps: people, participation and productivity. First, the simplest way of addressing labour or skill shortages is to import them – that is, immigration. Generally speaking, though, there is only a handful of countries with immigration rates that come close to having a material effect on sustaining the WAP. It includes the US, Canada and Australia, France and the pre-Brexit-referendum UK. The political climate for immigration, though, has turned markedly more hostile, and coupled with a historical opposition to immigration in many countries, including China, other coping mechanisms have better potential.

Second, we can try and compensate for the weakness in the WAP by encouraging people who are generally under-represented at work to go to work, or stay on. Typically, these people tend to be women and older citizens. In China, where, according to Mao Zedong's dictum, 'women hold up half the sky', women used to participate much more in the workforce than they do nowadays. Getting more women into the workforce is a possibility, but it is more problematic than simply providing better maternity and childcare benefits, which in China are already quite generous. The government needs to focus on other barriers to child-bearing such as the high cost of education, healthcare and housing. It ought to be possible for older worker participation to rise too, but here China has to get to grips with a very low retirement age – officially sixty for men and fifty-five for many women – and make rapid strides towards the kind of service-oriented economy in which older workers find more conducive opportunities to work longer.

Third, the most enticing but also the hardest way to compensate for the weakness in the WAP is to get tomorrow's workers to be more productive, so that less is more, so to speak. As we know, though, productivity cannot be turned on as if it were a switch, and for China this option is of the utmost importance. As the working-age population declines, China will have to focus on the expansion of tertiary education and upgrading of skills. Rebalancing and the eventual deleveraging of finance and the economy will, in any case, mean looking for new sources of economic growth, with productivity the elixir in China, as indeed everywhere else.

China's baby bust

China's demographics are perhaps best known because of the one-child policy, introduced in 1979. This policy has the dubious reputation of being one of the starkest examples ever of the state's interference in the reproductive habits of its citizens. It was scrapped formally in 2015, after several years in which some restrictions were eased. Reflecting on the policy, we wonder what must have gone through the minds of the people who devised and implemented it. It achieved very little and saddled China with premature ageing. In other words, it created a major distortion to the age structure of society from which the country will never recover.

The devastating demographic effects of the famine from 1960 to 1962 during the Great Leap Forward crushed China's fertility. The famine claimed 40–45 million lives and was responsible for chronic starvation and malnutrition, especially among mothers and their progeny. China's fertility rate had been as high as 6.4 children per woman in 1957, but it collapsed to 3.3 children by 1961. In the years following the retreat from this disaster, fertility recovered as China had a baby boom from about 1963 to the early 1970s. During this period, the fertility rate recovered to around 5.8 children.

In 1973, amid Malthusian concerns about the high birth rate, China introduced new family planning policies that sought to prescribe later marriage, longer intervals between births, and smaller family size. By the time the one-child policy was introduced, the fertility rate had more than halved to reach 2.3 children, not all that much above the replacement rate.

During the period of the one-child policy, China's fertility rate carried on falling. In the 1990s, it went down to 1.45 children, before picking up a bit in the 2000s to about 1.5–1.6 children.

In urban areas, the one-child policy was implemented as a strict form of social control, for which compliant residents were compensated by means of pension arrangements at their place of work. Rural residents were not so fortunate, even though work–life patterns depended more on children helping out with work and familial care. In the 1980s, the state allowed them the right to bear another child if their firstborn was female. In 2013, driven by the growing awareness of the weakness of China's demographic outlook, all couples were allowed a second child, if they were both single children.

Whether the one-child policy had a marked role in lowering the fertility rate, in contrast to other factors, is a moot point, given the stance of public policy before the one-child policy was introduced.[3] In any event, rising living standards still rank as one of the best forms of contraception. Consider that many places that never had a one-child policy have the same or lower fertility rates than China. These include Hong Kong, Singapore, Taiwan and South Korea, Germany, Spain, Greece, Portugal and Italy, Russia and most of eastern Europe, and Iran.

One thing that the one-child policy certainly did achieve was a serious gender imbalance. Compared with a global birth average of about 107–8 boys per 100 girls, China's gender imbalance was about 116 boys per 100 girls during the 1990s, rising to over 121 boys in 2004. At second or third births, the imbalance was as high as 130 boys. Since then, the average has fallen back to about 116–17, though it dipped to 113.5 in 2015.[4]

The announcement at the third plenum in late 2013 that the one-child policy would be ended was followed by its final demise in 2015. The impact was immediate, if brief. The National Health and Family Planning Commission reported a rise in births of 16.6 million in 2016 – a rise of 11.5 per cent – pushing the fertility rate up to 1.7 children. The National Bureau of Statistics, using different data, reported a rise of 8 per cent, or 17.9 million, of whom nearly half were second children. This was the highest number since 2000, and the biggest annual rise for thirty years, but in 2017, the number of new births fell back to 17.2 million.

Official hopes that the abandonment of the one-child policy would spark a new baby boom proved exaggerated. China's demographics are not propitious for an enduring rise in fertility. The number of women aged twenty to twenty-nine is predicted to drop 37 per cent by 2025 to just over

71 million, and by nearly half by 2050, according to United Nations Population Division statistics. The number of slightly older women, aged thirty to thirty-four years, is expected to hold steady at around 48–50 million for the next few years, but then drop by a quarter to about 36 million by 2050. Ultimately, though, the reasons for China's low fertility are the same as elsewhere, and hinge around rising levels of income, access to better social security, higher levels of female literacy and educational attainment, and urbanisation.

It is most likely, then, that China's fertility rate is going to remain somewhere around current levels of 1.6–1.7 children, or perhaps weaken still further. According to Yi Fuxian at the University of Wisconsin-Madison, Chinese officials may have been overestimating births for many years, possibly by about 90 million between 1990 and 2016. Although the official fertility estimate for 2015, for example, was 1.6 children, he suggests it was more like 1.05 children.[5] If this is even broadly correct, then China's WAP and total population over the next twenty to thirty years will be significantly smaller than expected. This would mean that China is ageing even faster than we currently think, with further and faster increases in old-age dependency leading to more troublesome economic implications.

China's demographic dividend is banked

In 2012, China's WAP fell for the first time, by 3.45 million people, and the rate of decline is going to accelerate significantly after 2020, with the biggest annual losses (around 7 million a year) occurring between 2025 and 2035. From a current level of just over 1 billion people, the WAP is predicted to decline by 213 million by 2050. This equates to an average drop of 0.7 per cent per year, which feeds directly into lower trend GDP growth, which may be no higher than 3, possibly 4 per cent.

As the WAP declines, the number of older people will continue to rise relentlessly. Those aged over sixty, numbering around 209 million in 2015 (just over 15 per cent of the population) will increase to 294 million by 2025 (21 per cent of the population), and 490 million (36.5 per cent) by 2050. By then, there will be nearly three times as many older citizens as children.

The old-age dependency ratio, which is the number of over-65-year-olds as a proportion of the WAP, is predicted to rise from 13 per cent today, to over 20 per cent in 2025 and 47 per cent by 2050. Put another way, the 7.7 workers who support each older citizen today will be just 2.1 workers by 2050. China's old-age dependency ratio will still be less than that of Japan and South Korea by then but significantly higher than the US (37 per cent), let alone India (20 per cent).

It is an intriguing question as to why China is ageing so rapidly, especially in relation to other emerging and developing nations. As suggested, though, the combination of the family planning policies adopted in the 1970s and the one-child policy brought the demographic dividend to China much earlier. They lowered child dependency sooner, and have now left the country with premature ageing by comparison. While India's demographic dividend phase is only just starting – a third of the population is aged under fifteen – China's began in the early 1970s, and achieved its maximum effect in the quarter century to about 2012.

We can judge premature ageing by comparing China with some of its Asian neighbours when they had China's current income per head many years ago. For example, China's age structure – or the ratio of over-sixties to those aged 0–14 – is two to three times as high as it was in Japan, South Korea and Taiwan. Moreover, the size of China's working-age population today is significantly larger than it was for these countries, meaning they were able to look forward to further demographic dividend years. China's potential for future growth, therefore, is much less by comparison, because the share of younger workers in the economy is substantially lower, and China's WAP is now declining.[6]

Another indicator that China's demographic dividend has been banked is the pattern of unemployment, which has probably been rising. There is a problem of measurement here because, like other emerging countries, China lacks a robust system for recording employment and, especially, unemployment. Neither figures prominently in macroeconomic planning and management, which still tend to be overshadowed by other quantitative, and often political, targets. Until 2018, the Chinese unemployment rate had been recorded at about 4 per cent, with small variations either side, for the last sixteen years, before which there were no data. The unemployment data are of course a political construct, but also statistically flawed, largely because of a significant under-estimation of the labour force itself. They also exclude urban workers without hukou registration,[7] who do not qualify to register with local employment service agencies, and don't allow for the generally weak incentives to register because unemployment benefit levels are very low.

There is, nevertheless, some evidence to suggest there was a marked change in the rate of unemployment after the mid-1990s, before which the labour market was still tightly regulated. From the 1980s until then, which coincides with the emergence of the demographic dividend, the unemployment rate averaged 3.9 per cent, according to one study. From the mid-1990s until 2009, though, reforms to state-owned enterprises, privatisation and increased labour-market flexibility constituted an altogether different backdrop, against which the unemployment rate almost certainly rose, slowly at first, but reaching about 10.9 per cent in the period from 2002 to 2009 that ended with the financial crisis.[8]

A decade on, unemployment is lower, but it is also quite likely that it is, to some extent, hidden. Jobs are being lost in coal, steel and other sectors where overcapacity is being tackled. It is not unreasonable to think that rural unemployment has been in double digits for a long time. We know, moreover, that investment is trending down. According to a 2012 survey, the unemployment rate may have been around 8 per cent.[9] A new survey of job seekers, started in 2018, estimated unemployment at just over 5 per cent.

In future, though, ageing should tend to soak up unemployment, as labour and skill shortages develop. Yet, this isn't always as simple as it seems. Fewer young people are entering the job market, for example, as we would expect given the demographic profile of the labour force. While new employment opportunities are constantly being created, particularly in the service sector, many of these new jobs are poorly paid, insecure and require employees to work long hours in often unfavourable conditions.[10]

The robotics revolution, on the other hand, could threaten job creation and the absorption of even lower numbers of new working age people. In 2011, for example, Foxconn, the Taiwanese company that supplies Apple, Samsung and Sony, made headlines by announcing that it anticipated replacing many of its workers by installing 1 million robots over the following three to five years. Progress hasn't been as rapid as that, but the company reported in 2016 that it had already replaced 60,000 jobs with such devices.[11]

This is the tip of the iceberg. Over the last five years, China has bought more industrial robots than anyone else, including Germany, Japan and South Korea, and over a quarter of the total sold worldwide in 2015. China still had only 36 robots per 10,000 manufacturing workers in 2016, compared with 292 in Germany, 314 in Japan and 478 in South Korea, but there is no question about China's direction of travel.[12] The industrial policy, Made in China 2025, incorporates a bet by China's policymakers that the threat to jobs from machine intelligence will be outweighed by other factors.

The next few years will represent a test, then, as to whether this bet is going to pay off. Ageing may produce labour and skill shortages. New technologies may restrict those shortages to the highly skilled and educated, with resulting unemployment or poor labour market conditions for many citizens in the countryside, and less skilled workers in towns and cities.

Is China running out of workers?

The end of China's demographic dividend, and the gradual exhaustion of surplus labour in the countryside, are changing China's labour market dynamics slowly, but inexorably. In the process, China will have to turn its attention to the only thing that matters in the long run to economic growth and living standards – the growth of productivity.

For decades, migrant workers have been moving to towns and cities, adding to the urban workforce and working in more productive factories and construction sites. But there comes a point when that flow of workers slows down, and then pretty much stops. It is known as the Lewis turning point, named after the Nobel-Prize-winning development economist Arthur Lewis.

In an economy with abundant labour in low-productivity agriculture, people move from farms to factories where productivity and wages are higher. The influx of labour is associated with higher investment and employment, leading to higher profits and wages. Lewis observed, though, that as the agricultural labour surplus dwindles, industrial wages rise still faster, dampening down both profits and investment, and leading to a slowdown in overall economic growth. This then raises a key demographic question, which is whether China has reached the Lewis turning point. Put another way, are the faster growth in Chinese wages and the slower growth in the economy compatible with the idea that China is running out of workers?

At first glance, the labour supply in the countryside doesn't look to have been exhausted. There are still over 600 million people classified as rural inhabitants, and United Nations Population Division estimates suggest that as urbanisation proceeds, their numbers will fall to 500 million by 2025 and 335 million by 2050. Look a little more deeply, though, and it appears that China may be a lot closer to running out of productive workers than meets the eye.

The slow or limited progress in relaxing urban hukou eligibility in large cities, to which rural migrants want to go, is one constraint. The shortcomings of land reforms and other measures that might give farmers and rural migrants greater financial security when they left the countryside is another. Demographic factors constitute still further reasons for caution. According to the IMF, the core of the WAP, men and women aged twenty to thirty-nine, has already started to shrink, very likely depriving China of most of its supply of low-cost workers quite soon, probably between 2020 and 2025.[13]

Moreover, the labour market in the countryside is in flux because the main characteristics of the population are changing. People are getting older – the average age of farmers is now in the late fifties – and less mobile in an environment where physical work is arduous. They tend to be more set in their ways, more disinclined to work because of age or family care responsibilities, and more unsuitable for work because of age, disability or illness. The restrictions of the hukou system also tend to impede the flow of labour, especially of women, who often return home to care for older family members. It is estimated, for example, that about 80 million older citizens, or roughly 60 per cent of the total in China, live away from cities and better healthcare facilities. About a fifth of them have incomes below the official poverty line – a phenomenon often related to the cost of meeting healthcare and hospital expenses.[14]

These developments underscore the necessity and urgency for economic and political reforms to change the way China's economic model works, and to boost productivity growth and labour force participation growth. Immigration into China is very small, and it is impossible to anticipate any meaningful or politically acceptable level of immigration that would make a difference to China's shrinking working-age population. In 2016, China made it known that it was thinking about setting up its first ever immigration office to attract foreign talent to boost the roughly 600,000 foreigners living in China. In a country of 1.4 billion people, this makes Japan's 2.17 million foreigners in a country of 127 million look almost plentiful.[15] Such is the Chinese wariness of immigration, though, that nothing has been formally announced as yet.

Labour force participation data are sparse in China. The World Bank has reported that labour force participation in China fell from about 75 per cent in the 1990s to about 65 per cent.[16] About a third of the decline was attributed to the rapid expansion of tertiary education with college enrolments rising sevenfold since 1990. Thus, the largest falls in participation occurred in the 15–24 and 25–34 age groups. In and of itself, this is no bad thing, especially if higher skilled and educated young people enter work later, but with the opportunity to contribute much more.

For the rest, the bulk of the fall in participation was due to the earlier withdrawal of women from the workforce, especially in urban areas. Women aged 25–34 in particular have tended to leave the labour force – a trend that may have been attributable to various factors, including the consequences of state-owned enterprise reforms and subsequent restructuring, which were generally more favourable to male employees, a decline in the amount of publicly funded childcare, gender wage differentials, and discrimination.

By the time women reach the age of retirement at fifty-five, or fifty for women in blue-collar jobs, only 20 per cent are still in work. This is a much greater rate of withdrawal than exists in South Korea, Indonesia, the US or the UK, for example. It is hard to say whether this is strictly because of the low age of retirement, the ease of earlier withdrawal from the workforce, the gender wage gap which is quite stark, or simply cultural issues. Men, by contrast, retain much higher rates of participation by the time they retire at sixty.

The age of retirement, though, hasn't changed since the 1950s, in spite of the steady rise in life expectancy, and change is long overdue. The government plans to raise it in future, starting in 2022, although it hasn't said exactly when or by how much. It seems likely that a step-by-step approach will gradually lift it to around sixty-five years, though if speculation that it might take thirty years is correct, the benefits would not be realisable for a long time. In principle, a higher retirement age would slow down, but not reverse, the decline in the WAP, but this would still be a helpful contribution in managing the ageing transition.

Age-related spending, pensions and healthcare

Until now, we have considered how ageing affects the real, as opposed to the financial side of the economy. However, the almost fourfold rise in the old-age dependency ratio will subject China to a substantial fiscal burden. The development of coping mechanisms can help to mitigate the burden, but China will also have to make difficult decisions affecting taxation and spending to keep public debt on an even keel.

In their seminal work in the wake of the financial crisis, Carmen Reinhart and Kenneth Rogoff asserted that economic growth slows sharply, or even falls, once the ratio of public debt to GDP breaches 90 per cent.[17] While the mechanical implication here has been disputed, and may in any case be uncertain in a state-driven economy, economists are right to say that the debt to GDP ratio cannot increase continuously without important economic implications, even if precise thresholds of risk are hard to define. Age-related spending in the next twenty to forty years, though, will bring this chicken home to roost. China's broadly defined public sector debt, excluding off-budget and contingent liabilities, and the debt of state-owned enterprises, is roughly 60 per cent of GDP. There is some room, therefore, for government debt to absorb some of the costs of age-related financing, but not that much.

China spends about 7 to 8 per cent of GDP on pensions and healthcare, or roughly 3.5 per cent and about 4 per cent, respectively. There is no question that these proportions will grow significantly if China is to match the kind of pension and healthcare services offered by advanced countries today, as its own population structure changes rapidly to become more like theirs. Or China will err on the side of caution, and end up with inadequately financed healthcare programmes, poor health outcomes, and rising pensioner poverty.

The richer Organisation for Economic Co-operation and Development (OECD) nations typically spend around 8 per cent of GDP on pensions, ranging from 2 per cent in Mexico to 16 per cent in Italy. They also spend roughly 7 to 8 per cent of GDP on healthcare, though again there are large variations, with the US, for example, spending half as much again. On average, then, OECD countries spend about 16 per cent of GDP on pensions and healthcare, and a range of long-term studies by the IMF, OECD and European Commission suggests that this proportion will rise by between 3 and 12 per cent of GDP by the middle of the century.

An even longer-run study of age-related spending based on current laws, including residential care costs, and covering more than a hundred countries going out to the end of the century argues that richer countries will have to boost spending from 16 to about 25 per cent of GDP. US spending would have to rise to 32 per cent of GDP, and spending in the EU and Japan would have to increase to 24 and 28 per cent, respectively. These increases are predominantly related to healthcare, because pension reforms in recent years have already contained expected outlays.[18] China's pension and healthcare expenditure are predicted to rise from 7 to about 20 per cent of GDP. These predictions are, if anything, on the low side, and are highly sensitive to fertility and mortality assumptions. Consequently, if the expected stabilisation of fertility at around 1.85 children falls short, and/or if life expectancy rises further, then these estimates will be overshot.

Another way of trying to get a handle on what these numbers mean is to look at estimates of their net present value, a technique to discount all known future obligations back to a sum that can be understood in today's cash terms. According to the IMF, the net present value of pension and healthcare spending in China out to 2050 amounts to 83.7 per cent, and 47.1 per cent of GDP, respectively, or roughly 132 per cent of today's GDP.[19] This estimate also chimes with another actuarial forecast that suggests the current social security system has a financing gap of RMB 86 trillion, which equates to about 122 per cent of 2017 GDP.[20]

The fiscal consequences of ageing for China, then, look quite forbidding, in spite of the fact that the state has worked strenuously in the last fifteen years to improve and broaden the provision of age-related spending. While China is not unique in this regard, there is a difficult structural barrier in the shape of the state's reluctance to provide comprehensive welfare and pension support for all citizens, especially rural residents, partly due to the long-institutionalised rural–urban divide, and partly because of the equally traditional role of families as the main source of welfare and support.

Logically, the case for expanding the social safety net, and for the central government to establish the basis and rules for expansion, is compelling. Health and education are important contributors to productivity and improving the quality of human capital. Modern social security and healthcare systems have to address, in any event, the huge transformation in demand for new and better healthcare delivery systems occurring as a result of the shift in the burden of disease towards non-communicable diseases.

Stronger social and health insurance would also go some way in helping to reduce high household savings. In China's case, for example, the IMF has estimated that every 1 yuan of incremental public spending on health translates into an additional 2 yuan of urban household consumption, and that every 1 per cent rise in the share of GDP accounted for by health, education and pensions translates into a rise of 1.25 per cent in the share of consumption in GDP.[21] Stronger social security systems, then, would help to spur rebalancing in the Chinese economy.

After the so-called 'iron rice bowl', under which state enterprises provided cradle-to-grave care, was dismantled in the 1990s and 2000s, the government introduced a new social security system built around individual employment contracts. Employees and/or employers were made responsible mainly for contributions to pensions and unemployment, medical, disability and maternity insurance. Former president Hu Jintao, who emphasised ageing as a top policy priority, codified a number of previous laws and regulations in the 2011 Social Insurance Law as China moved to extend social insurance, especially pension rights, to people previously excluded, such as farmers, migrant workers and hitherto ineligible urban residents.

The current multiple, regional pension schemes that pay benefits to government employees, salaried workers in the enterprise sector, and non-salaried workers, including migrants, provide almost universal coverage for older citizens. They are mostly unfunded, or pay-as-you-go schemes in which employers and employees both contribute, but some schemes report pension surpluses, that is an excess of assets over liabilities, and others report deficits. Often these correspond to the demographic make-up of provinces. The 13th Five-Year Plan aims to bring them all into a single, unified, national scheme, although the plan faces resistance from some regional governments which fear they may either have to subsidise less well-off peers or face restrictions in accessing pension funds to finance favoured projects.

From a demographic standpoint, the main problems with China's pension system are the low pensionable age, high contribution rates for current workers, who are paying for the current elderly who never contrib-uted, and low benefits. While coverage for urban workers is now around 80 per cent, it is only about 25 per cent for migrant workers.

In other social insurance schemes, employers and employees contribute variously to housing and unemployment and medical insurance funds, while employers only contribute to disability and maternity insurance funds. The Hong-Kong based NGO China Labour Bulletin maintains, however, that 'enforcement of the Social Insurance Law, even its most basic provisions, has been very lax, and the majority of workers are still denied the social security benefits they are legally entitled to'.[22] In trying to resolve disputes, the authorities have tended to use new schemes and compliance orders rather than using the law.

A strong and equitable healthcare system is an integral part of people's sense of well-being, but also an essential input into high rates of labour force participation and, therefore, economic growth. China has taken vigorous steps to improve access to healthcare by dramatically increasing insurance coverage. The coverage rate rose from 200 million people in 2004 to virtually the whole population by 2014. In rural areas, coverage rose from around 20 per cent a decade ago to almost universal coverage in 2017. The policies pursued over this period amount to perhaps the largest expansion in healthcare insurance coverage ever recorded.[23]

Yet, despite spending a lot more, the IMF's judgement a few years ago was that the Chinese healthcare sector as a whole retains high elements of inefficiency, is fragmented, and offers inadequate and unequal protection for the population. Only 18 per cent of migrant workers have health insurance in urban locations where they live and work. Many are required to return home to claim benefits through the Rural Cooperative Medical Scheme, though the government did announce at the end of 2016 that patients could claim reimbursement in the location where they were being treated. There are not that many general practitioners in China compared with OECD countries. The IMF noted that while the latter typically have general practitioners accounting for between 10 and 40 per cent of licensed physicians, in China, the proportion is only 3.5 per cent.[24] Medical care is expensive for individuals too. Out-of-pocket expenses for healthcare have fallen in recent years thanks to government subsidies, but they nevertheless remained around 30 per cent of total health spending in 2015.

China's healthcare system is also still misaligned with the burden of disease. The key health-related issue in ageing is the epidemiological shift away from illnesses associated with maternity, children and communicable diseases to non-communicable diseases. According to the World Health Organization, more than 100 million of China's 202 million older citizens in 2013 had at least one non-communicable disease. It also reported that in 2012, 80 per cent of deaths of people aged over sixty were due to such causes, and that it expected a 40 per cent rise in non-communicable diseases by 2030, in men in particular. It predicted that three times as many people would be living with at least one such disease.[25]

China will soon have to make a big push into the expansion and improvements of pensions and healthcare, because the historically and culturally important familial care system is becoming more complicated. The structure of Chinese families is changing. Whereas once China had traditional family structures comprising a couple of generations living under one roof, so to speak, now it has 'beanpole' families, which are characterised by multiple generations, separation, and families with few or no siblings and cousins. In urban areas, younger generations are better educated than their parents, more white-collar, have a stronger sense of individualism, and are more mobile. This phenomenon has increased both physical and cultural distance between family members. Rural families, by contrast, tend to be relatively more traditional but the burden of care for children, parents and generations of grandparents falls on fewer, mostly female, shoulders, especially in families with one child.

The government needs to address the geographical and economic constraints that face all families in a rapidly ageing society, especially as parents and grandparents become ill or disabled. The better off may be able to buy domestic help or pay to admit relatives to private care homes, but most people will need more and better access to an improved social safety net.

If China wants to address the ageing population trap it is going to cost a lot of money, raise public debt, and require a fairly urgent and comprehensive rethink about how to structure, provide and pay for a more modern and generous welfare system. China will have to consider how to evolve coping mechanisms best suited to itself when it comes to labour force participation and the organisation of work. Ultimately, like all other ageing economies, it will have to look to productivity growth. This takes us directly to the issue underlying the fourth red flag, the middle-income trap.

7

MIDDLE-INCOME TRAP

In a notable book about economic development, entitled *Why Nations Fail*, authors Daron Acemoglu and James Robinson set the scene by introducing us to the city of Nogales.[1] To the north of the fence that divides it lies the American city of Nogales, Arizona. To the south lies the Mexican city of Nogales, Sonora. The geography and climate either side of the fence are identical. The ethnic make-up of the population is the same with inter-related families that go back a long way. Yet, on the US side of the fence, living standards, life expectancy and the quality of life indicators such as crime, corruption, and public facilities and services are significantly higher than they are on the Mexican side. This introduction to the book paves the way for the authors' contention that the reason for the differences, and ultimately for why nations fail, is because of differences in the nature and inclusivity of political and economic institutions.

Institutions are the legal, competition, and regulatory organisations and rules in a society that shape, govern and constrain human behaviour and interactions. They include the organs and agencies of government and law-making, labour unions and employer organisations, media, education and health, non-governmental organisations, and lobby and pressure groups. The role that institutions play goes to the heart of the process of economic development. The topic is never far from the surface of discussion about China, whether it relates to the past, present or future.

It is central to a long-running argument as to why the origins of the Industrial Revolution are traceable to an obscure Shropshire village in northern England called Coalbrookdale on the periphery of what was once the global system, and not the Yangtze delta, which had been at the heart of China's most populous and dynamic region. Joseph Needham, the celebrated Cambridge scientist, historian and Sinologist, gave his name to the 'puzzle' or 'question', which was why Europe and not China developed modern and innovative scientific research and applications, given that China's technological prowess and expertise had been established for considerably longer. Needham did not fully work out the answer though he spawned an industry of explanations ranging from the stultifying impact of a complex bureaucracy to the absence of a merchant class that would foster commercial competition, and the predominance of totalitarianism and rigid institutions in China compared to the rivalry and technological competition between European states.

Institutions, too, are central to the reasons for China's radical economic transformation from the 1980s to recent times, and also to the important debate as to how China's economy might evolve in the future, especially in view of the tightening grip of President Xi and the Communist Party over the economy and society. It is incumbent on us to ask whether China runs a risk of an institutions deficit, and therefore of falling into what development economists call a middle-income trap. Premier Li Keqiang warned specifically of this in his speech to the National People's Congress in 2016, though in more recent times he has become both less prominent and less vocal about China's future prospects.[2]

The verdict hangs in the balance because China hasn't been a middle-income country for long enough yet. On the one hand, ambitious plans for leadership in artificial intelligence and other advanced technologies might be a game-changer for productivity growth. On the other hand, we don't know if China's digital authoritarianism is appropriate to harness fully what is most likely the world's newest general-purpose technology. By the 2020s, we should know whether China is going in the right direction. Or, indeed, whether, despite everything, it is headed for a situation in which the rising share of global GDP and surging income per head stall or get trapped.

Defining the trap

The term 'middle-income trap' was coined in 2005 by two World Bank economists, Indermit Gill and Homi Kharas, who used it to describe economies that were being squeezed between low-wage and poorer competitors, and high-wage, richer innovators. It referred to a stage of economic development, usually measured by income per head or expressed as a proportion of

US income per head, where relative economic progression slows down or gets stuck.

Economists don't always agree on whether such a trap exists. Some think it misses the point about economic development, which is not so much about 'making it' from one level of development to the next, but more about a continuum on which countries have to learn to do increasingly complex tasks related to the organisation and production of economic activity. As a result, economies are like roller-coasters, slowing down and speeding up in alternating cycles, in which speed and time vary, depending on circumstances.

The two originators of the term, reviewing their work a decade later, said that their principal purpose was not to say that middle-income countries were doomed to become trapped, but to emphasise the existence of a trap that could catch middle-income countries if policymakers lacked the vigilance to do the right things, assuming (wrongly) that past economic success would guarantee future success. World Bank colleagues, arguing more recently that the middle-income trap might be a myth, were careful to note that policymakers had to be aware not only that the transition from middle to high income was a lengthy process, but also that they could only expect to succeed by pursuing consistently sound policies designed to boost productivity.[3] All economists can agree on that, and the quest to boost productivity in China lies at the heart of this chapter.

The evidence for the middle-income trap suggests that growth in middle-income countries tends to slow down initially as income per head moves into a range of $10,000 to $11,000, and then again at levels around $15,000 to $16,000 (measured in 2005 purchasing power parity to US dollars).[4] Indeed, over the course of any decade since 1950, only about a third of emerging countries were able to grow by 5 per cent or more each year, less than a quarter kept high growth going for two decades, a tenth managed to do so for three decades, and a select few – Malaysia, Singapore, South Korea, Hong Kong, Taiwan and Thailand – were able to do so for four decades.[5] Eventually, though, growth slows down everywhere.

China managed to sustain seven years of double-digit growth from 2003 to 2010, and, setting a slightly lower bar, an impressive twenty-three years of growth of 7 per cent or more. However, the economy has now locked onto a lower growth path. It is officially reported still at around 6 to 7 per cent but, as I explained in the Introduction, not all of this is what we might call 'good growth' since a large part is attributable to malinvestment, for which there will be a payback sooner or later. Even so, the outlook is for weaker economic growth in the years ahead. Using the measurement standard just cited, China's income per head may reach around $15,000 to $16,000 in 2018, precisely the point at which we would expect economic growth to decline over the medium to long term.

We know that there is a big difference in policy requirements when comparing low-income economies wanting to escape poverty and middle-income countries wanting to get rich. In the early stages of development, countries need to harness and organise physical labour and capital, produce labour-intensive, low-cost products and acquire technical and technological help developed abroad. Later, as physical labour and capital are more or less fully exploited, the economic model has to change and productivity gains have to come more from the quality of labour and capital inputs. There is a greater focus on innovation, higher education and skill formation, advanced infrastructure, and institutional arrangements such as property rights and the rule of law.

There are also big differences in economic circumstances when comparing countries that were once middle-income and became rich, such as Ireland, Israel, South Korea and Spain, with others that didn't and stayed middle-income, such as Argentina, Brazil, and now perhaps Turkey, Thailand and South Africa. Brazil and South Korea, for example, had similar economic and demographic attributes in the 1960s and achieved comparable growth of around 5.5 to 6.5 per cent per year until the 1980s. Yet South Korea went on to chalk up two decades of only slightly lower growth and to develop an innovation-based industrial sector, but Brazil managed neither. South Korea is now a high-income country, but Brazil's income per head, allowing for inflation and exchange rate changes, is not so different from what it was fifty years ago.[6]

Looking back to the end of the Second World War, the story of economic development has vindicated another recent World Bank view that 'contrary to what many growth theories predict, there is no tendency for low- and middle-income countries to converge toward high-income countries'.[7] Perhaps it should have said 'general tendency' and 'converge fully'. In one study of 124 countries between 1950 and 2010, 35 of 52 middle-income countries became trapped.[8] If we look at the World Bank's 167 member countries in 2016 (excluding the 48 oil-producing countries and low-population, high-income island states), there were 31 low-income nations (less than $1,045 of income per head), 51 lower-middle-income countries ($1,046 to $4,125), 53 upper-middle-income countries ($4,126 to $12,735), and 32 high income countries, which were all members of the OECD.

This structure hasn't changed very much according to the widely quoted 'China 2030' study done by the World Bank and the Chinese State Council's Development Research Center in 2013. It noted that of the 101 countries or territories classified as middle-income in 1960, only 13 became high-income countries, most successfully adapting their economic development models and institutions as they matured. This select group comprised Hong Kong, Japan, Singapore, South Korea and Taiwan, along with Equatorial Guinea, Greece, Ireland, Israel, Mauritius, Portugal, Puerto Rico, and Spain. Development economists nowadays ask important questions not only about what countries such as Brazil, Argentina, Venezuela and Russia have to do to spring their traps, but also whether the list of trapped countries might also now extend to countries such as Chile.

What about China, then, which only became a low-middle-income country in 2001 and a high-middle-income country in 2010?

The key is total factor productivity

China certainly has all the ingredients of an economy facing a structural growth slowdown. It has had an unusually long period of high growth that's ended. Debt has accounted for a lot of growth in recent years, and this cannot continue forever. In any event, there are many things that China has proved successful at doing in the past, but which it can no longer repeat because they were one-off accomplishments. For example, China could only join the World Trade Organization once. It could only embark on a massive real-estate ownership and investment boom once. It could only enrol all of its children in secondary school once. Exploiting the demographic dividend, benefiting from rural–urban migration, and raising the share of employment in industry and manufacturing to peak levels were all achievements that could only happen once. Riding the wave of powerful globalisation during the 1990s and 2000s was a bonus, but we don't know when those go-go days are going to return, if at all.

Put simply, complex upper-middle-income countries such as China have, by definition, exhausted much if not most of the potential to get growth by deploying and exploiting physical capital and labour. Rebalancing requires a switch in focus, policy and resources away from investment and credit towards efficiency and innovation, human capital and productivity, and coping mechanisms to deal with the consequences of ageing and new technologies.

In a nutshell, China, like many countries, is faced with the challenge of having to boost its total factor productivity (TFP). A brief explanation would be helpful here because TFP isn't actually measurable. It is in fact a residual in GDP growth accounting, once we have accounted for the more measurable contributions made by changes in labour and capital inputs. It is, basically, an efficiency term that captures the impact of technical progress and institutional arrangements that enable total GDP growth to exceed the sum of its labour and capital parts. Think, for example, of things like changes in knowledge and 'know-how', as opposed to information; the impact of new technologies on new products and processes; competition rules, the operation of the rule of law, and the security of contracts; the way factories or offices are organised; business processes and management techniques; and the effects of high levels of trade and commercial integration. These things all enter into economic accounting gymnastics, and are subsumed under TFP.

The Nobel Prize-winning economist Paul Krugman famously drew attention to the concept of TFP when discussing the outlook for dynamic Southeast Asia in 1994 in an article entitled 'The Myth of Asia's Miracle'.[9] Krugman's argument was that Asia's economic success could only be properly understood and assessed by distinguishing additions to from improvements in labour, capital and technology. Or, by separating out perspiration from inspiration. Krugman's view was that there was at the time no evidence of a strong efficiency factor in Asian growth, and that the West had nothing to fear from the proposition that Asia would steal a march on the West in technology, or demonstrate the superiority of more authoritarian economic regimes. Remember this was in 1994 – China was still finding its feet after Tiananmen and Deng's Southern Tour. Almost on cue, from Krugman's point of view, Asia collapsed in crisis three years later.

Krugman's propositions were contentious then, but even more so today, partly because of the damaged reputation of the West's economic model, and importantly because of the exceptional rise of China. His point about the sources of growth, though, was right at the time and still is. Many countries in Asia are outward-looking, financially stable, and have a sharp focus on trade, innovation, infrastructure and technology. At the same time, however, they have the challenge of ageing, under-utilisation of women at work, and inadequate social safety nets. There is a weak culture of entrepreneurship, and bankruptcy regimes are often poor. Other shortcomings include human capital formation, distortionary trade and state-owned enterprise policies, and inadequate attention to the rule of law.[10] China fits many, if not all, of these descriptions. It has definitely arrived at the point where it needs to push up its TFP growth in order to re-energise the momentum needed to avoid stagnation in the future, relatively even if not absolutely.

In the past, China's TFP has occasionally been remarkably strong. The first such period, Deng Xiaoping's 'Reform and Opening Up' years, was the early 1980s, when it grew by nearly 5 per cent per year and accounted for almost half of China's growth. After this, it slumped in the period spanning the Tiananmen protests, but then surged again between 1991 and 1995 to over 7 per cent a year as state-owned enterprise reforms were pursued and migrant flows from farms to factories picked up. During this phase, TFP was generating about three-fifths of Chinese growth. Later, in the wake of accession to the WTO, TFP moderated to about 4 per cent per year (about two-fifths of economic growth) until 2010. Since then, however, it has been anaemic, growing by about 2 per cent per year until 2015, and subsequently a little less.[11]

The point is the association of fast rates of TFP growth with rapid and liberal economic reforms, and weaker TFP growth with stalled or weaker reform efforts.[12] It is also interesting to note how fluctuations in TFP growth correlate with the efficient use of capital, measured by the 'incremental capital–output ratio (ICOR)', which I discussed in Chapter 3. So, for example, in the early 1980s and 1990s, when TFP was robust, capital efficiency rose significantly. In these periods, the ICOR fell from about 4 to 2 and 1.5, respectively. In other words, less capital was needed to generate each additional unit of output. Again, after WTO entry, TFP growth was solid, and the ICOR dropped from 6 to 2. At other times, and since 2010, however, weaker TFP growth has gone hand-in-hand with higher capital inefficiency. In 2014, for example, the ICOR rose to 9, according to the National Bureau of Statistics, and while it probably fell back during and immediately after 2017, it remains historically quite elevated.

The key challenge in future, then, is to strengthen TFP growth, and that means efficiency improvements in the allocation of resources and capital, and putting some new backbone into economic reform. Chinese leaders talk about reform all the time, but, as I have already explained, when Xi's China talks about reform, it does not mean what we in the West mean, and it is certainly not liberal, market-oriented reform.

Curbing financial excess and avoiding financial instability are unequivocally good things to do to mitigate the risk of bad economic shocks, but they don't boost TFP, as such. More regulation may actually stifle it. Limiting excess capacity in coal and steel permanently and persistently will help the viability of some heavy industry state-owned enterprises (SOEs), but it won't transform the Chinese economy. Reducing inequalities and cleaning up the environment are also good things to do, but a transformative productivity boost needs much more.

The optimistic view is that with Xi Jinping in situ for the foreseeable future, and China fully focused on new technologies, including artificial intelligence, the economy will be allowed to experience some ups and downs, and productivity benefits will emerge to boost TFP. A more pessimistic view is that the political environment under Xi Jinping is significantly different from what it was during previous transformative reform periods in the 1980s and 1990s, and after WTO membership. The strong emphasis on the personal power of the president, the much strengthened role and function of Party control, and the sharper social and political repression have certainly raised the bar for success.

It is not hard to see China's authoritarian economy succeeding in some of its new industrial endeavours, but it is impossible to know if it can and will deliver enduring productivity gains. The Soviet Union, for example, was no slouch when it came to science, space, engineering and research and development. Neither was ancient China. And yet, these were not enough. We should at least consider, therefore, how important robust institutions and governance are to realising sustained productivity improvements. And also just what so-called general purpose technologies entail, how they differ from run-of-the-mill innovation and invention, and whether they can fulfil their potential in a state- and target-driven model.

Governance, institutions and Xi's new authority

China faces an important governance challenge. Some believe it is about whether the Communist Party system is strong enough to survive or derive continuous legitimacy, but its status and prestige are, for the foreseeable future at least, not in question. President Xi Jinping, whose power derives from his positions as general secretary of the Chinese Communist Party and head of the Central Military Commission, was secure even before the constitutional changes in 2018 that included the abandonment of presidential term limits.

Political scientists will scrutinise the consequences of Xi's emperor-like status, including the possible risks from adversaries, and the eventual circumstances of his succession. The concern here is more about a different aspect of governance, namely whether it is sufficiently robust and adaptable to meet the demands of an increasingly complex, upper-middle-income economy.

Good governance is widely recognised as central to successful economic development and the fulfilment of a stable and prosperous society. High standards of governance derive from the institutional and bureaucratic framework, and rules and mechanisms needed to produce well-designed policies that advance the interests of society as a whole and that are implemented fairly, efficiently and transparently.

Investors and companies, for example, making long-term economic commitments, are more likely to feel confident about investment and growth in a system where property rights are firmly established. Earlier in the book, we saw how important this was to China, to a degree under Mao but much more so later. The rule of law, to which Chinese officials often refer even though they actually have a system of rule by law, is central to the security and neutrality of contracts and rights, and to the independent adjudication of disputes. Where legal systems enforce and protect private property rights and contractual arrangements, savers and investors are much more likely to be willing and able to channel money into the financing of companies and longer-term projects, and financial markets are more likely to flourish.

As economic development proceeds, and especially as countries become more complex, good governance is essential in addressing challenges and weaknesses. In China's case nowadays, these include rising debt dependency, imbalances in the economy and in the distribution of wealth between the private and state sectors, income and regional inequalities, education and healthcare, and the environment and water scarcity. Governance issues, therefore, pervade agriculture, education, finance, labour markets and social protection, and even the collection of statistics, protection of intellectual property rights, and banking and tax collection. Governance structures encompass the role of the state, relationships with local and provincial governments and SOEs, and the broader framework of institutions that sets the balance between the state- and Party-oriented versus market-oriented allocation of resources.

The claims of effectiveness in favour of China's bureaucracy have rarely been in doubt. A bureaucratic and administrative machine that is unencumbered by democratic institutions and processes should be able to make decisions and implement policies. Consider, for example, the way in which China developed town and village enterprises, as explained in Chapter 2, as the agents of investment and economic growth, regardless of the fact that they were owned by local and provincial authorities. They were publicly owned but this was overshadowed by the fact that they partnered with private entrepreneurs in a 'de facto' property rights arrangement in which the threat of expropriation was deemed less likely by virtue of the partnership.[13]

Throughout the last twenty-five years or so, China's bureaucracy has continued to adapt, and experiment with, and test aspects of, the 'capitalist mode of production' on a trial-and-error basis. It introduced a vast body of law, even though it is subservient to the Party and the state. It established and pursued a number of market pricing mechanisms and liberalisation initiatives while phasing out many quantitative economic controls and targets. It privatised many SOEs, while retaining and rebooting others at the heart of the economic system. It modernised and liberalised the financial system at home and its interaction with foreign finance systems up to a point, even if the last few years have seen some back-pedalling as the implications of liberalisation became difficult to absorb and accept. The bureaucracy was highly effective as China prepared and implemented its response to the 2007–8 financial crash, for example.

At different points in time, China, like many other countries, has always had to assess where the shifting structural and institutional barriers to economic progress lay, and what to do about them. Before Deng Xiaoping came to power, the main obstacle to progress was the absence of any market-based system for resource allocation and production incentives. Under Jiang Zemin, it was the domination of SOEs and the stifling effects on the private enterprise sector. In the roaring 2000s, Hu Jintao's focus was largely on the household sector and the reconstruction of a social safety net.

President Xi has an altogether different set of challenges and circumstances, which are in many ways greater and politically more awkward. His task was and remains to change China's growth model and incentive systems, accept permanently lower growth, rebalance the economy, and re-establish a new economic, social and political contract with an increasingly middle-class and technologically aware citizenry. Xi is well schooled in Marxist dialectics, and has surely figured out that China's major contradiction, from the standpoint of development, is the tension between this agenda and the changing nature of the aspiring middle class. The answer, as he sees it, is through the re-emphasis of ideology. Yet ideology instead of pragmatism, and greater authoritarianism of the Party instead of rule by state institutions, raise important questions of governance effectiveness and sensitivity.

Even before the constitutional changes that took effect in 2018, China did not rank very highly in commonly followed measures of governance. The World Bank publishes an annual report, 'Governance Indicators', which assess numerous data points, according to six dimensions of governance: voice and accountability, political stability and absence of violence, government effectiveness, regulatory quality, rule of law and control of corruption. The higher the percentile in which a country falls, the higher the standards of governance. In 2016, China was situated in the 68th percentile for government effectiveness, and the 49th for control of corruption. These were both categories in which significant improvements had occurred over the previous decade, but elsewhere, rankings were lower or significantly lower, and had neither improved much nor regressed.

In the annual Corruption Perception Index, published by Transparency International and covering 180 nations, China ranked 77th in 2017 with a score of 40 on a scale of 0 (highly corrupt) to 100 (very clean), compared with an average of 43. The highest-ranked countries – Denmark, New Zealand, Finland, Sweden and Switzerland – scored well on things such as press freedom, access to information about public spending, standards of integrity of public officials and independence of judicial systems. These are areas in which China is most unlikely to improve its rankings. China's anti-corruption campaign was certainly noted but with the caveat that its effectiveness in the absence of transparent and independent oversight was questionable.

The Fraser Institute's Human Freedom Index ranks 159 countries according to 79 data streams spanning the rule of law, security and safety, several freedoms (of movement, religion, association and civil society, expression and information, identity and relationships), and policies covering the size of government. This looks at the extent to which countries rely on political processes to allocate resources, goods and services, the legal structure and security of property rights, sound money policies, freedom to and of trade internationally, and the regulatory environment in credit and labour markets, and business. Relative to 2008, China's ranking dropped from 120th to 130th, though the latter was slightly higher than the previous year, and it ranked higher at 112th in economic freedom only. Overall, China ranked just below Vietnam and Russia, and considerably below India in 102nd place.

The Chinese view may of course be that these governance measures are of no consequence, and that its own governance model has hardly done a poor job until now. While true, 'until now' is an important qualifier. Governance might well be described as firm and disciplined nowadays, but it is also more controlling, interfering, Party-dominated and Leninist, especially in the wake of the constitutional changes agreed in 2018.

One of the major changes, the abandonment of the two five-year presidential term limits, inscribed in the state constitution in 1982 to prevent the rise of authoritarianism and institutionalise an orderly succession of power, was an audacious move and means that one-man, dictatorial rule has returned to China within one generation. Similarly, the incorporation into the constitution of the newly formed National Supervision Commission represented a massive change in governance and a major reversal of four decades of practice in which Party discipline and the state's judicial functions were at least nominally separated. Arbitrary and discretionary powers over Party discipline and the criminal justice system have now been handed over to the Party.

The two-term limit change means that President Xi will not only stay in power after 2022, when his second term would normally have expired, but that he could stay on as president for life. It is possible to conjecture that this will allow Xi to implement tough economic decisions in the next few years without having to fret about the succession, but it is hard to pretend that this is a positive change in and for the governance of China. One-man rule makes China's political system and economy more vulnerable to instability. Inevitable errors and miscalculations will be made, without institutions and perhaps individuals willing to stand up to a strong leader. Eventually, he might become more detached, as many long-serving leaders do. Moreover, with the orderly succession of leaders now abandoned, there is a much greater risk that Xi's opponents and adversaries, who are understandably lying low, will rethink their options. They may not want to bide their time for an indefinite period.

Another major change, the establishment of a National Supervision Commission, formalises and takes on the task of fighting corruption at every level in the state bureaucracy from ministries down to provinces, cities and counties. The commission will be able to extend its powers of discipline and control to all public servants, and not just those who are Party members, which was as far as the Central Commission for Discipline Inspection could go. As a Party organ, rather than state authority, it will not be subject to interference by any administrative agencies, courts, public organisations or individuals.

The funnelling of control and decision-making back into the Party at all levels had already been under way in Xi Jinping's first term, when he gave additional emphasis to Leading Small Groups (LSGs), which are policy bodies with roots going back to the revolutionary period. Largely disbanded or reorganised in the 1980s, many continued to be a forum for discussion about policies and the formulation of guiding principles.

Under Xi Jinping, they acquired a new lease of life as policy-making bodies. Xi increased their number by about a third to eighty-three.[14] Around twenty-six are Party LSGs, the remainder are State Council bodies. These groups involve different and sometimes competing parts of the bureaucracy, and operate across a broad universe of economic, social and other policies. Yet, in many respects, they have effectively drawn power and accountability away from technocrats and ministries. As much as they may have facilitated decision-making and implementation, the track record on reforms leans strongly towards the view that the relevant groups must also have acted as a deadweight, sometimes stifling reforms, sometimes rendering processes too cumbersome. Macroeconomic, financial, industrial and other policy decisions have not always been followed through by actions and effective implementation, nor have they always been mutually coherent and compatible. Market-oriented reforms in the financial sector, for example, have sometimes been poorly sequenced and run far ahead of reforms in the real economy. Reforms in the real economy, especially regarding SOEs much trumpeted in 2013, mostly gathered dust.

Other radical changes in the structure of government institutions were unveiled at the National People's Congress in 2018. In addition to the National Supervision Commission, and the merger of the Banking and Insurance Regulation Commissions referred to in Chapter 4, LSGs on cybersecurity, reform, economics and finance and external affairs are being upgraded to commissions, a move that also underlines the transfer of authority away from state institutions and ministries. A new Market Supervision Administration will deal with business regulation and competition policy, a rebranded and reorganised Ministry of Agriculture and Rural Affairs will manage rural development and try to boost its productivity, the Ministry of Environmental Protection will have an expanded remit over pollution and climate change, a new Resources Department will have oversight over land use and urban planning, and local and tax bureaus will be merged in an attempt to re-organise fiscal responsibilities, and possibly, though we have heard this often before, introduce a property tax. The Party's Department of Propaganda is going to take control of film, news media and state publications.

Enterprising and administratively positive as these changes could be, we should not presume that organisational change itself will break new productivity ground. China has never been backward in making big organisational changes. The trick, though, is to build inclusive institutions that enable and incentivise people to feel involved, do, and think about, things differently, and carry them out with greater efficiency. Whether the all-powerful, controlling Party will prove adept at these tasks is a moot point.

China's biggest vested interest is itself

Authoritarian and repressive governments do not necessarily lack legitimacy, especially if they are perceived by citizens as benign. In this sense, even Xi's authoritarian China could certainly change and improve its governance model if it were seen to be delivering justice, a better environment, income redistribution, better health and education and so on. The provision of public goods, in other words, can be the quid pro quo for even benevolent dictators and kleptocrats to remain in power and popular. It's hard to think of many examples, but people sometimes cite Turkey's Mustafa Kemal Atatürk early in the twentieth century, and in more modern times, Singapore's Lee Kuan Yew comes to mind. They are, however, almost certainly exceptions to the rule.

Xi Jinping's personal and political control should mean that he can implement reforms without interference or pushback. Economic reforms will be much less about liberalisation and market reform than those that focus on prices and tariffs, administrative and organisational changes, and regulations. They will be designed to allow demand and supply interactions to determine who participates in markets and where they are, the composition and logistics of goods and services to be supplied, and the incentives offered to both buyers and sellers. They may also be tailored to deliver financial stability, greater efficiencies and competition for local enterprises, and a favourable environment for national champions in key sectors and new technologies. All outcomes, though, will be in the context of meeting the Party's political goals and objectives.

It is not normal, however, to change and improve things, or to kick-start needed productivity growth, without experiencing sometimes painful disruption, the outcomes of which involve both winners and losers, and the conquest of interests that are hostile or have something to lose. In his seminal writing, the US economist Mancur Olson emphasised why, in the ascent to industrial leadership, states had to prevent vested interests, such as the military, steel magnates, railroad tycoons, bankers and so on, from blocking structural change in the economy and society.[15] He called these vested interests 'distributional coalitions', and said that they tend to have crowded agendas, have difficulties reaching effective decisions in a timely way, have recourse to increasingly complex regulations, and build layer upon layer of government. These special interests create a sort of institutional sclerosis that inhibits change and lowers long-term economic performance.

It is China's misfortune that the biggest vested interest opposed to disruptive and fundamental reform is the Party itself. It was not always thus, but seems increasingly so in Xi's China. Leaving aside economic and commercial decisions within the state and government sectors, SOE decisions, for example, have to be approved by Party committees in the firms. According to a State Council document issued in 2017, moreover, the Party is also seeking to influence decisions made by private, including foreign, companies, by establishing Party units or cells in or close to their operational management. Many larger private companies are legally private, but they either have complex ownership structures behind which are state entities, or they are what might be called 'political insider' enterprises to the extent that their owners and senior managers have close Party connections and enjoy political as well as commercial relationships with top Party officials.

The key issue underlying the vested interest conundrum derives from the Party's structural conflict of interests. Curiously, this was laid bare in a 2015 research paper on the financial sector, produced by the State Council's Development Research Center and the World Bank, but with broader economic implications.[16] The report was made available online, but the concluding and sensitive Section 3 was removed a week later. The official explanation cited clearance procedures but at the time there was a strong view that its removal was more about political sensitivity.[17]

Section 3 was essentially about shortcomings in China's governance and institutional structure that were hindering the kind of reforms needed to sustain growth, rebalance the economy and address wasteful investment and excessive debt.[18] It highlighted the central role of the state, which is misaligned in a hierarchy in which its role as a strategic promoter dominates both its role as an owner, and in turn, as a regulator. Put another way, the state is at the heart of a fundamental conflict of interests that cannot be resolved as things stand. In its role as promoter, the state intervenes extensively and directly in ways that have no parallels in mixed economies. It has a pervasive and conflicting ownership role that is even sharper at subnational government levels, because many local and provincial governments are simultaneously not only owners and regulators but also among the most egregious debtors.

The report's strong conclusions had no chance of being accepted by Beijing and it is not surprising that Section 3 was removed. It argued that China needed to wind down or lessen the state's role as an owner of institutions in general – which would necessitate privatisation of state assets – and of the main regulatory agencies in particular. In its role as promoter, the state could continue to intervene in many areas but its role should be to nurture, encourage and facilitate change rather than to take responsibility for it completely. Only this way, the report said, can the state's regulatory role be released from conflicts of interest.

It is pretty clear that the Communist Party will not sanction any such outcomes. On the contrary, it is moving precisely in the other direction. Yet the curious tale of Section 3 serves to underline an important governance weakness, which is the conflicted role of the state. We can see the relevance of this and other governance issues by taking a detailed look at one of the exciting areas that could help China to generate new productivity gains in future and circumvent the middle-income trap: technology.

Going all out for technology leadership

In March 2016, Lee Sedol, a South Korean master of the ancient and complex board game Go, was defeated by AlphaGo, a Google computer program. Two months later, AlphaGo was deployed in China to take on the world's leading Go player, Ke Jie, and won. The event is alleged to have had profound consequences on the thinking of leading Chinese scientists and politicians, who were taken aback by the cutting edge in artificial intelligence (AI) seemingly shown by the US.

Speaking to the 19th Congress in 2017, President Xi said: 'We need to speed up building China into a strong country with advanced manufacturing, pushing for deep integration between the real economy and advanced technologies including internet, big data, and artificial intelligence.' In April 2018, speaking at the National Cyberspace Work Conference, he alluded to the now popular narrative that, having missed out on the Industrial Revolution and ended up subject to the rule of foreigners, China has to seize the historic and rare opportunity to grasp the new technological revolution so as to realise the Chinese Dream.

No one should think that China isn't deadly serious about this, or that Chinese innovation nowadays is mostly about copying Western ideas more cheaply. China and the West both want to be tech leaders, and will probably have to settle for sharing the spoils. This is no ordinary tech race, though, and what sets it apart is that the ultimate prize is the full exploitation and commercialisation of what is almost certainly our newest general-purpose technology (GPT). Following in the footsteps of steam, railroads, electricity, the internal combustion engine and the internet, this GPT will also be distinguished not by big data or AI, specifically, but by the hundreds of other innovations and changes that they spawn in many other sectors, products and processes. In a nutshell, new technologies enable multiple and unpredictable uses and applications, which tend to empower consumers, raise competition and productivity, and lead to significant changes in regulations.

China's challenge is not just to be world leader in AI, robotics or driverless vehicles, but to encourage the disruptive changes wrought by GPT and so harness the productivity benefits across the board. The fundamental issue is whether a centralised and authoritarian political system is what is needed to guide innovation, disruption, and creative industries, or whether it is the antithesis of what makes these things happen. One could argue the case both ways, but in the end what matters is not just scientific and industrial expertise, but also the quality of human capital and ingenuity from top to bottom in frontier companies. It remains to be seen, of course, but where the interests of senior executives and political and state bureaucrats are closely aligned, it is reasonable to assume that politics hold sway over the commercialisation, funding and financing of worthwhile and profitable innovation.

China's focus on new technologies goes back a long way. In 2006, the National Medium- and Long-Term Plan for the Development of Science and Technology (2006–2020) served as a blueprint for their development. It came with the hope that it would bring about the 'great renaissance of the Chinese nation' and turn China into a technological powerhouse by 2020 and a global leader by 2050. The authors lamented China's shortcomings as an economic power principally because of 'our weak innovative capacity' and hatched a new policy that carried the now common term 'indigenous innovation'.

It seemed innocuous enough, even praiseworthy as a strategy to encourage Chinese enterprises and researchers to develop home-grown technologies. Yet, over time and for foreign firms especially, indigenous innovation came to be associated with various forms of protectionism and favouritism for local companies, unfair trade and commercial practices, and the leveraging of Chinese technical progress on the back of imported technology either from acquisitions abroad or through foreign companies operating in China. According to a US Chamber of Commerce report, indigenous innovation came to be considered by many international technology companies as 'a blueprint for technology theft on a scale the world has never seen before'.[19]

The financial crisis that followed soon after and then the fractious Party backdrop to Xi Jinping's coming to power in 2012 may have drawn attention away from China's focus on innovation and technology, but only fleetingly. The 13th Five-Year Plan (2016–2020) sets out ambitious plans to develop modern manufacturing and new technologies. It aims to deliver significant results in innovation-driven development, flourishing business start-ups, and total factor productivity. It says that science and technology should become more deeply embedded in the economy, and lays out a number of goals which will help China become a talent-rich 'country of innovation'.[20]

The launch of the State Council's industrial policy Made in China 2025 (MIC25) in 2015 and subsequent announcements took many of these initiatives further. Their focus is on key sectors, including advanced rail, ship, aviation and aerospace equipment, agricultural machinery and technology, low and new-energy vehicles, new materials, robotics, biopharmaceuticals and high-end medical equipment, integrated circuits, and 5G mobile telecommunications.

Taken aback by AlphaGo's victory, as noted earlier, China stepped up a few gears to formalise and launch nationally an ambitious AI strategy, already underway at the local government level. A year after the match, the State Council set out the Next Generation AI Development Plan with the goal of boosting China's AI status, from being in line with competitors by 2202, to world-leading by 2025, and the world's primary source by 2030. During this period, the industry is supposed to increase in value from RMB 1 to RMB 10 trillion, or from \$150 billion to \$1.5 trillion. This plan was followed in quick succession by a report from the National Natural Science Foundation entitled 'Guidelines on AI Basic Research Urgent Management Projects', the announcement by the National Development Reform Commission of an AI Innovation and Development Megaproject, and a three-year Action Plan by the Ministry of Industry and Information Technology.

Weighing up the tech wheat and chaff

Judged by statements, and published plans and reports, then, it looks as though China just has to join up the proverbial dots to fulfil its ambitions.

Yet you might be forgiven for asking whether it is really all that simple. In several respects, China really is making waves, and unquestionably enjoys strong competitive advantages deriving from the sheer size of its market and population – especially where large data collection and processing are involved – and from the absence of privacy and confidentiality laws, at least relative to Western countries. There are over 1 billion mobile phone users and about 730 million internet users. Mobile payment volumes were about $5 trillion in 2016 and rising, a huge multiple over the US. Yet, there are also many caveats, and it is not enough simply to acknowledge uncritically China's alleged Midas touch in new technologies.

High-speed rail is one of the sectors commonly cited as an example of the transformation from reliance on foreign to Chinese manufacturers. In telecommunications, Huawei has earned its spurs as a global player. Several other companies are well known internationally, such as ZTE, which is also in telecommunications, and China Telecom, China Unicom, and China Mobile in broadband and communications. Xiaomi, which designs and sells smartphones, mobile apps and laptops is a global top five company in smartphones. Alibaba, the e-commerce giant, has a cloud subsidiary that is working on smart cities. Tencent and Baidu, which are internet services companies, are exploring medical imaging and facial recognition, and autonomous vehicles, respectively. Lenovo computers, Air China, and Moutai, the beverage company, also exemplify Chinese companies that got big in China and turned their attention to foreign markets. A strong domestic focus and large home-market size have certainly helped these and other companies, and there's no question that they have excelled in more efficient production and in adapting imported technologies and products to local consumer tastes.

In 2017, China's first commercial airliner, the Comac C919, made its maiden flight, and China hopes it will be able not only to meet the demand for its own significant domestic air traffic growth, but compete with Airbus and Boeing internationally. For now, though, the only major parts of the plane made by local companies are the wings and the tail. It is hoping to make an even bigger splash with the C929 long-haul aircraft, which it is building together with Russia, and which is scheduled to make its first flight between 2025 and 2028. Nevertheless, it is still expected that foreign companies will be required to supply key and complex parts of the jet.

China is increasingly looking further up the value chain of technology nowadays, including AI, big data and robotics, 3D-printing and nanotechnology, alternative energy and driverless vehicles, biotechnology and biomedicine, and aerospace. It aims to have a nation-wide 5G network by

2020, and is also pursuing its own space programme, which has included the launch of manned missions, cargo spacecraft, space stations, and a number of satellites and measuring and observation systems. China is also a major player in some of the more sophisticated technologies, including quantum computing, cyber-defence, DNA sequencing and gene-editing medical treatments.

Impressive as all these things are, they don't yet add up to a watertight case for significantly higher productivity growth. So where are the weak spots, and are they surmountable?

The role and appeal of foreign technology are not yet spent bullets by any means in China's quest for technological leadership, but the intensification of trade and technology disputes with the US will inevitably hasten China's aim to lower or eliminate its dependence on foreign technological expertise. It is fair to point out that it is no longer appropriate to charge that China is always a 'copycat innovator' or lacks the prowess to do its own thing.[21] A lot of capital, moreover, is going into start-ups and smaller companies, with estimates that the size of venture capital infusions into small-scale technology firms rose from $12 billion between 2011 and 2013 to $77 billion between 2014 and 2016.[22] On the other hand, China still looks to foreign technology to drive a lot of its innovation, high-tech exports and advances in key modern sectors. In 2014, nearly 90 per cent of Shanghai's high-tech industry output, for example, were traceable to foreign enterprises, despite the policy of 'indigenous innovation', and in Chongqing, which makes over a third of the world's personal computers, the industry is almost completely linked to foreign investment.[23]

In AI, it is argued that China still lags behind the US, for example, in several important indicators, including advanced 'university AI programs, qualified faculty, overall numbers of AI companies, and companies capable of producing cutting-edge semiconductors for AI applications. In fact, China's leaders are soberly aware that their nation risks remaining behind in developing potentially transformative technologies.'[24]

China has not yet developed strengths, for example, in semiconductors, which it has been trying to develop, unsuccessfully, since the 1960s. A policy switch in the 2000s from central planning to equity investments has gained some traction, but ended up with over-capacity at the low end of the sector and weakness at the high end. It lags behind the US in university-led research. It falls considerably short when it comes to AI engineers and scientists. It does not have the same business-facing software capacity, or high levels of integration between its technology and industrial sectors.

Chinese firms tend to be less digitised, and do not yet really compete when it comes to commercialising technologies overseas or setting global standards. A recent study of China's AI potential judges that it is about half as advanced as that of the US, according to an AI Potential Index, designed to approximate AI capabilities in key drivers of overall AI development. China's one lead is in access to data.[25] These things can change, but at the same time, it would be naive to think that the US or other Western companies are going to stand still and allow their competitive edges to be eaten away.

It is also important to note that when it comes to human capital, or the quality of education, and to research and development, there are weaknesses that remain to be addressed. Human capital improvement is a critical determinant of economic development. While bright Shanghai schoolchildren with high PISA (Programme for International Student Assessment) scores regularly command attention, especially in Western countries, it is rarely pointed out that they are not as representative as is often made out. They are accurate readings of a sample of children, but they sit at one extreme of a rural–urban educational attainment chasm that is of enormous social significance for the chances of avoiding the middle-income trap.

All of the countries (excluding oil and island states that are not strictly comparable) that managed to become high-income since 1945 managed to establish developed country-wide education standards, defined by the proportion of working-age people who completed secondary education. China's position in this respect shows that much remains to be done. Although China has high secondary school enrolment rates, it also has high drop-out rates, such that only 24 per cent of working-age people completed their education.

This is a rather astounding fact, and as Scott Rozelle has pointed out from research into rural education in China, the completion rate is lower than the average 32 per cent for middle-income countries, and compares with 41 to 42 per cent in Brazil and Argentina, 36 per cent in Mexico, 31 per cent in Turkey, and 28 per cent in South Africa.[26] Although more than 90 per cent of urban children finish secondary school, only about a quarter of children grow up in prosperous cities. A third or more of rural children don't even complete junior high school.

Rozelle has predicted that a further 400 million or so working-age Chinese people are 'in danger of becoming cognitively handicapped'. The heart of the problem is poor paediatric health, with anaemia, intestinal worms, uncorrected myopia, and poor parenting and stimulus in infancy all contributing to weak learning skills and poor educational attainment levels. While, in principle, this ought to be a fixable problem, Rozelle is concerned that overall standards of healthcare for children have not improved in spite of significantly higher expenditure and coverage. The hukou residential permit system remains an important barrier to narrowing the rural–urban divide, and neither the schooling system nor local government administrations are incentivised by institutionalised rules to address many of the underlying problems.

Over time, the central government could make resources available and pass laws to lift standards of child health and educational attainment. This would put China in a much more favourable position to broaden and deepen the educational attainment levels needed to avert the middle-income trap. It should be a major priority for Xi Jinping's administration.

Moreover, while China would like its universities to figure at the top of global rankings, we should remember that the education system is also now expected to incorporate more Marxist and Maoist teaching, and it is thought that postgraduate education, especially at the doctoral level, is inferior to that of developed countries.[27] China has had just nine Nobel Prize winners, three of whom had foreign passports, and two were honoured for Peace and Literature. Even India, which is much poorer, can boast one more Nobel laureate.

According to the Conference Board, the share of Chinese workers with tertiary education was about 17 per cent in 2015, and the share of highly skilled workers in manufacturing was just 10 per cent in 2013, compared with 47 per cent in the US.[28] The OECD has estimated that only 10 per cent of Chinese adults aged twenty-five to sixty-four possess tertiary education, which is less than one-third of the average in OECD countries.[29] This high skill gap in the workforce is probably a major reason for the emphasis on robotics in the Made in China 2025 plan, though this is unlikely to resolve the issues raised by low educational attainment levels.

Turning to the corporate world: only about 5 per cent of Chinese companies spend money on research and development, and gross expenditure on research and development, while up from 1.3 per cent of GDP in 2005, hasn't deviated in more recent years away from about 2 per cent of GDP. By comparison, in 2016 the US spent 2.7 per cent of GDP, Germany 2.9 per cent, Japan 3.5 per cent and South Korea 4.2 per cent. Moreover, there are recurring doubts, usually expressed by foreign observers and international bodies, about the quality of products and processes emerging from China's innovation system.

China is often cited, for example, as being a global leader in patent registration, just thirty-three years after its first patent law was enacted. Over time, subnational governments have been enthusiastic backers of patent registration, often providing financial incentives and targets for successful filers in a system that has traditionally favoured SOEs. Allegations of plagiarism and duplication have never been far from the surface. Nevertheless, in 1999 China was filing 50,000 patents, equivalent to 4 per cent of the world total, rising in 2016 to 1.3 million patents compared with a world total of 3.1 million. The vast majority of China's filings are so-called utility patents, designed to protect a new or improved product or process, as opposed to design patents, which protect the way an article or process is used or works.[30] That said, China has been doing more of the latter in recent years.

The registration of patents abroad is an important, and often overlooked, property of the significance of patent data. It corresponds to the institutionalisation of the intellectual property protection, and reflects the desire and ability to commercialise technology in foreign markets. Because the value of such patents is higher, companies like to register abroad if possible. Most are design or invention patents. In 2016, US companies registered about half of their patents abroad, compared with just 4 per cent for Chinese companies;[31] Chinese companies filed just over 50,000 patents abroad, just 25 per cent of the volume filed by US companies.

Patent filing, often cited as a hallmark of Chinese innovation potential and intellectual property progress, is therefore only one – and not necessarily the best – indicator of China's technological prowess. The low commercial value of patent and intellectual property portfolios among Chinese companies is down to intellectual property abuse or theft, and the low quality of intellectual property enforcement.

The registration of patents by type and location are just two of the eighty variables measured by the World Intellectual Property Organization to determine how 127 countries stack up against one another in terms of innovation. In the 2017 Global Innovation Index, China ranked twenty-second, ousting Australia to become number six in Asia, but globally it was positioned just above the Czech Republic and Estonia, and just below Norway, Austria and New Zealand.[32] In some areas, for example, business sophistication and knowledge and technology outputs, China is unquestionably a top ten country. In several areas such as human capital and research, market sophistication, creativity and infrastructure, it is ranked along with the lower half of OECD nations. It benefits from the Global

Innovation Index focus on engineering degrees, infrastructure and patent filing.

Yet, interestingly from the perspective of this chapter, China's weakest ranking is in its institutions. Separated into political, environmental and regulatory institutions, China's overall ranking was seventy-eighth, highlighting that this is the biggest single drag on China's potential to excel at innovation. In the Innovation Index, China didn't do that well in engineering students' creative abilities, or the institutional linkages between infrastructure and technology.

This all brings us neatly back to the earlier discussion about governance and institutions because AI, say, and machine learning are at the heart of what is probably the most important GPT since the internet and information and communications technologies. The various components of the GPT make a direct contribution to the economy, businesses, and the earnings of those who patent them. Yet there is a broader and more pervasive aspect to a GPT, which is the more indirect contribution it makes as an enabling mechanism of hundreds of complementary innovations and new products and processes in other industries and sectors. These could change the way factories and offices are structured and work, the entire transportation infrastructure in the case of driverless vehicles, business processes and corporate governance, skill structures and educational attainment, the organisation of preventative and social care, the location of manufacturing and much more.

The essential point about these complementary changes is that they are disruptive, unpredictable and prone to trial and error, experimentation, and failure. These are things that sit much less comfortably in a bureaucratic, top-down and authoritarian governance structure, whose weaknesses have been outlined earlier, than in a more open, flexible and bottom-up system that encourages disruption and research-driven ideas.

Since the GPT in question is new, we should perhaps not be overly prescriptive, but a lot of it all boils down to risk-taking, disruption and instability. China's governance system and the structures in place to evaluate and incentivise scientists and engineers, projects and methodologies of instruction and research tend not to be compatible, by and large, with these phenomena. Will China be able to break the mould by showing that autocracy and repression and transformative innovation can coexist?

If so, Xi Jinping's China will not do it by invoking liberalisation or Western reform programmes. The kind of reform and governance changes which I have raised and examined in this chapter may be familiar in Western thinking as the way forward to avoid or avert the middle-income trap, but there is no realistic chance that China will embrace them. It will evolve its own agenda, putting the Party at the forefront. It will reform in its own ways, but focus mainly on administrative and bureaucratic measures designed to increase the operational efficiency of enterprises, and organisational changes to make various levels of government work better.

We shall have to reserve judgement as to whether China's way will succeed in keeping a balance sheet recession at arm's length indefinitely, and in developing industrial and engineering successes into transformative and commercialised technologies that set global standards. My hunch is that it will come up short. Conscious that this sceptical view will not find favour everywhere, we can, however, all agree that if China succeeds in avoiding the middle-income trap, it would be the first authoritarian country or dictatorship to do so.

8

TRADE DOGS OF WAR

When Mark Antony utters the words 'let slip the dogs of war' after the assassination of Julius Caesar, he is thought to be referring to devices in civilised societies that allow or inhibit war. For a long time, China and the US have had spats over specific trade issues, or sometimes currency matters, which never really threatened the fabric of their relationship. In 2018, this all started to change, not least because beyond the headlines about trade lay the sensitive issue of new technologies and their ubiquitous applications as much in defence as in commerce. The phrase 'dogs of war' then seems an appropriate way to think about trade, and the nature of trade relations between China and the US in particular, and the West in general.

Although the world's two biggest economies enjoy a relationship marked by a high state of interdependence in economics, commerce and finance, the new tension between them when it comes to trade and investment is remarkable. The tension is best captured by the geo-economic thinking of the political scientist Edward Luttwak, for whom trade is the 'logic of conflict in the grammar of commerce'.[1]

The meaning is self-evident, and while his 1990 writing was about the aggressive export-led growth of Japan and the Asian Tigers, and the impact of the creation of the European Economic Community, the essence of the commercial conflict he was describing is equally applicable today. Fundamentally, it is about the conversion of economic clout by China into regional and global political influence, where the US, the incumbent and dominant power until now, has held sway.

At the end of 2017, a new national security strategy review did not mince words about the adversarial role in which the US now sees China. Citing China as existential economic competition to the US, it vowed stricter enforcement of trade violations, which is diplomatic code for tariffs. China wasn't the only country in the crosshairs of the White House, but it is the major one, and one with which the US runs a large deficit. President Trump's view about trade is that it is a zero-sum game in which there can only be one winner. China's view about trade is ostensibly much more aligned with that of other advanced economy and international organisations, but Xi's China is certainly not blameless in allowing trade tensions between the two countries to reach boiling point.

The rest of us look on with curiosity and concern at both the Trump administration and China. The US says it supports the multilateral trade system in principle, and yet it is simultaneously pulling back from its long-standing Asian and global commitments. China tells the world that it wants to champion globalisation, maintain a free and open trading system, and open up to foreign firms and capital, and yet pursues policies that are the exact antithesis. It is precisely as Edward Luttwak described.

Trump's gift to China

In 1944, as the tide in the Pacific War turned in favour of the United States, Nicholas John Spykman's book *The Geography of Peace* was published posthumously. In the book, he emphasised the strategic and maritime significance to the US of what he called the 'rimland', or the countries and islands on the rim of the continental powers of the US, Europe and what was then the USSR. The geography of the rim ran from southern Europe and the Maghreb, east through the Persian Gulf, into the Indian Ocean, across to the South China Sea and up to Japan and the north west of China. Drawing attention to the population residing in the Asia-Pacific region in particular, along with its resources and industrial development potential, Spykman argued that whoever controlled this rimland would rule Eurasia, and the destiny of the world.

This judgement, underlying the US commitment to defeat Japan in the Second World War, remained firmly embedded in US military, foreign and international economic policies, especially as China emerged from backwardness to become a regional power and global force. In 2011, President Obama's chairman of the Joint Chiefs of Staff, General Martin Dempsey, noted that 'all of the trends, demographic trends, geopolitical trends, economic trends, and military trends are shifting toward the Pacific. So our strategic challenges will largely emanate out of the Pacific region, but also the littorals of the Indian Ocean.'[2]

President Obama himself was touring Asia at that time to assure allies of America's geopolitical commitments, and its determination to promote deeper trade links. A key part of his strategy – otherwise labelled the 'pivot to Asia' – was to sign Asia-Pacific countries up to the Trans-Pacific Partnership (TPP), a free trade bloc that was eventually signed by Australia, Brunei Darussalam, Canada, Chile, Japan, Malaysia, Mexico, New Zealand, Peru, Singapore, Vietnam and the US. These countries represented 40 per cent of global GDP. The TPP was crafted as a new type of free trade agreement, covering rules and regulations for service industries, intellectual property, the internet and data movement and access, environmental and labour standards, and investment (including by state enterprises). Deep in the details of the TPP were also requirements for free bargaining and trade unions, prohibitions on human and wildlife trafficking, and regulations governing the treatment of guest workers.

Strategically, the TPP was designed to solidify America's economic, political and military influence in Asia, and even though it excluded China, it was thought that it might nevertheless spur reform-minded politicians in China to sustain the drive towards liberalisation and economic reforms. China had, after all, opened up as a precondition for and consequence of its joining the World Trade Organization, and the TPP might continue that trend. As it turned out the emergence of Xi Jinping and the change in Chinese politics finally exposed such hopes as wishful thinking. President Trump, though, had earlier warned he was going to withdraw from the TPP anyway.

On his first day in office in 2017, he did just that. He also served notice that he would renegotiate the North American Free Trade Agreement (NAFTA) with Canada and Mexico. In abandoning the TPP and promoting the America First slogan, he turned Spykman's judgement on its head. More specifically, he abandoned the economic and commercial links and trust on which America's allies have grown to depend, and threw away a valuable tool the US had in its geo-economic arsenal for shaping the Pacific region and for putting pressure on China to change its import, industrial and foreign direct investment regimes. Trump's insistence that the TPP was another useless multilateral agreement in which the US would lose out to others, and his failure to see the TPP as an opportunity for major nations to come together in ways that could wield leverage over China, were two sides of the same catastrophic coin.

To the uninitiated, Trump's exhortation of America First might have sounded like traditional patriotism but to American allies as well as to China, it resonated precisely with the slogan used by isolationists during the 1930s, a time characterised by severe trade conflict around the world. Trump's predecessors may have barked about trade fairness, and in the 1980s they were genuinely bothered about Japan's commercial superiority, but none of them called into question the role that America played as the champion of a liberal, rules-based trading system. Donald Trump was the first winning presidential candidate since 1945 to threaten and then to initiate measures leading to American withdrawal from this essential function. He used language alluding to the 'rape' of American jobs, the protectionism that would bring great prosperity and strength, and welcomed a trade war as something that America would win. Trump is much more interested in Americans as suppliers of a narrow range of products, not the economy's broader interests, let alone those of the world trade system.

It came as no surprise, therefore, that President Xi Jinping felt able to give a tour de force address to the global elite of policymakers and business people at the annual meeting of the World Economic Forum in Davos a few days later. He told them how China had been hesitant about joining the WTO but summoned up the courage to do so, adjust, and make a virtue of free trade. Taking on the role of defender of globalisation, Xi said: 'Whether you like it or not, the global economy is the big ocean that you cannot escape from. Any attempt to cut off the flow of capital, technologies, products, industries and people between economies, and channel the waters in the ocean back into isolated lakes and creeks is simply not possible. Indeed, it runs counter to the historical trend.'[3] A sufficient number of people present and those reporting on the forum were impressed enough to report that the world had a new globalisation champion.

No one could deny that China had been a major, perhaps the biggest, beneficiary of globalisation over the last twenty to thirty years, and yet this interpretation of China as the champion of globalisation and free trade was naive, even rather sycophantic. Trump may have done China a huge favour, but he is not completely wrong about China, its approach to trade, or about its gaming of the world's commercial and investment arrangements. His views are petty and misinformed, and the focus on Chinese exports to the US misses the point about the US–Sino relationship. Yet he is right to call China out on substantive issues such as China's import tariffs, inward investment rules and regulations, protection of local businesses and enterprises, and now state-driven innovation strategies, all of which put foreign firms at a disadvantage.

China in the world trading system

China's external surplus peaked a long time ago, in 2007. Its trade surplus has fluctuated between 2.5 and 3.5 per cent of GDP since 2011, while the current account surplus, which includes trade in services and transfers, has fallen more sharply to around 1 to 2 per cent of GDP. Much of the reason for the fall in the latter may have been due to tourism, and disguised capital outflows.[4] Even though China ran a small deficit in early 2018, it is likely to continue to generate modest external surpluses unless there is a material decline in national savings by households and companies that goes beyond any decline in the rate of investment. Yet the global circumstances for a big realignment of Chinese investment and savings are not that good.

The world trade environment faced by China is nowhere near as benign as it was in the past. After growing more or less in line with world GDP for decades, world trade subsequently increased twice as quickly between 1985 and 2007. Yet, after 2008, it barely managed to keep pace with GDP. Between 2012 and 2016, trade grew at about 2.5 per cent a year, which is less than half the rate of growth over the previous thirty years, and 1 per cent below global growth. There are few historical precedents in the last fifty years for such weak performance, and none for such prolonged sluggishness.

The global recovery that planted firmer roots in 2017 was accompanied by stronger world trade, which returned to a 4 per cent pace, a little higher than global growth. This shift unquestionably benefited China, whose exports responded positively after having fallen for almost two years. While a welcome development, the global trade environment remains fraught with risk, and the outlook to 2020 and beyond is sober.

Global trade liberalisation has been dormant for some time. The Doha round, the last truly global attempt to liberalise world trade, died in 2015, fourteen years after it was launched, although it had been comatose since 2005. The climate for multilateral trade liberalisation is now quite different and less benign.

Protectionist trade measures are on the rise. Global Trade Alert, a monitoring organisation, reported that since it started work in 2008, over 6,000 protectionist measures have been introduced by G20 countries.[5] The main tool used to restrain trade was not tariffs as such, but rather a variety of so-called non-tariff barriers, such as state aid, financial favouritism of local firms, tax incentives for exporters, bail-outs, and trade defence measures such as anti-dumping duties, which are levied on imports that recipient countries think are priced below fair market value or what exporting countries charge in their home market.

The number of free trade agreements (FTAs) has been sliding. According to the Design of Trade Agreements Database, while there were around thirty FTAs per year in the 1990s, there were twenty-six per year in the run-up to the financial crisis in 2008, and just ten annually since 2010.[6] US withdrawal from the TPP, and the stalled Transatlantic Trade and Investment Partnership (TTIP) between the US and the EU, extinguished hopes that there might be a revival of big FTAs, though the non-US signatories to the TPP, including Japan and Canada, have agreed to a slightly narrower-in-scope Comprehensive and Progressive Agreement for Trans-Pacific Partnership.

Meanwhile, China is patching together its own free trade agreements. It has nineteen bilateral deals under construction, of which fourteen have been signed, including those with Australia, South Korea and New Zealand, but its most important agreements are with the Association of Southeast Asian Nations (ASEAN) countries. In 2018, it was in the fifth year of negotiating a new regional deal, called the Regional Comprehensive Economic Partnership (RCEP), which will cover sixteen countries: China, the ASEAN group of Brunei Darussalam, Cambodia, Indonesia, Laos, Malaysia, Myanmar, the Philippines, Singapore, Thailand and Vietnam, plus Australia, India, Japan, New Zealand and South Korea. The RCEP is no TPP. It spans countries accounting for half the world's population, 30 per cent of global GDP, and 28 per cent of world trade. It is less ambitious than the TPP when it comes to goods liberalisation and tariff reductions, more limited when it comes to services trade, and doesn't really embrace the contentious issues of data and privacy, state enterprises, and protections for labour, human rights and the environment.

Sino–US trade tensions

While a more pedestrian world trade outlook is one which might cramp China a bit, its significance for China should be lessened to the extent that China becomes more a consumption- and services-focused economy. Yet it would be bad news if China became ensnared in much greater trade friction or a trade war with the US. In spite of the rhetoric on both sides as the rumblings of trade conflict grow louder, no one wins a trade war. The strategy is to inflict greater losses on the other side, and to this extent, countries that run trade surpluses probably have more to lose than those that run deficits.

US Census Bureau data show that US imports from China amounted to over $500 billion in 2017, compared to US exports to China of $130 billion. Yet, this $370 billion US trade deficit with China is not all strict bilateral trade, because China, as Asia's prime supply chain hub, finishes off a lot of products shipped there by, say, Japan and South Korea. According to the value-added trade data of the Organisation for Economic Co-operation and Development (OECD), which allows for this sort of effect, the US trade deficit with China was just $150 billion in 2017, and once you allow for the US surplus in services sold to China, which includes tourism and commercial services, the total deficit was about $110–120 billion. This doesn't mean the Americans don't have legitimate arguments about Chinese trade and investment practices, but it is important to bear this in mind in assessing the bluster that often passes as trade policy.

The argument that deficit countries have less to lose than surplus countries rests on the idea that China's surplus adds to its economic growth, jobs and welfare, while America's deficit subtracts from its economic growth. If its deficit fell, it might have a mathematically positive impact on GDP, but the US would also pay a heavy price in terms of lost economic growth, higher costs and prices, and unemployment. Yet China has more to lose. Looked at another way, US exports and imports together amount to about 28 per cent of GDP, whereas in China, they account for over 40 per cent of GDP. China is, therefore, a more open economy and more sensitive to world trade and what its major trade partners are doing. The bottom line is that US exports to China amount to barely 1 per cent of US GDP and 8 per cent of total exports, while China's to the US amount to 4 per cent of Chinese GDP and a fifth of total exports.

Most of what America sells to China is made up of aircraft and parts, soya beans and other agricultural products, cars, semiconductors, industrial and electrical machinery, and oil and plastics, whereas China ships the other way mainly mobile phones and household goods, computers and accessories, telecommunications equipment, toys and games, furniture and bedding, toys and sports equipment and footwear and clothing. In services, the US has a distinct advantage, exporting around $50 billion of mainly tourism, intellectual property and transportation services, compared to its purchases from

China of $16 billion of services. Trade in services between the US and China is growing much more rapidly than in goods. Compared with 2001, when China joined the WTO, US service exports have risen ninefold, while China's services exports have risen fourfold. As China's economy changes, and if rebalancing succeeds, China's appetite for services and America's expertise in providing them could make for a good match. Politics and regulations permitting, it would make sense to explore these avenues of cooperation.

There isn't anything positive that can be said in favour of a trade war. Yet, the drumbeat of trade tensions has been getting louder. Some of this we can put down to political histrionics, issued primarily for domestic consumption. Such is the nature of trade rhetoric. Some, however, is for real and reflects the fact that Trump has chosen to make an issue of Chinese technology, and trade and investment practices that previous US presidents have not. Since Trump is learning from the autocrat's playbook, and Xi Jinping is an established player, we would be wise to look on with justifiable concern.

When Donald Trump took office in 2017, many people thought the trade rhetoric emanating from the White House and the president's top advisers meant that a trade war with China might be imminent. It didn't happen in the way people had feared, and in fact when President Xi visited Trump in Mar-a-Lago in April 2017, China agreed, after sitting on the issue for a long time, to resume beef imports from the US (after a fourteen-year ban), and also to raise natural gas imports, and open up its financial services markets to US payment system providers, asset managers and credit-rating agencies. When Trump visited China later in the year, the US side made hay over $250 billion of trade agreements.

Both sides had an interest in hailing breakthroughs, but little of substance was achieved. The Obama administration had actually agreed the resumption of beef imports. China's appetite for natural gas is limited because vertically integrated coal to chemical companies are much more likely to burn coal. Although China ostensibly welcomed the admission of credit-card companies, and credit-rating agencies, and the easing of limits on foreign ownership of financial services companies, its enthusiasm and tolerance are much less than its rhetoric. In any event, few companies are likely to establish majority stakes in Chinese financial companies soon, if at all, and most of the big trade deals announced were non-binding, and those that could happen will take years of negotiation.

Sino–US relations, book-ended by these high-level meetings, became frostier. The US resumed arms sales to Taiwan, and periodically sent naval warships close to contested islands in the South China Sea. The relabelled Comprehensive Economic Dialogue ended without any substantive agreement, or the usual joint policy statements and press conferences. When the new vice premier and overall head of economic and financial affairs, Liu He, visited Washington in early 2018, partly to restart the dialogue talks, he returned home empty-handed.

After launching a wide range of investigations into trade with China, the US administration began in 2018 to take steps against the Chinese. The first announcement concerned tariffs on imported solar panels and washing machines from all sources, but the Office of the US Trade Representative singled out China for trade practices of particular concern. China's response was to open anti-dumping investigations into sorghum imports from the US. Sorghum is America's third largest cereal crop, and China takes almost 80 per cent of US exports.

Next, the US decided to impose tariffs on imports of steel and aluminium at 25 and 10 per cent respectively, under Section 232 of the Trade Expansion Act 1962. Typically, US workers, companies or industries have pushed for trade cases to be investigated in the US, and so for the government to initiate such an action was rare.[7] The last time the US government did so was in 2001, also on steel. Invoking national security as the basis for levying these tariffs runs some big risks of retaliation or other dispute actions involving not just China but America's allies too.

Steel has been a sensitive issue for the US, China and other countries for a long time, and one can understand the politics in the US, for example, by considering that employment in the US steel industry fell by a third between 2000 and 2016 to 87,000. Yet steel accounts for a tiny proportion, 0.1 per cent, of US non-farm jobs. It also accounted for about 1.4 per cent of total US imports, and China doesn't even figure as a major source, for half was imported from Canada, Brazil, South Korea and Mexico. Vietnam, to which Chinese steel firms have shipped some of their production, accounted for 3 per cent of US steel imports, while China itself accounted for barely 1.5 per cent.

These measures were more noise than substance as far as US–China trade was concerned. In March 2018, though, the administration stepped up a gear, following investigations into China's intellectual property policies under Section 301 of the Trade Act 1974. It said it would impose new 25 per cent tariffs on $50 billion of imports from China targeted at the ten sectors China has prioritised in its Made in China 2025 industrial policy. These sectors are: information technology; numerical control tools and robotics; aerospace equipment; ocean engineering equipment and high-tech ships; railway equipment; energy saving and new energy vehicles; power equipment; new material; medicine and medical devices; and agricultural machinery. The real significance of these measures was not so much the short-term economic effect, because in these modern sectors China's exports, including to the US, are still small to non-existent. Rather, the purpose was to emphasise to China America's intention of targeting China's key industrial and technology sectors via trade measures specifically but also in broader and more enduring ways.

A high-level US government delegation went to Beijing in May 2018 with demands that were both clear, and, as far as China's industrial strategy was concerned, impossible for China to agree to. They included a $200 billion reduction in the bilateral trade deficit by 2020, and an array of measures under which China would cease market-distorting subsidies in Made in China 2025 sectors, and eliminate or change a number of policies related to intellectual property protection, cybersecurity intrusion and theft, joint-venture technology transfer stipulations, tariffs, and China's requests of and capacity to retaliate under WTO rules. Unsurprisingly, the US delegation returned to Washington without anything to show except that the two sides were still willing to talk. Over time, if trust prevails, China could step up purchases of US goods and services to help lower the deficit, and ease some conditions under which US companies operate in China. Yet, it cannot be expected realistically to subordinate its industrial strategy to American demands, especially to the extent that these violate many of the rules and regulations that underlie the global trade and investment governance structure.

By July 2018, Trump was prepared to go beyond the tariffs on $50 billion of imports from China to widen the scope to two further actions, each worth $200 billion. China had vowed to retaliate in kind to the exent that it could. China will be careful not to over-react, not least because its DNA is programmed to avoid instability. It was only in 2015–16 that it experienced financial shocks in which capital flight posed a major threat. Trapped capital in China, and private companies and households already pressured by a more politically repressive government, might only need the instability of a trade war to find ways of exiting China again. This is not to say that China would not participate in more vigorous trade war actions, but its interests are certainly to manage and to minimise the risk.

The main problem with the US tariff strategy is that it won't work. It will raise prices at home, and end up undermining more jobs than it preserves. In any case, since the Trump administration and Congress agreed to substantial cuts in taxation in 2018 and 2019, a much wider fiscal deficit will emerge. This is the equivalent of a fall in US savings, and since the external deficit is the outcome of the relationship between savings and investment, it follows that the wider fiscal deficit will simply expand the external or trade deficit. Tariffs will achieve nothing except make US allies and adversaries angry. If the US government went too far, moreover, there would undoubtedly be more vocal opposition at home both from Republican law-makers and US businesses.

Further, if China felt pushed or humiliated, or if it could no longer engage in tit-for-tat retaliation because it imports so much less from the US than the other way round, it could yet target or discriminate more against US companies operating in China. In this latter respect, China has form. Remember, for example, that in March 2017, China restricted tourists wanting to go to South Korea as a protest against Seoul's adoption of a controversial US-supplied missile shield. Previously, in November 2016, angry about the visit of the Dalai Lama to Mongolia, it imposed punitive fees on the country's commodity exports. In 2012, the Chinese government encouraged anti-Japan protests and actions against Japanese companies as tensions rose over the disputed Diaoyu or Senkaku Islands, and it also curbed tourism to and banana imports from the Philippines over the disputed Scarborough Shoal in the South China Sea. In 2010, China acted against imports of Norwegian salmon over the Nobel Prize award to Chinese dissident Liu Xiaobo, and implemented a rare-earth export embargo on Japan and other Western nations, partly related to an earlier dispute over the Senkaku Islands. It seems reasonable to assume that Beijing has not been idle since Trump came to power, and has developed some ideas about companies and products that might be the object of retaliatory action.

It could target companies where the domestic effects would be zero or negligible, or where there are alternative foreign suppliers. It could, for example, cancel orders for aircraft built by Boeing, whose Chinese sales generated about 12 per cent of the company's global sales in 2015. Airbus provides a ready substitute. It could target semiconductor manufacturers such as Qualcomm and Broadcom, most of whose revenues come from China. It could penalise US companies with big China operations, such as Apple, General Motors, Walmart and Starbucks, all of whom do big business there and are looking to expand. Yet this sort of strategy aimed at US companies could become highly risky for China, threatening not only

Chinese jobs and the livelihoods of citizens, but also the remnants of whatever trust exists between the US, its companies and China. That is a price China may simply be unwilling to pay, except in extremis.

Even though America's focus on China's trade practices is not without justification, the unilateral imposition of universal tariffs and similar punitive measures is misinformed and could easily backfire. Instead, it should look to persuade China to open up its markets to a wider range of US exports including cars, a product on which China has agreed to cut tariffs from a lofty level of 25 per cent. Over 90 per cent of automobiles sold in China are produced locally, and Chinese producers had a market share of about 43 per cent in the first eight months of 2017.

The US should seek a dialogue with China about circumstances under which the latter might be willing to amend its industrial policies in its own interests, for example by allowing improved market access in non-politically sensitive commercial and service producing sectors beyond finance. The US has a strong case when it alleges that China persists with discriminatory policies that favour local companies and penalise foreign firms. These apply in several areas, including intellectual property rights, the free flow of information, cybersecurity regulations, technology transfer requirements, the ability of technology companies to operate freely, and service industry regulations and protection. They have dominated Sino–US talks for many years, but remain key to the chances of sustainably managed trade between China and the US, and to the specific goal of lowering the bilateral trade deficit.

The Comprehensive Economic Dialogue is an appropriate forum to recognise that the dependency relationship of the US and China is not as one-way as is often portrayed. The US, in other words, has leverage that it could deploy without necessarily coming across as bellicose. China depends on a vibrant US economy and on being able to sell goods into it. It wants to be able to acquire US companies with good growth prospects and technological know-how. It depends a lot on the technology transfer that US companies are able to, or are required to, provide when they set up in China. Above all it values enormously the status quo of the international trade and investment systems.

China also wants 'market economy status' (MES), which it believes it was promised on the 15th anniversary of joining the WTO, which occurred late in 2016, and to which the US and EU both objected. China filed a complaint on which the WTO will eventually rule. A country with MES means that its trade partners accept that domestic prices, including, for example, of steel, are set by open competition rather than by the government or diktat. A country without MES is more likely to be accused of 'rigging' the market, making it more vulnerable to anti-dumping and other countervailing duties.

China without MES thus continues to be an easy target when it comes to steel and other products where China has overcapacity, and where other countries maintain that China uses non-market methods to export into world markets. Under US anti-dumping law, in the Tariff Act 1930, the Department of Commerce is responsible for determining whether a country is a market economy for the purpose of anti-dumping investigations, and whether MES will apply to the whole country or to specific sectors or enterprises. The US could commit to China to work towards MES in exchange for at least some of the more important changes in Chinese trade and investment policies that it would like to secure.

Xi's China, moreover, is most unlikely to be drawn seriously into the instability that a trade war would bring, unless the bilateral political relationship had already become toxic. In any event, as I have pointed out, trade is merely the wrapper around a conflict of interests that are really about technology and the terms under which US and Chinese companies invest and operate in one another's countries. Some of these interests are so fundamental to both sides – spanning defence and national security to economic strength and commercialisation – that agreeing to changes in trade arrangements seems almost easy by comparison. We need, therefore, to examine, investment tensions too.

Investment tensions

Beyond trade itself, investment relations are also contentious. China would like to do much more investment business in the US, if it could and if it were permitted. China's stock of investment in the US, measured officially in the US at $14.8 billion in 2015 (the latest year for which figures are available) was just a fifth of the stock of US foreign direct investment in the US.[8] Estimates made by the research and analysis think tank Rhodium Group suggest, rather differently, that in 2015 China's stock of investment in the US was almost $64 billion, and climbed a further $45 billion in 2016, while the stock of US investment in China was $228 billion.[9]

Yet Chinese flows into the US have been slowing down significantly, partly because the authorities in Beijing clamped down on outward investment, but also because CFIUS, or the Committee on Foreign

Investment in the United States, is becoming increasingly restrictive about Chinese investment in the US.

The Rhodium Group reported, for example, that Chinese direct investment deals completed in the US fell by 35 per cent in 2017 to $29 billion, largely because of restrictions emanating from China. These numbers are still historically high, but include previously announced direct investment deals. In terms of new activity, the decline was significantly larger – a 90 per cent decline to around $9 billion.[10]

CFIUS is authorised, under the auspices of the US Treasury, to review foreign transactions that could result in control of a US business from the standpoint of national security, but it doesn't disclose details of specific transactions in order to protect the parties involved. Until recently, and over three decades, it had only ever blocked two transactions, but since 2016, it has blocked four: the proposed acquisition by Chinese-owned Grand Chip GmbH of Aixtron SE, a German company with a California-headquartered subsidiary; the $1.3 billion acquisition of Lattice Semiconductor Corporation by Chinese-funded Canyon Bridge Capital Partners; the $1.2 billion acquisition of money transfer company Monogram by Alibaba's affiliate, Ant Financial; and the acquisition of the semiconductor testing company Xcerra by an affiliate of Sino IC Fund, a state-backed fund set up to develop integrated circuit and electronic technologies. Other Chinese companies have also had plans disrupted or blocked as the US has become more anxious about the activities of China's high-tech firms. Both Huawei and ZTE have been the subject of Department of Commerce investigations and proposals to restrict the capacity of US companies to do business with them.

CFIUS is concerned not only by the surge in Chinese investments, especially in strategic and high technology firms, but also by what it perceives as an increasingly mercantilist China, evident in various manifestations of industrial policy plans, such as Made in China 2025, newer strategic goals involving artificial intelligence, and the increasingly onerous restrictions placed by China on foreign firms doing business in China. Several US politicians have considered drafting bills to give CFIUS more authority, especially in food security, economic security and national security-related areas. Now that more and more Chinese investment abroad is probably going to have a greater state-driven technological thrust, CFIUS is likely to become a lot busier. The same goes for the European Commission, which has proposed a new screening law designed to exercise increased national security oversight over Chinese foreign direct investment in the EU in the light of concerns that SOEs lack autonomy from the

Chinese government when it comes to corporate strategy, planning and financing.

US trade deficit, China trust deficit

With trade and investment relations under some duress, is it even possible that the world economy could do without US leadership? Could we in fact look to China to fill the vacuum that the US might leave if it retreated further behind its America First banner?

Leaving aside the rhetoric from President Xi Jinping in front of the Davos elite in 2017, China has demonstrated both a willingness to engage more deeply with the rest of the world, and to project its interests more forcefully. These are themes that I will pick up in the penultimate chapter of this book, but it would be churlish not to acknowledge its attempts to replace its spaghetti of bilateral trade deals in Asia with proper regional agreements such as the RCEP, the initiatives to set up the Asian Infrastructure Investment Bank and the New Development Bank, or BRICS Bank, and the Belt and Road Initiative. China's objectives are to try and draw Asian countries more closely into its orbit by presenting itself as a more reliable economic and trade security partner, and to establish China as the pre-eminent Eurasian power.

Displacing the US economically, however, is a major challenge, even if the US itself is acting for now as a willing participant in the process. To be the leader of globalisation, as the US has been, you need to have willing followers, who will not so much pay you tribute, as have respect for and trust in your statecraft and diplomacy, and look to you as the provider of generosity and shared ideals. There are some exceptions, but for most countries, China falls short of these criteria even if they nevertheless regard China as a magnet for commerce.

Although about 32 per cent of people polled in thirty-eight nations by Pew Research said that China was the world's leading economy, 42 per cent continued to maintain it was the US. Interestingly, most countries in Asia and Sub-Saharan Africa, as well as all in Latin America, subscribed to this latter view. Even though the gap between China and the US has narrowed, most people in most countries had a negative view of President Xi Jinping, albeit slightly less so than of Donald Trump, and there was a strong negative view about China's position on human rights.[11]

Trust, for example, which goes to the heart of the rule of law, and other institutional phenomena discussed in Chapter 7, runs through economic and commercial business, international agreements and treaties, and the veins of soft power. China's authoritarian and state capitalism model has checked boxes when it comes to economic development, high-value products and science and technology, and resonated for more nations now than in the past. This wins respect, but not necessarily trust.

Indeed, the gaining of trust in China and in the West is different. Western culture is more individualistic, and people have to develop skills to build alliances and networks to get things done, based on the giving and gaining of trust. Chinese culture is more about existing relationships and networks within which there is trust, but not necessarily about venturing outside these networks. Trust is given only if new relationships preserve, and don't threaten, these networks.

To be a leader in globalisation and a champion of free trade, you have to give and gain trust, and fulfil a complicated role in which self-interest and global interests may not always be well aligned, but which are for the greater good. Many of the global elite assembled at Davos in 2017, who applauded the Chinese president's defence of globalisation, may have done so hearing what they wanted to hear, but they didn't recognise that a global leader would have said something quite different.

Xi should have acknowledged that faced with new and possibly stressful circumstances in the global trading system and economy, including America's intent to lower its deficit, China would address the structural causes of its own trade surpluses, and work to reduce them, so as to help both itself and the rest of the world. Otherwise, world trade could falter again, and quite possibly tip the world economy into another quite avoidable recession. The reason is simple. If the rest of the world wanted to look to China as a new leader in trade, countries would want it to provide either more of its capital without strings or to import more goods and services. Put another way, they would want China to abandon its capital controls or run trade deficits.

Just for comparison, the US has fulfilled both roles. From the First World War until roughly the 1960s, the US satisfied the world's need for savings and investment mostly by running trade surpluses, the counterpart of which was sustained exports of US capital and US dollar liquidity. Surpluses were especially pronounced in the decade to 1952, after which smaller surpluses or balanced trade over several years continued until the 1970s. America's agenda in the post-Second World War period comprised the reconstruction of the post-war economy, especially in Europe, trade liberalisation and the promotion of the Bretton Woods institutions.

Throughout the period, capital flows, which were subject to controls for the most part, continued from the US. This suited both the US and the countries of war-ravaged Europe, which were desperate for US dollars to finance more trade.

Over time, though, as Europe and Japan recovered their economic poise and embarked on successful export-led growth strategies, US trade deficits started to rise. Concerns about shortages of US dollars gradually gave way to concerns about a glut. The build-up of US dollars in the rest of the world gave rise to doubts as to whether the US had the gold reserves ultimately to back the supply of US currency at the fixed price at the time of $35 an ounce. The eventual breakdown of the Bretton Woods system of fixed exchange rates and the subsequent liberalisation of capital flows around much of the world would then transform the US balance of payments position. Larger trade deficits became common from the 1980s onwards, and the trend was underpinned as emerging markets also took up their positions as export-led economies from the 1990s.

The US function in the global system necessarily changed. In the immediate post-war years, it mainly supplied US dollar liquidity via capital outflows. Since the advent of floating exchange rates, it has done so mainly via trade deficits, the counterpart of which are net inflows of capital from other countries, including China. The bottom line, however, is that US imports played a key role in greasing the world's demand for US dollars and sustaining global economic growth.[12]

There is no question that the US dollar has survived as the premier global currency – contrary to repeated warnings – with its reputation for stability, safety and liquidity largely intact, but not wholly. The challenge of ordering a stable global monetary system revolves around managing acceptable levels of trade surpluses and deficits so as to keep economic growth stable, what to do about capital sloshing around the world in quantities that dwarf trade, and how to lessen the dependence on a single currency, in this case the US dollar.

No one realistically imagines the US dollar won't play a key role in the world's monetary and trading systems for a long time to come, but could China and the Renminbi complement, if not supplant it?

The world can't access China's capital easily enough because it maintains restrictions on capital exports. This doesn't look likely to change. China is not enamoured with the prospect of substantial offshore holdings of Renminbi or open capital markets, and is happy to remain in a position of control over the actions of Chinese residents. In any event, a world that is awash with capital doesn't need China's capital nearly as much as it needs China to import more, and so add more to global demand.

For China to import more, it would need to allow its balance of payments surpluses to change into continuing but manageable deficits. That would mean saving less, and consuming and importing more, as per the rebalancing discussed in Chapter 3. As the share of consumption in GDP also rises, and the high savings and investment shares fall, China would become a new engine of global growth, and lay claim to a stronger role in the global governance system.

The chances of China being willing to embark on such a momentous shift in macroeconomic policies and management, though, are slim. Like it or not, the US and the US dollar remain the linchpin of our global trade and investment system, warts and all. The trade dogs of war may have been unleashed, but while Trump's America may have ceded political advantage to Xi's China, the US remains at the heart of the global system, nevertheless. Cooperation between the US and China may now be much harder, but this doesn't necessarily mean the two are destined to confront one another in a mutually destructive stand-off. There is still room and potential for them to develop a tense relationship characterised by robust competition to win support for their ideas, politics and political beliefs, and to demonstrate the appeal of their respective democratic and autocratic systems as they develop and commercialise new technologies. However China and the US choose to address their differences and conflicting commercial interests, though, they also face a huge challenge to accommodate China's pursuit of its Belt and Road strategy, a topic to which we now turn.

9

THE EAST WIND PREVAILS OVER THE WEST WIND[1]

In January 2017, a freight train called the 'East Wind Train', pulling thirty-four containers packed with clothes and other consumer products, left Yiwu in Zhejiang province, about 280 kilometres south of Shanghai, making its way for the first time to London's Gateway terminal on the Thames Estuary. Transportation of goods along the 12,000-kilometre route went through ten countries, including Kazakhstan, Russia, Belarus, Poland, Germany, Belgium and France, and took seventeen days. The fanfare surrounding the arrival was remarkable, with the BBC, for example, exclaiming 'with the world's demand for consumer goods continuing to grow, all the ingredients seem to be there for rail to help the global economy steam ahead in 2017 and beyond'.[2]

On the return journey to Yiwu, several weeks later, the containers were laden with different products, including pharmaceuticals, vitamin pills, baby milk and Scotch whisky. The freight journey from China to the UK, though, was anything but exceptional. China has been running freight trains to Europe and bringing them back for four years. By 2018, about three dozen Chinese and the same number of European cities were connected.

These developments are occurring under the umbrella of China's so-called Belt and Road Initiative (BRI), more formally called the Silk Road Economic Belt and the Twenty-First-Century Maritime Silk Road, which President Xi Jinping announced in 2013 in Kazakhstan and Indonesia, and with which he is closely associated. At the time, he said that maintaining stability in China's neighbourhood was the key objective in Chinese diplomacy and that 'we must encourage and participate in the process of regional economic integration, speed up the process of building up infrastructure and connectivity. We must build the Silk Road Economic Belt and Twenty-First-Century Maritime Silk Road, creating a new regional economic order.'[3] The word 'neighbourhood' in this context is interesting, as I will point out, and Xi's claims are contentious, not least among other major countries, such as the US, Japan and India.

The long-distance freight train connections and journeys certainly appeal to China's Silk Road narrative, and to widely shared, sometimes romantic ideas about long-distance train travel. Yet running freight trains halfway across the world is probably more meaningful to rail enthusiasts than it is to the global economy and global commerce. Sending goods by train to Europe is faster than sending them by sea or road, but it is also twice as expensive and leaves bigger carbon footprints. It's much cheaper than sending goods by air, and there is a limit to what you can put in the hold of a cargo plane.

Yet, even though freight traffic between China and Europe is growing quickly from a zero baseline, it's small. It accounts for about 1 per cent of the volume of total trade. Trains have to stop many times along the way to switch locomotives and trucks to cope with different railway gauges and signalling systems. Trains are no competition for ships when it comes to the container loads they can transport, and China has already indicated it will stop subsidising expansion of the freight network from 2020.

The trains, then, are largely symbolic. They are part of a much broader plan that is about China's ambitions, economic leverage and leadership, and a much more activist diplomacy as China looks to expand its influence throughout Eurasia – an area accounting for about a third of global trade and GDP, three-fifths of the world's population, and the bulk of the world's energy resources.

When Mao spoke over forty years ago about the east wind prevailing over the west wind, he was assuring his audience that the winds of change were shifting away from the 'imperialists' towards countries reclaiming or rebuilding their independence and towards capitalist countries with what he called 'neutral tendencies'. President Xi Jinping's language is different, but there is no doubt that he shares similar sentiments. In Xi's neighbourhood, China will dominate Asia, be prominent elsewhere, and set out its stall as an example for others.

In this sense, the BRI deserves to be taken seriously. China is capitalising on some important advantages, leveraging its own economic might and the relative economic dynamism of Asia. It is also taking advantage of

Donald Trump's America First thinking in which the US is retreating from allies and institutions. Further, many smaller and poorer countries hope to benefit from China's financing or construction of ports, railways, roads and so on. They might balk at China's politics, but not at the chance to have China finance or build development infrastructure.

We should not, however, take all the BRI hype at face value. I have emphasised other policies in which wide gaps emerged between slogans and facts or implementation. The Shanghai Free Trade Zone, for example, became more of a real-estate project than a hub for international business, and the inclusion of the Renminbi in the IMF's Special Drawing Rights was more about symbolism than reserve currency status.

Moreover, Xi's 'neighbourhood' has become geographically incoherent. Originally, it was about sixty-five states between the Ural Mountains and the Bering Strait, south of the Caucasus Mountains and east of the Bosphorus Strait and the Suez Canal, spanning most of Eurasia. But the BRI concept also extends, at least commercially, into Western Europe, Africa and Latin America. China has even outlined plans for a 'Polar Silk Road' in the Arctic, seeking access to Russia's backyard to take advantage of the thawing of Arctic ice caps to halve the shipping time to, say, Rotterdam, and exploit hydrocarbon and mineral resources.

The BRI is a big idea, but it is also a complex and vaguely defined concept that might easily fall short of the great claims made for it inside and outside China. Practically, it could give rise to new financial problems for Chinese financial institutions, and debt service problems for countries with weak credit ratings and debt capacity. Geopolitically, it could turn out to be an example of 'hubristic overstretch'.[4]

Where the rubber meets the Belt and Road

What, then, is the BRI? In a nutshell, it is a massive connectivity project comprising trade, policy coordination, financial links, people-to-people ties, but, above all, networks of infrastructure projects involving the construction of transportation systems such as railways, highways, bridges and airports, energy facilities such as power plants and pipelines, and telecommunications capabilities.

Projects that have already been started or agreed include high-speed rail links from Jakarta to the textile hub of Bandung in central Java, cutting the journey from 3 hours to 40 minutes; from China to Laos, a project that will link Kunming in China to Vientiane, and then via Thailand and Malaysia to

Singapore;[5] from Addis Ababa to Djibouti, allowing landlocked Ethiopia to access the coast on the horn of Africa; and from Belgrade to Budapest, linking the capitals of Serbia and Hungary. They also include the development of major port facilities, for example Gwadar in Pakistan, Port City Colombo in Sri Lanka, and the Greek port of Piraeus; the construction of power stations in Pakistan along the China–Pakistan Economic Corridor, Vietnam, and Mongolia; and the rail network system linking the Pacific seaports of eastern China and the Russian Far East to Europe, known as the New Eurasian Land Bridge.

Remember, though, that the BRI has become an umbrella term for all manner of construction and foreign direct investment projects, many of which pre-date the announcement of the BRI but which, nonetheless, inflate the number and value of the projects undertaken since. For example, the goal of linking the Chinese border with Pakistan to the latter's deep-water ports on the Arabian Sea along what is called the China–Pakistan Economic Corridor is a few decades old. Work on linking Kashgar in western Xinjiang to the port of Gwadar dates from 2002. The 6-kilometre Padma Bridge project in Bangladesh, linking the south west of the country to northern and eastern regions, was put out to tender in 2010, and was supposed to have been finished in 2013.

That's just one reason why no one really knows how large the BRI is or will be, but there is no question that significant amounts of money are involved. There is a lot of analysis and commentary oozing facts and figures designed to impress listeners and readers. Numerous estimates, some ranging up to $5 trillion, have been banded around to emphasise the seriousness of the BRI strategy, which is already much bigger than the US Marshall Plan to rebuild Europe at the end of the Second World War. The Marshall Plan amounted to about $130 billion in today's money, which is about how much China allocated to BRI projects and loans in both 2016 and 2017. Chinese officials have put a more modest tag on the BRI, pledging to commit $1 trillion over a number of years.

To add some perspective, the Asian Development Bank estimated in 2017 that forty-five nations in Asia, broadly defined, needed to build about $26 trillion of infrastructure by 2030, which equates to annual expenditure of about $1.7 trillion – more than double the current rate.[6] China's contribution will nevertheless be significant, even at current levels of financing.

China's current BRI project investment is running at roughly $120 billion a year, and could rise to about $170–180 billion a year by 2020.[7]

These numbers don't look out of order. Chinese commercial banks, of which Bank of China, Industrial and Commercial Bank of China, and China Construction Bank are the biggest BRI lenders, finance most project and foreign investments. Their BRI lending is just 5 per cent of domestic credit expansion, and so it helps to see it in this light. They have provided over three-fifths of BRI investment financing since 2016.[8]

The future scale of BRI financing is unknowable. Estimates made today of what Chinese banks are likely to finance take no account of the quality of the loans made to specific borrowers and projects, the borrowers' ability to service and repay loans, or the risk of political disturbances or disagreements in countries welcoming Chinese investment. Moreover, restrictions on outward capital movements from China, including on companies undertaking foreign investment and lending, could also restrain growth in BRI activities. That said, BRI infrastructure and construction projects will most likely receive priority in terms of approval over other 'frivolous' investment projects in, say, real-estate, hotels, luxury goods, entertainment and sports teams. If the domestic loan portfolios and bad debts of Chinese banks should deteriorate, for example, in a period of slower growth, their enthusiasm for large-scale foreign financing of projects to weak borrowers would doubtless wane.

For the time being, the bulk of investment that China does abroad (excluding Hong Kong) is with countries that aren't or will never be part of the BRI. The only major destinations for investment in the BRI neighbourhood are Russia, Indonesia and Kazakhstan. The other major destinations for Chinese investment abroad comprise OECD countries with large markets and sophisticated technologies, such as the US, Singapore, Australia, the Netherlands, the UK, Canada and also offshore financial centres in the Caribbean, used as financial and fiscal conduits. These aside, much Chinese direct investment abroad has been undertaken in search of raw materials and energy, in countries such as Venezuela, Angola and the Democratic Republic of Congo. As of the start of 2016, BRI countries accounted for 17 per cent of the stock of Chinese investment, and in 2016, China announced that 8.5 per cent of direct investment that year had gone to these states.[9]

Similarly, the lending abroad by China's policy banks is overwhelmingly to non-BRI countries. At the end of 2016, China Development Bank and Export Import Bank of China together reported total overseas loans at $675 billion, of which 15 per cent were to BRI countries, with larger volumes earmarked for countries in Latin America and Africa.

It is a never-ending challenge to evaluate and value the BRI. At the Belt and Road Forum in Beijing in May 2017, President Xi claimed that investment in BRI countries since 2013 had already exceeded $50 billion.[10] This, though, was almost certainly a reference only to foreign direct investment by Chinese companies, including mergers and acquisitions, which, as I just suggested, account for a small proportion of Chinese foreign investment abroad – perhaps no more than 9–10 per cent on an annual basis – and also a small proportion of the much larger amounts disbursed via direct project investment, that is, financing linked specifically to projects.

Under this sort of financing, a Chinese state enterprise (typically) bids for a project and, if successful, gets Chinese financing, completes the project, operates it and takes revenues for an agreed number of years. The cumulative total of project investment may be roughly $400 billion since 2013 but this includes both announced and completed projects.[11] Of these, half may have been completed and half simply announced. This is important because the latter projects flatter current financing totals even though they may take many years to be completed.

It is also hard to get an accurate handle on the size and scale of BRI spending and financing because it is a huge project which demands persistent and unusually high levels of coordination between multiple layers of government and administration. These include most of China's thirty-two provincial governments pitching their preferred lists of projects and industries. In 2014, it was incorporated into the national economic development strategy. The National Development and Reform Commission is the lead agency and also China's most powerful central institution, but the State Council, the National Security Commission, the Ministries of Commerce, Finance and Foreign Affairs and the Small Leading Group on Comprehensively Deepening Reform also have significant interests. There is an additional Leading Small Group for the BRI based at the State Council, currently chaired by Zhang Gaoli, a Politburo Standing Committee member, and with four very senior Party deputy chairs.[12]

In addition, there are fifteen other ministries and agencies that seek to influence projects, often with conflicting commercial and financial objectives, while provincial governors and state-owned enterprise (SOE) chiefs, who often outrank ministers within the Party, also tend to push for their preferred policies. If the bureaucracy involved was not problematic enough, the BRI has been incorporated not just into the 13th Five-Year Plan, and local and provincial government economic plans, but also into the Party constitution.

BRI incubates both commerce and confrontation

Politically and strategically, the BRI raises important questions. Some think, for example, that it is primarily a Eurasian development project, in which China, unusually, is assuming a leadership role in supplying public goods and improving economic welfare in large tracts of the world economy. Others accept this but also think that it is a major Chinese economic, foreign policy and international relations project designed to benefit mainly China.

The distinction is quite important. A Eurasian development project would suggest that China is taking on a strong leadership role, and pursuing regional and global objectives to which Beijing would, if necessary, subordinate its immediate national interests. History offers no assurances that this is likely. It is true that China's participation in the Asian Infrastructure Investment Bank, in which it is the biggest shareholder and has an effective veto, entails its being willing to subscribe to an internationally accepted governance structure. Yet, as the core of China's international relations, it would be strange if the BRI were not principally a China First strategy.

Aside from the Asian Infrastructure Investment Bank, there are other institutional arrangements that dovetail or tie in to the BRI. China's Silk Road Fund provides capital to the policy development banks. The Shanghai Cooperation Organisation (SCO), the twenty-one-member Asia-Pacific Economic Cooperation group, the Regional Comprehensive Economic Partnership, and an array of bilateral trade, currency swap and trade agreements comprise important parts of the institutional infrastructure in which China is active, but none of them is BRI-specific. The SCO is a political, economic and security grouping set up by China in 2001 with four Central Asian republics, but which now includes India, Russia and Pakistan as full members.

Unlike America's financial and global policy thinking at the end of the Second World War, reflected in the Marshall Plan, the BRI comes with no proposals for a new international architecture. The BRI provides for no formal institutions with members or a secretariat drawn from participating countries. There are no formal commitments to established criteria, designs, financing principles and safeguards in the implementation and operation of projects. Little or no attention is paid to corruption, human rights and labour or environmental standards, and there is no transparency or accountability. The lack of institutional infrastructure may not matter to commercial and financial decisions affecting project infrastructure, but it could be a major shortcoming in relations between China and some of its larger neighbours and other powers.

Economics and geopolitics: drivers and dividers

Early in 2018, Chinese warships entered the Indian Ocean, some headed for the beautiful Maldives which was in the middle of a constitutional crisis. Its president, Abdulla Yameen, had opened the door to extensive Chinese port and other infrastructure financing and construction, handed the main port over, signed a free trade agreement, and signed up to the BRI. India was not pleased, especially as it had regarded the Maldives as part of its own sphere of influence. China's naval force was sent to deter India from getting involved, in spite of an invitation to do so from the islands' main political opposition. Here, then, in the BRI's infancy, was a microcosm of how confrontation in the BRI might be just as likely as commerce.

Perhaps this is not so surprising, for the two are closely connected, and both have evolved out of China's rising economic weight in Asia and the world economy. Consider first the main economic drivers of the BRI.

China is, after all, the hub of a huge regional and global production system, much as Japan was between the First and Second World Wars, and for a while in the 1960s and 1970s. Since China is the world's largest export nation – accounting for almost 15 per cent of world exports – its domestic economic and political needs and priorities have taken on an increasingly global significance. So much so, in fact, that it needs to engage and participate globally in ways that both protect and shape the environment in which Chinese business and trade function.

China relies heavily on imported energy, raw material and food for its economy and citizens, and it depends on important supply chains for trade. It has also built up extensive investments abroad, and millions of Chinese either work, study or travel abroad. Though slightly dated, the number of enterprises established abroad is estimated at more than 20,000, and the number of 'outbound' Chinese at more than 100 million.[13] The breakneck speed of China's economic development, moreover, has generated major inequality problems not only between rich and poor, but also between rural and urban populations, and between poorer western and central provinces on the one hand, and the richer coastal provinces on the other.

Western provinces record income per head that is on average roughly half of what it is in the coastal provinces. In 2016 in Shanghai, income per head was almost four times as much as it was in Gansu in northwestern China. Western Chinese provinces and cities tend to be the most significant recipients of financial largesse from Beijing and from banks, and have the highest concentration of SOEs. The flagship development of the China–Pakistan Economic Corridor, in the southernmost part of which is Gwadar, is intended to develop parts of Xinjiang province, which is 5,000 kilometres from China's east coast and home to both a large Turkic-speaking Muslim population and China's major security and separatist threats.

The BRI is intended also to help reboot Chinese manufacturing industries, and spur the development of newer industries, such as advanced manufacturing, high-speed rail, telecommunications and green energy, including in China's more economically backward provinces. The 13th Five-Year Plan, the Made in China 2025 industrial strategy and the most recent plan to be a world leader in artificial intelligence by 2030 all aim to make China shape and influence advanced information and digital systems 'with Chinese characteristics' rather than continue to take them off the shelf from the US and other Western companies and countries.

China, in effect, is aiming to use its expanded global footprint to establish its own technologies and product standards – which it wants recognised and branded abroad – and, in turn, to contribute to greater commercial and reputational success. Chinese high-speed rail may not be representative across the spectrum of modern industries and technologies, but it does serve to illustrate what China is after. If China can gain acceptance of its product and technical standards externally, then a much wider and deeper market position might have positive spillover effects not just for the high-speed rail industry vis-à-vis Japan, for example, but also for constituent manufacturers and suppliers. China's Ministry of Industry and Information Technology believes that high-speed rail success could boost demand for high-end industrial exports from countries in Southeast Asia as well as Central and Western Asia. Indonesia, for example, which chose China rather than Japan to build the Bandung to Jakarta rail link, has in effect opted for Chinese technology and equipment, construction and management.

There is no question that China will develop its efforts behind a web of discriminatory industrial policies. This isn't a uniquely Chinese phenomenon because other Asian countries, such as Japan and South Korea, industrialised behind protectionist barriers too. Yet times were different then and they had the protection and encouragement of the US. China does not. Indeed, China's practices, for example in industrial procurement, product standards, information security, tax and competition rules, and intellectual property requirements are viewed with increasing concern not just in the US but elsewhere too.

SOEs are now being asked to do much more than in the past, when their main task was to search for and gain access to natural resources and trade opportunities. They still do this to support urbanisation, infrastructure, energy and other construction programmes, which require iron ore, bauxite, copper and other metals from Africa and Latin America. Yet SOEs are also at the heart of China's foreign investment and project-related work, and at the cutting edge of state-to-state infrastructure and trade deals, financial assistance arrangements and loans, and education and training opportunities.

The BRI is expected to relieve the pressure on sluggish heavy industries suffering from excess capacity, notably coal and steel. Affected firms might export that excess output to BRI countries directly by dumping coal and steel abroad, or by moving the physical capacity itself into other countries. The latter seems more likely. It is planned, for example, to migrate 20 million tonnes of Hebei province's large surplus steel capacity (as well as cement and pleat glass) to Southeast Asia, Africa and Western Asia by 2023.[14] This foreign direct investment strategy may reduce the supply glut in China, but add to it elsewhere. Exporting, one way or another, will not solve the problem from a global standpoint.

What suits China economically might not always bond well with other countries' economic interests. While most people probably take it as read that smaller countries, especially poorer ones, welcome China's financing and infrastructure, there are important caveats and qualifications. Some countries may simply not be able economically, or be willing politically, to absorb the sheer scale of China's excess capacity or integrate big new construction projects well. They may lack the political resilience and institutions to keep corruption at bay. Poorer countries with below investment grade credit ratings are constrained from getting access to important sources of finance, such as co-financing from official development agencies. Because major infrastructure construction projects are frequently characterised by corruption or poor governance, restricted access to financing could prove especially damaging.

Countries receiving BRI financing and projects, moreover, may need unencumbered borrowing capacity to support the full exploitation of big projects. They may need to provide complementary below-the-radar improvements in ancillary services. For example, bigger and better road and rail links between two major points won't necessarily live up to expectations if there is no finance to build supporting and spur links, or provide efficient customs and administration procedures, legal infrastructure for loading and unloading, and storage and distribution facilities.

While BRI headlines are normally about new contracts and project progress reports, it is worth noting that there is also a flurry of reports detailing disputes, cancelled contracts and delays. At the end of 2017, Pakistan withdrew its request for the Diamer-Bhasha dam in northern Pakistan to be included in China's BRI projects in the country, ostensibly because of financing conditions but amid complaints about Chinese ownership conditions. Meanwhile, Chinese construction and acquisition of Sri Lanka's Hambantota port, and the Port City Colombo project, have brought claims that Chinese behaviour threatened Sri Lanka's sovereignty, resulted in large excess capacity at a brand new airport and excessive debt financing.

In Africa, allegations of colonialism have accompanied greater Chinese involvement and engagement with the continent, and the arrival of Chinese companies, workers and finance.[15] Both the Nairobi to Mombasa railway line, which opened in 2017, and the previously completed major rail project from Addis Ababa to Djibouti, linked Indian Ocean ports to natural resource deposits, and put the sponsoring governments under great financial strain. The response in these cases, as well as in other countries including Tanzania and Namibia, was to allow Chinese entities to take controlling stakes in companies in finance, real estate and resource management. Although African nations are getting infrastructure that is financed, built or operated by China, the terms to some Africans look eerily familiar to those extracted under colonialism.

In Pakistan, the Economic Corridor runs through tribal areas in which China is financing about $60 billion of infrastructure and where there have been outbreaks of unrest and terrorism. Political and commercial disputes have arisen also in Nepal, Myanmar, Thailand and Sri Lanka. In Malaysia, the new government, elected in 2018, moved quickly to suspend four large China-backed rail and pipeline projects deemed to have been rife with corruption and over-spending.

Looked at economically, then, the BRI seems to be much more a China-centric strategy from which small countries might benefit, though, as suggested, some countries, including those with weak debt carrying capacity, are quite likely to find the price includes financial stress and the navigation of big political sensitivities. According to one study of BRI financing, over-reliance on China as a creditor, and the peculiarities of Chinese as opposed to multilateral agency financing, threaten twenty-three BRI countries with some form of financial distress, and eight of them with serious debt sustainability issues.[16]

Geopolitical drivers are important, and the BRI is not just about the romance and myths of the old Silk Road. It is also about China's presenting to the world an alternative, authoritarian model, and trying to influence the political environment in its expanded neighbourhood in its favour. China is already the leading or a leading trade partner for many countries, and it has developed extensive programmes of cultural and educational exchange with several nations, in Asia in particular. It is self-evident that just as colonial powers and later the US sought to establish political influence in countries within their commercial sphere of influence, so too does China.

Yet, Eurasia includes countries and states in which regional distrust and fear of Chinese domination go back a long way, and we do not have to look too far below the surface to see how and where edgy and even confrontational situations might emerge.

The South China Sea carries about 30 per cent of global sea-borne trade, and contains enormous fishing grounds that yield about 12 per cent of the world's annual catch.[17] Six of China's largest ten ports are on the East China Sea. These commercial interests have to be protected and it is consequently natural for China to aspire to be not just a naval but also a maritime power. China wants to build warships and submarines to equip its navy, and is expanding its navy faster than any other country. But it also wants a whole range of military land, sea and even space-based assets, a coast-guard, extensive port infrastructure, merchant shipping and fishing fleets, and a shipbuilding industry. Chinese shipping companies carry more cargo than those of any other country, while China itself is home to five of the world's top ten container ports, the largest maritime law enforcement fleet, and a more than 200,000-strong fishing fleet.[18]

Yet, in pursuing this goal, frictions with other countries have inevitably arisen, and for many nations China is pushing its claims too far. It has run up against the US and Japan, both of whom assert interests in seas and islands that clash with China's. China wants to keep the US Pacific fleet as far away from China as possible with an immediate focus on the so-called 'first island chain', comprising islands off Russia's peninsula of Kamchatka down past Japan to Taiwan, and then to the Philippines and Malay peninsula. Eventually, we might imagine, China could seek to extend its naval influence further and perhaps as far away as Indonesia or even Australia. It has already clashed with Japan over uninhabited but strategically placed islands it calls the Diaoyu but which Japan calls the Senkaku.

It has also asserted sovereignty over the seas, islands, rocks and reefs that fall inside the so-called Nine-Dash Line in a questionable Chinese map of the South China Sea. China claims historical rights over the entire area bounded by this line, which looks like a giant U-shape, starting off the coast of Vietnam and running all the way down to Malaysia, where it turns north, passes Brunei and goes up to the northernmost part of the Philippines. Since 2014, substantial dredging projects have been undertaken to reclaim land on around a half-dozen or so reefs and turn them into sea-based runways, ports and anti-aircraft and anti-missile battery systems.

In 2016, an international tribunal in The Hague ruled decisively in favour of the Philippines in a case against China, ruling that rocky outcrops claimed by the latter could not be used as the basis of territorial claims, and that China had violated the Philippines' sovereign rights in those waters by interfering with its fishing and petroleum exploration and by constructing artificial islands. China never recognised the court's jurisdiction, and rejected the verdict. *Xinhua News*, for example, attacked the ill-founded ruling that was 'naturally null and void', while the Communist Party's *People's Daily* said that the tribunal had ignored 'basic truths' and 'trampled' on international laws and norms.[19]

Soon after, President Duterte came to power in Manila and pursued a policy of rapprochement with China, later taking China's side by arguing that China's activities in the South China Sea were aimed not at regional states, but the United States. Other states have not been so easily won over.

China's maritime interests are not, of course, restricted to the South and East China Seas. The construction of and access to ports on the Arabian Sea and Indian Ocean, notably Gwadar in the Pakistani province of Baluchistan, gives China commercial and naval proximity to Oman and the Persian Gulf, which are a mere 380 kilometres away. This means China doesn't have to ship oil all the way around India, across the Indian Ocean, through the Straits of Malacca in Southeast Asia and then north to its eastern coast. The 880-kilometre-long Straits of Malacca, which are 2.5 kilometres wide at the narrowest point and through which 80 per cent of China's sea-traded oil comes, are potentially a chokepoint on a 12,000-kilometre journey from the Gulf to, say, Shanghai. Gwadar, moreover, offers the Chinese Indian Ocean fleet a perfectly situated naval base where naval craft, including submarines and aircraft carriers, will be able to dock for repairs and maintenance, and Chinese naval missions can be supported.

Central Asia, including Russia, including many of the former Soviet republics, constitutes the immediate geography for China. The terrain is rugged, though the region is rich in energy and comprises a strategic conduit between western China and Europe and the Middle East, but it is nether populous nor at the cutting edge of global development.

China sees Russia essentially as peripheral from an economic standpoint. The dependency relationship is tilted heavily in China's favour. President Putin has spoken welcomingly about China's BRI, and Russia and China liaise in the Shanghai Cooperation Organisation and other Eurasian forums. Putin's main focus is to establish ties between the BRI and his own Eurasian Economic Union, comprising the former Soviet countries of Russia, Kazakhstan, Belarus, Armenia and Kyrgyzstan. Given Central Asia's importance regarding energy and for transit of pipelines and railways, commercial cooperation looks more likely than commercial clashes. Relations with Russia do not look especially volatile.

Though Southeast Asia is highly developed, BRI commercial opportunities reside in rail transport projects in Indonesia, Malaysia, the Philippines and Thailand. For the most part, though, China's projects in this part of Asia are with smaller, poorer countries such as Cambodia, Myanmar, Nepal and Vietnam. Again, however, these have not been without largely unreported incidents. At the end of 2017, Nepal scrapped a $2.5 billion contract for a hydroelectricity project, accusing the Chinese company of financial irregularities. Myanmar, which halted a $3.6 billion Chinese-backed dam in 2014, also withdrew from a big hydroelectric power project.

China's interests in Africa extend from East Africa, especially Kenya, Ethiopia, and the naval facilities in Djibouti, to Egypt, the Democratic Republic of Congo, Morocco, South Africa, Cameroon and Togo. Opportunities are limited, however, by low absolute levels of development and debt capacity, and the weak state of private sector activity.

Europe is potentially a major BRI prize, but most of China's BRI activities have centred around Poland, Hungary, Bulgaria, Slovenia, the Baltic and Balkan countries, and Greece. However, the EU has quite mixed views about Chinese investment. It has investigated China for public tendering violations, and has deep-seated issues about China's public procurement, reciprocity, market access, data and privacy laws, among other commercial and investment matters.

The jewel in the BRI potentially for China, then, is southern Asia, where China is already heavily involved with its long-standing ally, Pakistan, as well as with Sri Lanka and Bangladesh, but, of course, not with India. India, along with Japan and the US and Australia – bigger, richer or more populous – are starting to push back against China, possibly with important implications. If closer cooperation between these four nations materialises, it could send an important signal to the countries in the Association of Southeast Asian Nations (ASEAN), which are already closely tied to China commercially. They did over $500 billion of trade in 2017, which was almost as much as China did with the EU, but many are also natural political and/or military allies for the US. A more cohesive and inclusive approach to ASEAN by India, Japan, Australia and the US could help member states out of a difficult strategic predicament.

Japan is important, not least because of its history with China, and a lingering mutual distrust. For most of the post-1945 period, Japan played a secondary and supportive role to the US in Asia. Yet, in view of US policies under Trump, Prime Minister Abe is leading a Japanese rethink about alliances, national interests in Asia and beyond, and above all from a Japanese perspective, defence budgets and strategy. Japan's ambiguity about the BRI can be seen from the warm words of welcome and cooperation pitched towards China, balanced by other policy developments and initiatives in which Japan is trying to stake out a new, more assertive Asian role.

In 2016, Abe outlined a new development and security plan for Asia as a sort of riposte to China, which included Tokyo's own proposals for 'quality' infrastructure creation in the region. He insisted that it was vital for infrastructure to be commercially viable, especially for host countries, to be open to use by all, and to be developed through procurement that was transparent and fair. These qualifications seemed designed to distinguish Japan's approach from China's in Tokyo's eyes. Japan has also embraced and signed up to the Comprehensive and Progressive Agreement for the Trans-Pacific Partnership after the US withdrew from the original agreement.

Japan's infrastructure strategy was articulated in the Ministry of Foreign Affairs announcement in 2017 that Official Development Assistance would be used to promote a Free and Open Indo-Pacific Strategy. According to the policy document, Japan will 'enhance connectivity between Asia and Africa to promote stability and prosperity across the regions'.[20] Whether Japan acts alone, in conjunction with other nations or through the Asian Development Bank or Asian Infrastructure Investment Bank, its policy is bound to be seen as a counter to the BRI. Japan may be an ageing nation with a slowly falling population, but for the foreseeable future it would be surprising if it did not seek to leverage its economic and commercial significance against a China that still harbours deep historical resentment.

India was the only country invited to China's Belt and Road Forum in 2017 in Beijing that didn't show up, and it has not been shy in expressing rather negative views about the BRI. Although Prime Minister Narendra Modi's visit to Xi Jinping in 2018 was seen as a new China–India rapprochement, both sides had reasons not to emphasise tensions, and the meeting did nothing to detract from them. The underlying problem for India with regard to China is also a pervasive sense of mistrust, historical baggage from a military defeat by China in 1962 clashes, and China's courtship of Pakistan, in particular of disputed lands in Kashmir and Gilgit-Baltistan. India's former National Security Adviser, Shivshankar Menon, echoing what his prime minister, Narendra Modi, had told President Xi on a visit to Beijing two years earlier, said in 2017 that the China–Pakistan Economic Corridor was 'not acceptable to us'.[21]

Further, India sees China as encroaching on its natural sphere of influence in Sri Lanka, Nepal and Bangladesh, as well as on territorial and water claims in shared border areas in the Himalayas, and as surrounding it with the so-called 'string of pearls' – naval and port facilities that encircle India and link China to Myanmar, Bangladesh, Sri Lanka, Pakistan and Djibouti. Undeterred by its own relative lack of economic strength and infrastructure reputation compared to China, India is embarking on closer ties and cooperation with not just its regional allies and countries and islands in the Indian Ocean, but also with both the US and Japan. It is working with Japan to develop energy, power, port and transportation infrastructure in Sri Lanka, Bangladesh and Myanmar. India is also engaged in a four-way dialogue with the US, Japan and Australia to develop an alternative strategy, designed to appeal to Asia as a counterweight to the BRI.

Locking horns in Eurasia

Such is the significance of the BRI in China that it has produced English-language videos in the form of a children's bedtime story. In one of the videos, an American father says to his five-year-old child: 'It's China's idea, but it belongs to the world.'[22] This soft-soap version of the BRI is in keeping with a Chinese narrative that looks back fondly to the era of the ancient Silk Road, and recasts it as Xi Jinping's recreation for the good of the world.

Speaking to the first Belt and Road Forum in Beijing in May 2017, President Xi reminded the 29 foreign heads of state and representatives from more than 130 countries and 70 international organisations that over 2,000 years ago, 'our ancestors trekking across vast steppes and deserts, opened up the transcontinental passage connecting Asia, Europe and

Africa, known today as the Silk Road'. He went on to refer to the sea routes that later evolved linking the East with the West, and noted that the ancient silk routes 'opened windows of friendly engagement among nations, adding a splendid chapter to the history of human progress ... and embody the spirit of peace and cooperation, openness and inclusiveness, mutual learning and mutual benefit'.[23]

Unsurprisingly, the narrative reads differently in the West. No one disputes that once upon a time China was rich, relatively sophisticated and very active in private trade conducted by merchants and craftsmen. The idea, though, of 'friendly engagement, openness, and inclusiveness' and so on constitutes a bit of poetic licence. China never had to engage with other countries or civilisations that came even close to it in scale or sophistication. This was no doubt partly because of China's geography, bounded by the Himalayas and the Tibetan plateau to the south, the vast, arid deserts of Central Asia to the west, and enormous distances to Persia, Babylonia, and ultimately the Roman Empire. Moreover, there was never any government or state-sponsored trade and diplomatic strategy, as such, and the Chinese were rather dismissive about what the rest of the world had to offer them. According to Henry Kissinger, 'trade with China was so prized that it was with only partial exaggeration that Chinese elites described it not as ordinary economic exchange but as tribute to China's superiority'.[24]

The BRI, as constituted, has no historical precedence other than in rhetoric. The ambition to encircle India by land and sea is new. So is the creation of a financial and resource exchange system for power, transportation and infrastructure development in central Asia, the Middle East, parts of Europe and Africa. Likewise, the formation of trade and security relationships designed to keep the US away from Asia, or at least stifle its reach.

China's approach to global engagement today is different from that of previous leaders over the last six decades. Deng Xiaoping urged China to keep a low profile, and even after the fall of the Soviet Union in 1989, he still exhorted comrades and compatriots to 'coolly observe, calmly deal with things, hold your position, hide your capacities, bide your time, accomplish things where possible'.[25] Deng's approach to international relations, which held sway for twenty years or so, has been transformed by the establishment and entrenchment of Chinese economic power. Indeed, with economic power comes a sense of entitlement, capability and ambition, and even a demand for deference and respect from others. This moment certainly seems to have arrived in China around the time of the financial crisis in 2007–8, and since. It was inevitable that this would unsettle the US.

Twenty years ago, Zbigniew Brzezinski, former counsellor to Lyndon Johnson, and National Security Chief under Jimmy Carter, emphasised that all historical pretenders to global power originated in Eurasia, which he called the world's 'axial supercontinent'. He wrote that whoever controls Eurasia has decisive influence over two of the world's three most economically productive regions. Worried as he would have been at the time about an unstable Russia and a Central Asian cauldron of ethnic conflicts and great power rivalries, he warned 'the US will not have a Eurasian strategy unless a Sino-American political consensus is nurtured'.[26]

For the most part, with occasional friction, the US and China have sought to build that political consensus. Under Bill Clinton, China was designated a strategic partner. Under George W. Bush, China became a strategic competitor, but his deputy secretary of state, Robert Zoellick, famously urged China to become a 'responsible stakeholder' in the international system. In President Obama's first term, Secretary of State Hillary Clinton said that while some believed a rising China to be an adversary, 'we believe that the United States and China can benefit from and contribute to each other's successes. It is in our interests to work harder to build on areas of common concern and shared opportunities.'[27] In the same year, Obama and Chinese president Hu Jintao established the high-level U.S.– China Strategic and Economic Dialogue, a series of regular meetings between officials to discuss economic, financial and commercial issues of mutual interest.

In the wake of the dislocations and consequences of the financial crisis, however, an economically exhausted and politically compromised US, confronted by a still economically confident China, changed tack. In 2013, it began to pursue a new policy, the 'Pivot to Asia', spurred partly by an emerging discussion about the Beijing consensus, or Chinese-style development model as an alternative to the hitherto dominant Washington consensus. American policy was doubtless driven by concerns not to allow a Beijing consensus to plant irretrievably strong roots in Asia. According to a former national security official, Michael Green, 'American policy in the Far East has for a long time been driven by its reluctance to tolerate any other power establishing exclusive hegemonic control over Asia or the Pacific.'[28]

Things have moved on under the Trump administration. After some wavering in approach as the US sought China's good offices as an intermediary in its dispute with North Korea, the administration gradually re-asserted a more adversarial position. At the end of 2017, the National Security Strategy portrayed China as a top threat that was becoming more powerful at the expense of the sovereignty of others. It charged that China exploited trade on an unprecedented scale, looked to spread authoritarianism, was building a well-funded military capacity, and sought access to America's innovation economy.

The foundations of political consensus between China and the US look shakier than for many years as they interact in the shadows as partners, but in the headlines increasingly as adversaries and rivals. For the time being, the east wind certainly appears to be in the ascendant, but nothing is preordained.

We must hope that future US administrations remain committed to engagement as well as to fairness in developing relations with China, and preferably after reconnecting with allies both in Asia and beyond, and by working again to nurture institutions of collaboration and cooperation in monetary, economic, cybersecurity and information-related forums. For all its economic weight in the world, China still lacks what Joseph Nye famously called 'soft power', or the means by which 'a country gets others to do what it wants'. The relevance here is not so much with respect to smaller and poorer countries but to large and powerful peers. Its transaction-oriented approach has entailed commercial practices that have reflected badly, such as bankrolling Venezuela, and exporting its workers to countries with plenty of unemployed or poorly employed people along with its capital. Western values, which are much derided in China, still count for something in large swathes of Asia and the wider global economy, even if there is disappointment and disillusion about free market economic thinking itself.

Henry Ford is reported to have said: 'When everything seems to be going against you, remember that the airplane takes off against the wind, not with it.' Just because the Communist Party and others say the BRI will change the world order and global economy, doesn't mean it will be so, or that we can predict the responses of others who will be affected, or have their own vested interests.

10

XI JINPING'S CHINA

About 6 kilometres west of the iconic Oriental Pearl TV Tower in Shanghai lies a modest building at 76 Xingye Road in the Huangpu District. Now a museum, it was the location of a 1921 meeting of a dozen writers and political activists for the first Congress of the Chinese Communist Party. It had a membership at the time of several hundred. Today the Party has about 85 million members, and they are looking forward to celebrating its centenary in 2021.

The same year also marks seventy-two years of Communist Party rule, matching the longevity of Soviet Communist Party rule from 1917 to 1989. Xi Jinping and other prominent politicians, whose biggest nightmare must be the risk of following the Soviet Communist Party into oblivion, have often referred to its demise as an example of why China's Party members, along with their leaders and the military, must be forever vigilant about discipline, obedience and loyalty.

Together, they could then go on to celebrate another important centenary, of the founding of the People's Republic, in 2049, when the Party has set the goal for China to be a Great Power. Halfway between these two centenaries, in 2035, the Party has set an intermediate goal for China to have become a 'moderately prosperous society'. Xi Jinping's continuing status and influence in the Party are assured. If his health holds, there are no adverse events with which he is associated, and his opponents permit, Xi, who turned sixty-five in 2018, could remain president for much of this period.

For China, Asia and the West, the consequences of Xi Jinping are going to have profound effects. We will have to wrestle with three fundamental issues, which I have tried to emphasise in this book.

Putting politics back in command

First, although Xi is not the source of authoritarianism in China, the concentration of power and control around him has created a 'dictatorship' that marks a new chapter in China's contemporary history. Some people liken him to Mao, but, whether or not this is accurate, he has, to use a Maoist phrase from the Cultural Revolution, put 'politics in command' in ways that recall the Mao era. Xi's politics are the Party's politics, and the Party alone, rather than collective institutions and technocrats, is going to shape domestic policy and international relations. The Party in fact is the defining feature of contemporary Socialism with Chinese Characteristics, and as omnipresent in education, the media and culture as it is in the economy and business.

I used the word 'Echoes' as the title of Chapter 1 as a sort of reminder that amid many centuries of change in China, some things stay the same or echo the past, and in this sense, the idea of Xi as a new emperor resonates. This raises two governance issues that have dogged China for millennia – the lack of any downward accountability, and the so-called 'bad emperor' problem, where orderly succession is not allowed for. Lacking institutions of constraint and consensus, it is not easy to predict what Xi's China will do or how it will behave, especially when it makes errors, missteps and miscalculations. There is no accountability system to remove a bad emperor, and the term limits that might have at least had Xi hand over the presidency to someone else in 2022 are gone.

We know that China perfected bureaucratic effectiveness, based on high standards of merit, long before anyone else, and has carried this through to modern times. Yet it has not saved China in the past from weaknesses and failures arising from remote or unresponsive emperors, and it won't in future. As general secretary of the Party, chairman of the Central Military Commission, and, should he so choose, president for life, Xi Jinping has attained exalted status. The power that resides and is concentrated around him personally, the Party and its agencies is a curious fusion of both strength and weakness.

A strong Party state can demonstrate coherence and consistency in the policies it pursues, and one could argue that in a digital and information-intensive society, there should be no excuse for top officials not to know what citizens want or are up to. The issue, though, is not so much what officials know, but rather if they are, in important ways, responsive – and all the more so since information itself empowers people. Coherence and consistency do not necessarily mean that policies are always good or well thought out.

Indeed, the concentration of power itself is a substitute for the institutionalisation and transparency of rules and procedures that normally govern society.

Governance and institutions, therefore, about which there were already reservations as far as China's twenty-first-century challenges are concerned, are now even more important. Unbridled power, the disincentives to argue with or reason against the leader, the heavy hand of state censorship and limitations on learning, the new suppression of dissent, and the incorporation into the state constitution of the National Supervision Commission are not ideal hand-maidens of dynamic reform and high economic aspiration. Political, regulatory and other forms of intrusion are being brought to bear in corporate boardrooms, including in the private sector, to which China owes much of its dynamism.

In Xi's China, politics, which have for so long formed a tailwind behind economic development, are now turning into a formidable headwind. The Chinese argument, also argued by some commentators outside the country, is quite the opposite. The strengthening of the Party-state is precisely what contemporary circumstances demand, especially in the wake of the perceived bankruptcy of Western economic thinking and performance. As to who is right, it is, as they say, too early to tell. Yet, even as we lick our wounds in the West, we have no reason to determine that China's model is going to succeed just because it is different.

A maze of economic contradictions

Second, China faces a confluence of economic challenges, which have been building for some time. Xi and his close advisers know that the economic model has to change, and that the principal contradiction facing them is the tension between modernity, markets and the implicit drive to adopt the rule of law on the one hand, and the structure of the Party-state on the other. In good old-fashioned dialectics, the synthesis for them is ideological commitment to the primacy of the Party in all economic and social matters. Yet there are no assurances this approach will suffice to deal with the four traps discussed in the book. Debt and the state of the currency loom in the next few years, and ageing and the middle-income trap do so over the medium term, and they are all wrapped in a more toxic trade environment and far more intrusive Party environment.

At the 19th Party Congress in 2017, the Party's formal 'central contradiction' requiring resolution was changed. Since 1981, it had been framed in terms of the conflict between the 'ever growing material and cultural needs of the people and backward social production'. It now reflects the conflict between 'unbalanced and inadequate development, and the people's ever growing needs for a better life'. The key difference, ostensibly at least, is a shift in government priorities from high economic growth at any cost (including to the environment) to financial stability, which is already the subject of a concerted regulatory campaign, improving the environment and pollution, lowering income and regional inequality, and strengthening the social safety net.

These priorities only make sense, though, if China lets go of its addiction to setting unrealistic growth targets. It isn't certain, at least yet, if this is going to happen, but it is a key question, the answer to which is important in trying to gauge what to expect from reforms, and how China will address the four traps highlighted in this book.

I referred to GDP targets in the Introduction to underscore how China's treatment of GDP as a target that has to be met differed from the Western system of measuring it as an outcome of random spending decisions. The problem with GDP targeting is that it is a licence to deliver bad GDP, that is, uncommercial, debt-driven and loss-making investment and loans that have to be paid for eventually with negative consequences for GDP later.

Targets look likely to remain in situ while the current commitment to double income per head between 2010 and 2020 is in force. The acid test, and this is the principal contradiction in China, will be whether the Party will change its tune in and after 2020, and whether it is genuinely prepared to accept significantly lower growth in an economy where it is pursuing less credit-oriented, and more people-focused, environmental and social goals.

A proper deleveraging of the economic and financial system would be hard enough without a material loss of economic growth, at least for a few years. But, when the authorities also have goals to lower heavy industry capacity, cut income inequality, clean up the environment, push the Party into all areas of commercial decision-making, and simultaneously manage a more testing trade environment, it is hard to see how growth cannot slide significantly. Would the government allow growth to slide to 3 per cent, which may be roughly where trend growth is now? If so, it would be a meaningful shift. If it didn't, and maintained an informal or covert target of around 5.5 to 6.5 per cent, then it wouldn't be so significant. It is all in the implementation, not the slogan. The government will probably remain highly sensitive to the cyclical performance of the economy, with a particular focus on jobs and social stability. I don't expect China to drop growth targets, formally or informally, for the foreseeable future, and this will complicate its capacity to deal effectively and smoothly with the debt trap.

Reforms, as I have suggested, will figure prominently, but not in the way that Western economics would prescribe. They may include measures to deliver financial stability and lower excess capacity in industries such as coal and steel, the liberalisation of some prices, subsidies or tariffs in designated products or sectors, the opening up of some opportunities to private, including foreign companies, and ambitious goals for new technologies. They will be incremental and stability-oriented, with a focus on administrative and regulatory arrangements between different layers and levels of government. They will happen behind nationalistic and protectionist barriers.

In finance, the government has already embarked on firmer regulatory policing of excesses in the marketing and accounting of financial products, risk-taking and the behaviour of a few conglomerates. And credit growth has slowed down, though it remains elevated. Policies, though, need to go further to lean persistently on the sources and principal users of credit, the funding structure of loans, ubiquitous guarantees, and the deleveraging of both financial institutions and state-owned enterprise and local government borrowing platforms. Effective deleveraging would involve asset sales, mergers, closures and bankruptcies, the winding down of guarantees and bail-outs, and the allocation of costs for bad loans that have to be written down or written off. It is doubtful the government will go this far, at least voluntarily. The test will come when economic growth slows down to levels deemed too low. If the government then steps again on the economic accelerator pedal, the risk of a more disruptive denouement of debt will be clearer.

The timing and pattern of the government's approach will determine whether the Renminbi trap opens sooner or later. The main argument here centres around the incompatibility of a softly pegged exchange rate with a financial system that prints assets out of proportion to the currency reserves that back them. If this continues, the reserves will eventually be viewed as inadequate. Yet, whether this happens or not, eventually China will have to inflate or deflate its way out of debt, both of which would entail outcomes in which capital would most likely try to flee China. Since China is susceptible to capital flight in spite of capital controls, we should expect the Renminbi to be weaker in future. The existence of capital controls buys China time, but not in perpetuity. In any event, because a significant liberalisation of outward capital movements is unlikely, and an external balance of payments surplus will persist for the time being, the often prop-agated belief that the Renminbi will become a major international or even significant global reserve currency is another example of the triumph of rhetoric over reality.

Over the next twenty years and beyond, Xi's China must find its own coping mechanisms to deal with a rapidly ageing population and declining labour force. These will play out in a quarter of the time that it took in most advanced economies, and at lower levels of income and wealth per head of population. The starting point in terms of pension and healthcare coverage is good, but benefits are not generous or well funded, and in cities rural migrant workers without urban registration are still discriminated against. It is sometimes argued that China is well served by a modest social system because it has learned from Western countries about the huge welfare costs of age-related spending. This sounds like a poor excuse for inertia, and weak governance when it comes to adequate welfare provision.

The ultimate proof of how and if China comes to terms with its prin-cipal economic tests will be whether it is able to avoid the middle-income trap. To do this, it will have to address and overcome leverage, debt, economic rebalancing and social policy issues, and re-energise productivity growth. By the 2020s, we should know much better how the wind blows. The consensus view among many observers and investors is that Xi's China is different from other middle-income countries because it has economic size, a vast market, unencumbered and controlling government, and a single-minded focus on success in new industries. We should certainly be mindful of these properties and characteristics, and not rush to judgement that autocratic states are doomed to fail.

Yet, as I have also tried to point out, economic, scientific and engineering achievements, laudable as they are, do not always imply broader economic success or print the ticket to unlock the middle-income trap. We should instead be aware of the significance of the quality, robustness and inclusive-ness of institutions and governance that act as enablers of new technologies to spark broad-based productivity growth gains. In this respect, Xi's China looks at best like a work-in-progress. It will doubtless score big technology successes, but, conflicted over the roles it occupies as owner, promoter and regulator in the economy and society, it is never going to be able to resolve the systemic contradiction in which the biggest barrier to enlightened reform and economic change is the Party itself.

New divergences

Third, Xi's China is going to open up new divergences between itself and the West, spanning political orientation and values, as already discussed, but also technological universes in which both aim for leadership, and international relations, in which China is going to throw down a gauntlet to the West.

One day, someone will rewrite Kenneth Pomeranz's well-known 2000 book, *The Great Divergence: China, Europe, and the Making of the Modern World Economy*. The new author's subtitle might read something like *China, the West, and the Making of the Modern Tech Economy*. Pomeranz's long historical focus on living standards, agriculture and natural conditions in the Yangtze and in northwestern Europe led him to the conclusion that Europe put China in the shade a bit more than two centuries ago because the availability of coal and its proximity to the New World allowed it to exploit resource-intensive and labour-saving technologies.

The case for a rewrite might one day be to examine a new divergence between China and the Western world, this time in China's favour. Or, it might be about why it didn't happen according to the inevitability that many people expected. The central focus, though, will similarly be on what happened to the development and exploitation of technology, including artificial intelligence (AI), big data and robotics, and a multitude of product and process innovations.

It will be a battle between China's experiment with state-directed digital authoritarianism and the West's more traditional experience of private sector technology nurtured and egged on by public agencies.

In the chapter on the middle-income trap, I highlighted the efforts and commitments that the Party is making to ramp up state support and financing, in close partnership with China's own tech giants and start-ups, for the development and integration of AI, 5G networks, big data, the internet of things (devices in objects that send and receive data), cloud computing, and the creation of new science parks and laboratories. It wants to show that the combination of government leadership, research and development spending, the establishment of clear policy priorities, and the exploitation of comparative advantage in large market size and data collection will fulfil ambitious global tech leadership targets. The absence of Western-style privacy laws is a further comparative advantage, up to a point, in the development of some tech applications, if not necessarily in their global commercialisation.

Chinese technology companies are already blazing a trail in the development of e-commerce, mobile device payments systems, unicorns or start-ups, and most recently, its 'social credit system' under which big data systems are using advanced facial recognition technology to create personal information sets about residence, travel and movement, social media, health and finance. The core elements of this system are being extended to monitor and keep track of the activities of companies too. China's tech giants, including Baidu, Alibaba, Tencent and Xiaomi, for example, while prospering behind protective barriers that keep out their US and other Western competitors, have already become highly valued and ambitious companies offering AI, social media, electronic payment, communications and e-commerce to a market of 1.4 billion people.

While there is sometimes a self-serving and often naive presumption that Chinese tech companies have already won the race to be global leaders, everyone can agree that Chinese tech companies are catching up fast, or even rivalling their US peers. Eric Schmidt, chairman of Alphabet, the company which owns Google, has opined that the future will belong to the countries that can surf the tidal wave of AI, and while Chinese efforts appear up to the challenge, he thought that the US seemed to be going in the wrong direction.

Indeed, the US National Science Foundation said in its annual report mandated by Congress for 2018 that while the US maintains a lead in research and development (R&D), venture capital, most advanced degrees, and production of high-tech manufacturing, its lead is slipping in certain important areas. The US is still ahead overall in AI technology, but Baidu, for example, is one of the top global firms in speech recognition. China was a good second to the US in R&D spending, and accounted for about half the US share of global venture capital investment and of knowledge and technology-intensive services provided to businesses. In both the latter cases, though, China's progress since 2012 has been remarkable, albeit from a low base. China's bachelor degrees in science and engineering have surged in recent years but it still lags the US in doctoral degrees. China may be making big strides, but its AI still faces limitations. According to a LinkedIn survey in early 2017, there are 50,000 AI professionals working in China compared with 850,000 in the US, a gap that amounts to a chasm when expressed as per head of population. Over time, of course, the gap could close but the relative shortcomings in China's tertiary level enrolment and attainment levels suggest that it could linger for a considerable number of years.

Hopefully the foundation will find the support in Congress and more widely in Washington to rail against President Trump's latest budget proposals providing for a 10 per cent reduction in Federal funding of its AI budget.

Even though they are in competition, Chinese and US tech firms do collaborate in large part because of a Chinese regulatory environment that includes bans on products and services offered by US companies, hostile anti-trust agencies and procurement policies, and joint venture regulations. Facebook has a tie-up with Chinese phone manufacturer Xiaomi to manufacture virtual reality headsets. Apple is developing a relationship with Guizhou-Cloud Big Data for storage of photos and messages. Telecoms giant Huawei, and Ant Financial, an affiliate of Alibaba Holdings, have agreements with Western companies as they look to bridge their two largely separate universes. Furthermore, US and Chinese tech companies compete both directly in emerging and developing countries, and indirectly by shaping their rivals' strategies and products even if their market share in one another's countries is limited.

Nevertheless, collaboration is overshadowed by rivalry, and we can already see a marked divergence developing between the ways in which China and Western economies are developing new technologies and integrating them into their societies. In the US, as I have already pointed out in Chapter 8, the government is looking with growing suspicion at Chinese investment in the US tech and other sectors through a national security lens, and certainly put ZTE and Huawei in its crosshairs in 2018. In China, new cybersecurity laws enacted in 2017 govern in particular the use and storage of data, and restrictions over the operations of foreign tech firms working in China, while in the US and EU, there is growing scrutiny over rules and regulations as they apply to privacy, which some industry experts think could become a new gold-plated benchmark for tech supremacy.

The EU General Data Protection Regulation, for example, that came into force in 2018, is designed to protect and empower all EU citizens' data privacy and reshape the way organisations across the EU collect, use and store data. An important implication is that non-EU countries will have to align with EU data provisions or else risk being shut out of one of the richest markets in the world with 500 million citizens. The EU is looking to set rules and standards, to which it hopes other countries will conform. This is an example of a very different kind of approach to digital technologies, with which Chinese entities may find it tough to compete in the EU and even in third countries.

The environment in which modern technologies emerge in China and the West will be quite different. China's digital authoritarianism revolves around a centralised, top-down direction and sponsorship of technology by the Party, and state enterprises and 'private' companies that work in tandem. Behind a wall of censorship, a surveillance state is developing rapidly that may be very effective at gathering information but also quite stifling in terms of creativity and disruption – phenomena in which the West has traditionally enjoyed strong advantages.

In contrast to their foreign counterparts, Chinese companies benefit from an array of public policy tools and instruments, including financial, interest rate and tax benefits, distinctive and favourable technological standards, advantageous competition and procurement conditions, beneficial market access for domestic producers, and special treatment regarding investment, trade and intellectual property rights. But Western companies are free to enter their own sectors, experiment and fail. They tend to be driven more by university research activities, small teams, and bottom-up pressure groups. China says that it is developing a greater tolerance for risk but the systems employed to evaluate and promote scientists, projects and methods of learning are not really compatible with at least the kind of risk encouragement and tolerance accepted in the West.

China expects its tech companies to play a central role in government industrial policies, and meet quantitative goals. These include specific targets for domestic market share, generally in the range of 70–80 per cent, by 2030. They apply to smart manufacturing, including robotics and components, cloud computing and big data, and information technology. Yet there is no empirical evidence that this sort of approach is successful in driving general purpose technologies, which are about both scientific achievement and complementary innovations across a wide range of sectors and applications that typically are unplanned and unpredictable. China certainly had scientific achievement in abundance before the original Great Divergence, but it wasn't enough. Nor was it for the USSR. It would be a curious twist indeed, given the 'wow' factor that pervades so much discussion about China's technological progress, if the next Great Divergence was determined not so much by achievements in new technologies per se, but by a combination of their broader and surprise innovation spin-offs, Chinese repression and hostility to the West's values and methods, and the enabling power of social media and information.

International relations divergence

Divergence between China and the West is also evident in the sharper differences in approach to politics and values. It is important to note, however, why this has happened and how in many ways it reflects not only the consequences of the financial crisis in the West, but also significant changes in Chinese domestic politics.

Under Mao, China was revolutionary, violent and isolated, and on a mission to put the Party at the core of everything. In terms of international relations, China's image was not so different, and while it enjoyed the USSR's backing for a while, and supported revolutionary movements in poor countries, it was more or less an outcast state in the global order. Under Deng Xiaoping, and pretty much until 2012, China was about 'Reform and Opening Up', engagement, collective leadership, the establishment of credible state institutions, a mission to leave poverty behind and realise steady economic growth, and, for a while towards the end, about the institutions of civil society. This was reflected internationally in a constructive and sustained attempt to participate in the global order, realise the status of a responsible player, and in a few respects, such as in the WTO, to go head-to-head on trade law with the US and the EU, and to do so successfully.

Yet, as the West's economic star fell to earth after 2008, and China's economic weight rose, it was inevitable that its confidence at home would spill over into foreign policy and international relations. Xi Jinping's leadership developed and cemented that confidence, encouraging citizens to believe in the Chinese Dream, and to capitalise on a world that he saw as changing to become more aligned with China itself. Freedom House, an independent watchdog organisation, has been documenting the rise of autocracies and strongman regimes in the world system for over a decade, and noted that more than half of the countries it monitors, comprising more than three-fifths of the world's population, have become less free. The post-crisis environment provided the ideal backdrop for Xi's narrative and, with the West in some disarray, China could stand proudly among the nations of the world. At the 19th Congress, Xi announced that China would become a leading global power, a role model for other countries, and build a world-class military that can fight and win wars.

It is true that China has not turned its back on global institutions such as the UN, WTO, the IMF and the World Bank. If anything, it wants to be heard more, and play a more prominent role, not least so that – instead of being accused of not playing by some of the institutions' rules – it can, by participating more, effect change to those rules. As I noted above, Xi Jinping's pitch to the global elite in Davos in 2017 was heavy on rhetoric and impression, but it also indicated that he wanted China to be seen as a partner.

Yet China has no truck with human rights or universal values, no qualms about supporting illiberal regimes, and has no doubt that the security of the state and the Party override all other forms of security. As I have noted in Chapters 8 and 9 on trade and the Belt and Road, respectively, it is quite willing to paddle its own canoe in terms of global architecture, for example by founding the Asian Infrastructure Investment Bank in which it retains a veto, and the New Development Bank, or BRICS Bank. It is trying to formalise the Regional Comprehensive Economic Partnership as a riposte to the revised Trans-Pacific Partnership, now relaunched without the US. It is a core member of the Shanghai Cooperation Organisation, the political, economic and security grouping in Eurasia.

The trade tension between China and the US merits particular attention because it represents sand in the gears of their economic interdependency. It is self-evident that US patience with China has run out, and that the Trump administration wants to hold China to account for what it sees as unfair trade and investment practices, especially as the technological race heats up in the next few years. It is not wrong to do so, but certainly mistaken to think that general tariffs and other measures, imposed unilaterally, and the alienation of allies are an appropriate response. The danger that this sort of behaviour could spill over into trade and tech wars with retaliatory actions perpetuating and deepening the tension is real. If calmer heads prevailed, the US would sit down with allies and try to work out a collective approach to China, using much more effective carrots and sticks, to address the treatment of foreign companies doing business in China, along with market access, technology and intellectual property transfer, and indigenous innovation policies.

There is at least an institutional architecture for that sort of engagement to take place, whereas in other areas, no such formal arrangements exist. The latest US National Security Strategy report claims that China seeks to displace the US in the Indo-Pacific region, expand the reaches of its state-driven economic model, and reorder the region in its favour. That is not wrong and conforms well to China's behaviour as a regional hegemony at least, and it is doubtful that China would privately disagree. China's military might and naval build-up, along with the militarisation of reefs and atolls in the South

China Sea, are not hidden, and nothing would please China more than to drive the US Seventh Fleet away from the island chains off China's coast and back across the Pacific. When Xi Jinping insisted on China's refusal to countenance 'separatism' at the National People's Congress in 2018, he was referring to Xinjiang and Tibet provinces, as well as to Hong Kong, and there was little question that this was also aimed at Taiwan. He has pledged to return Taiwan to the Motherland during his rule, and we are left to wonder how China might contrive to make this occur, under what circumstances, and what the implications might be for China and the US and others in the South China Sea.

Nor has China been shy about extolling its own economic success and economic strategies as examples for the rest of the world to follow. The reordering of the Indo-Pacific region is also, surely, a key part of what the Belt and Road Initiative is about. I argued that the BRI has both grown naturally out of China's economic heft, and emerged as a statement by China of the way it sees its role and influence throughout Eurasia and beyond. The BRI is a complicated and opaque strategy which doesn't always live up to the hype, but it is real in at least two particular ways.

It brings infrastructure to a lot of mainly poorer countries in China's neighbourhood, though not without financing, ownership and security problems, and it is a cause of serious security concerns to India, Japan and Australia in Asia and the US and the EU outside it. Since security is an umbrella term that includes not just military and political issues, but also trade, commerce and technology, it is not hard to imagine new and rising sources of tension, or even conflict, in years to come.

To mitigate this, Western thinking has to sharpen up and get smarter. We will first have to do a better job at understanding what Xi's China is all about and how Socialism with Chinese Characteristics determines the Party's behaviour at home and overseas. We have to dispel seductive narratives underpinning China's rhetoric about globalisation, the Belt and Road, and win-win situations, for example, and understand them for what they really are. Second, we have to acknowledge that it is proper and respectful to accord China a fair say in global governance institutions. We must tirelessly explore opportunities for cooperation and what we can call constructive competition. Third, we have to learn that hard as it might be to elicit favourable responses from the Party all the time, unity is strength. The West – US, EU, Japan, India and Australia – needs to coalesce around common agendas. Trump's America is not helping this cause at all. Fourth, while seeking to engage with China, we should make no excuses for the

Western values that we hold dear but which Xi Jinping rejects, or fail to point out that while the furthering of influence is something all powers do, the pursuit of interference – as highlighted by China in Australia, for example – is not acceptable. Fifth, and by no means finally, we should not only criticise China for the things we don't like, but spend time and money to strengthen the things we think we are good at, including higher education, research and development, disruptive technology, financial and modern services, and seek to rediscover the holy grail of productivity growth.

Will the east wind prevail?

The short and honest answer is that we don't know. I have tried to bring some balance to the argument, but am nonetheless sceptical. For all its past successes, impressive achievements and bold aspirations, China's four traps and a more fractious global environment represent a considerable challenge. The new ideological path on which Xi's China is set marks a break from the pragmatism that characterised China under previous leaders, and increases the likelihood of mishaps and, perhaps in the medium to long term, instability. Hence, my argument that Xi Jinping's China is in jeopardy.

Further, while no one would question China's dominant role in Asia, global leadership is altogether different. To be a leader, you have to have willing followers, and the reality is that few countries of significance would classify themselves as such. China has economic might, and growing military significance. One thing it lacks, though, is soft power.

It is no small matter that the distinctions between the Party and state, such as they were, that emerged from Deng Xiaoping onwards, are now being eliminated and that a more repressive ideology is planting roots. As the former Australian Prime Minister and long-time China student Kevin Rudd ably put it in a speech at West Point Military Academy in 2018, 'China's historical greatness, across its dynastic histories, lay in a strong, authoritarian hierarchical Confucian state. By corollary, China's historical greatness has never been a product of Western liberal democracy. By further corollary, China's future national greatness will lie not in any adaptation of Western political forms, but instead through the modern adaptation of its own indigenous political legacy in the form of a Confucian, communist state.'

If China, as such a state, succeeds in addressing its four traps and in becoming a high-income country at the same time, it will be a unique accomplishment, and from a Western standpoint, a deeply worrying prospect. China's long history is testament both to its capability for significant achievements but also to its susceptibility to failure and shortcomings. I have examined China's economic challenges, and in spite of what more cheerful analysts conclude, the case for a marked slowdown in economic growth that might in time become unstable is hard to refute.

Two known unknowns, to cite former US Secretary of Defense Donald Rumsfeld, remain to be added to the mix. One is how China's private sector, on which so much rests, will respond to the growing intrusion of and repression by the Party state. Uncertainty, or worse, disillusion about the economy is quite likely to manifest itself again at some point in capital flight and financial instability. The other is about the strength of China's social fabric, and how Xi's China might deal with future distresses, dislocations and demands of the fabled, rising and tech-savvy middle class as and when the economy slows down more significantly or runs into trouble. The intervention of technology in spurring change could be of great significance, as it has been to people and to regimes through the ages. The Party sees AI and digital technology as both a tool and a weapon of social control and surveillance. The middle class, millennials, and younger cohorts especially, might use it as an enabler of power in ways that no one expects today, or, echoing Mao's 1956 campaign to let arts and science flourish, a twenty-first-century opportunity to allow 'a hundred flowers to blossom'.

The east wind is surely blowing, but so are China's red flags. That they will have trenchant consequences for China and the world is not in doubt. They point to a brittleness in Xi Jinping's China which is not apparent when considering only the supposed omnipotence of the leader and the Party. That places Xi's China in jeopardy.

AFTERWORD

The paperback edition of *Red Flags* offered me the opportunity to do a couple of things in this new concluding chapter that I hope readers will find helpful. I have written in a little more detail about two ideas which I think have become more noteworthy since I submitted my original manuscript in the early months of 2018. The first comprises a challenge to the widely presumed inevitability that China will become the biggest economy in the world before too long. Since much of the narrative of the global economy and international relations takes it as a given that this outcome is a foregone conclusion, it follows that we should think carefully about the implications if it did not occur as expected. Second, I have also set out the gist of what some dissenting voices in China have been writing about. It is probably not an accident that these essays and commentaries have become more evident in the wake of the trade war with the US, and signs of economic difficulty at home.

I have elaborated too on several themes in the book, so as to bring readers up to date in light of the almost non-stop news about China in the last twelve to eighteen months. Much of this has focused on the trade war with the US, though it also spans other important – perhaps even more significant – aspects of the relationship between China and the US and, indeed, other Western nations. The escalation of the trade war to include commercial relations in general has been remarkable, notably the targeting of firms and especially technology companies, such as China's tech giant Huawei, for national security and other reasons.

I have also taken the opportunity to contextualise a little more and bring readers up to date with regard to the economy, how economic policy has been changing to counter downward pressures in economic activity, new information pertaining to the four traps referred to in the book, and what seems like a recalibration of aspects of the Belt and Road Initiative.

Why China might not become the world's biggest economy after all

During the second Belt and Road Forum that took place in Beijing in April 2019, I listened to an interview on the BBC's Today programme, the corporation's signature current affairs morning show, in which the anchor asked a minister of an EU member state about her country's support for the Belt and Road Initiative. She began her reply: 'Well, since China will soon be the largest economy in the world . . .' The remark went unchallenged, as is usual, because that's what we are constantly being told. Yet, this comment should at least be made with caveats, if not challenged, because it might not be right. In the past, we have, after all, made similar predictions about pre-1939 Germany, then the 1950s Soviet Union and, not all that long ago, Japan.

This is not to doubt that China has become and will likely remain a very large and important power, nor that the era of American primacy in the global system is over, at least as we have known it for the last century. However, it is not preordained that recent trends will continue.

Chinese economic growth is frequently viewed through a different lens from that used to see other countries. Even if there is some disbelief about official growth statistics, it is usually assumed that China's GDP will continue to grow at an elevated rate and without interruption. In other words, unlike the tiny printed warnings at the bottom of financial documents, the future will resemble the past. The nominal or monetary value of China's GDP will grow twice as fast as or more than in the US in perpetuity. If this happens then, as we are constantly told, there would be significant implications for China's economic and political heft, its relative place in the world and its military and commercial power, principally at the expense of the US and the West.

Incorporating the IMF's latest assumptions that China's GDP at market exchange rates will grow at a little over 8 per cent per year and America's at just over 3 per cent per year, the GDP cross-over point will come in or by 2030. For those familiar with the dark art of economics, China is already 13 per cent larger than the US, using GDP measured in so-called purchasing power parity terms. This method adjusts principally for the much lower prices of services and wages in poorer countries, so that we can better compare aggregate development across countries. But for all practical intents and purposes, including those of trade and commerce, savings and investment, and defence and politics, market exchange rates matter more.

Yet the notion that China is destined to become the largest economy in the world is a commonly presumed factoid. While it's possible that China will have a Midas-touch type of future in which nothing goes wrong, the chances of this happening are pretty slim. Indeed, it is equally if not more likely that over the next ten years or so, China's GDP relative to the US will not be so different from what it is today. And if that's true, then by the same reasoning as in the more optimistic predictions, China's outlook, relative position and so on would be quite different. Governments, corporate strategists, defence analysts and economists would all have to rethink their assumptions and implications.

To understand why this is a possible – even likely – outcome we have to consider two things: why China's future economic growth rate will slow down quite a lot; and the crucial and mostly overlooked role played by the Yuan exchange rate.

In the book, I have explained how China's economic growth of 6–6.5 per cent, or whatever the government says it is, has become dependent on credit creation. The government still thinks it can deleverage the economy and deliver high rates of growth. Yet, as China's experience since 2018 has shown again, slower credit growth and deleveraging in the economy and financial system lead inevitably to slower economic growth. To prevent economic growth from falling too far, as was the case in the winter of 2018–19, the government had to allow private and public indebtedness to expand again.

In short, China faces a rather unenviable choice between political stability and financial stability. It craves the former but this comes with unsustainable economic growth, rising indebtedness and the risk of currency depreciation. It believes also in the latter but the consequences would mean having to compromise on growth and employment objectives, for example, which could turn out to be politically risky. As the 2020s approach and China's capacity to support rising indebtedness, cash-flow constrained corporations and local governments, and rising non-performing loans dwindles, the choice will become starker: a growth crunch, or a financial crunch that would probably end up with slower growth anyway.

Waning growth drivers and a weaker Yuan

China's growth model is running into blockages everywhere. Its debt burden will have to decline sooner or later, and bad loans will have to be worked off and paid for. The aftermath of deleveraging, as is well known, is usually an extended period of low growth.

Trade hasn't been a significant growth driver in China since about 2010–12, which marked the peak of China's surge in global manufacturing trade following its accession to the World Trade Organisation. It is hardly likely to become stronger in the kind of global trade environment that now seems to be taking shape.

Investment in fixed assets, such as property, factories and infrastructure, was the principal growth driver following the big 2008 economic stimulus programme, but its share of GDP has slipped by 2–3 percentage points since 2016 and a further slide is most likely over time. Property and construction spending, which still account for about a quarter of GDP, remains important, but its contribution to growth has been slipping for the last few years. Tellingly, at the National People's Congress in 2019, the Party decreed 'housing is for living in, and not for speculation', and the government has established rules to restrict the latter, making life more difficult for land developers.

Consumer spending has become the mainstay of the economy, contributing a little over three-quarters of economic growth in 2018. Note, however, that this is happening in the context of a decline in the overall tempo of economic growth. China has an odd demand structure compared to most of its peers and nearly all developed nations. Consumer spending accounts for little more than 40 per cent of GDP, compared with 60–70 per cent in most OECD economies, and reflects both a relatively low share of wages and salaries in GDP, and a persistently high household savings rate. Since 2017, especially, growing household debt and debt service payments have also tended to crimp household spending. It is indeed an oddity that China's income per person is about the same as in Brazil, but consumption per person is no higher than it is in Thailand or Peru.

Imagine how China's prospects could be transformed if it could address this anomaly. Yet, this is easier said economically than done politically.

It is also interesting to note that while we read a lot about China's progress or leadership in developing mobile payment systems, e-commerce, and the sharing and digital economies, a lot of the weight of this 'new economy' activity is the result of having cannibalised the 'old economy'. In other words, it reflects how e-commerce, for example, has displaced physical commerce. Further, while users of information and communications technology have unquestionably become more engaged, the ICT-producing industry itself accounts for only about 5 per cent of GDP, or roughly half or less of the share in the US and other major developed economies.

The effect of slower growth overall, though, will probably be compounded by the likelihood of a hefty fall in the Yuan's value against the US dollar in the future.

Think about the simple maths. China's GDP in monetary terms, according to the IMF, amounted to about $12 trillion in 2018, compared to $20.5 trillion in the US. Suppose China's GDP grows over the next 10 years by 5 per cent per year, rather than the IMF's 8 per cent per year. It would be $20 trillion by 2028 ($26 trillion at 8 per cent compounded), compared with America's $28 trillion: still converging but more slowly. Now imagine that the yuan exchange rate is 15 per cent lower at just over 8 yuan to the US dollar. China's GDP would be $16 trillion in 2028, which would make its comparison with US GDP in proportion with that of today.

The reason this is not just possible but likely was explained in Chapter 5. Essentially, it is about the rapid growth in domestic financial assets resulting from expansionary credit and financial policies, and the growing threat this poses to the stability of the semi-pegged relationship the yuan has with the US dollar. Since China is still vulnerable to capital flight, despite the existence of controls on outward capital movements, and its foreign exchange reserves cannot be allowed to drop substantially, the 'peg' is unlikely to survive if domestic financial assets continue to grow apace.

Some pegged or semi-pegged exchange rates have survived, mostly in smaller and open economies, such as Hong Kong or Saudi Arabia, where the monetary authorities keep domestic asset growth in line with the underlying foreign currency reserve cover. Most though, especially in larger economies, have not done so, for example several Asian countries in the late 1980s and more recently Argentina, Ukraine and Venezuela. Empirically, when pegs in these and other larger countries have broken, they have done so with spectacular depreciations, leading to both financial instability and a big impact on GDP growth. China doesn't have to follow this path if it opts for and is prepared for the economic and social costs entailed in the financial stability–lower growth path, but would most likely fall into this second category of countries if it doesn't.

Pushback and criticism

It is unusual for the original texts of speeches made by China's top leaders to be published in their lifetime, but on 1 April 2019 long excerpts of a speech made by Xi Jinping early in 2013 to around 300 newly appointed members of the Party's Central Committee were made available.

In the speech, he advised that socialism would eventually triumph over capitalism but that the West still had significant economic and military advantages, and that China would have to both co-operate with and struggle against the West while building a superior socialist model. He warned delegates of the reasons for the Soviet Communist Party's painful collapse, and of the need to be vigilant against liberally minded and politically progressive thinking.

Why might the Party have wanted to remind people of the president's speech? China-watchers have speculated that the reason may have been to inspire Party members and citizens against the backdrop of a deteriorating economy, help strengthen the Party's backbone at a difficult time at home and abroad, and give confidence ahead of the seventieth anniversary of the founding of the People's Republic. The main message was that President Xi had correctly anticipated developments before being confirmed as head of state in 2013, and had been proved right in his strategy and thinking.

It is strange, though, to think that a supposedly all-powerful president and Party leadership would go to such lengths unless, of course, they sensed some unease – and that may not have been without foundation.

The US–China trade war had not had a marked impact on China's economy by the spring of 2019, and in so far as it had had an effect, it would have been offset by stimulus measures adopted to counter the effects of deleveraging. Yet its more notable impact, perhaps, was that it seemed to wrong-foot the government. China's relationship with the US was in the balance, and all of a sudden other questions over the direction of policy and leadership spilled over into the foreign policy and international relations aspects of the Belt and Road Initiative, the overall thrust of domestic – especially economic – policies, and wider issues relating to the narrative and strategy of the Party in relation to the role of the state versus the private sector. No one dared express criticism of President Xi directly, but it is clear he has been in the crosshairs in essays and letters which survived long enough online for the rest of the world to note.

One of the first noteworthy signs of dissent came in the form of an open letter written in July 2018 by a law professor at Tsinghua University, Xu Zhangrun, who criticised the abandonment of presidential term limits and government repression and ideology, asserted that the government had lost its way in the conduct of economic policy, and warned that China was going down a dangerous path in its pursuit of foreign policy. Xu has subsequently been suspended from his post while being investigated.

In early October 2018, Zhang Weiying, an economics professor at Peking University, wrote an article (subsequently erased by net censors) arguing that the narrative about the reasons for China's past success and potentially bright future was wrong. Instead of the central role of the Party, the state and top-down industrial policy, the focus was elsewhere, on marketisation, entrepreneurship and learning from the rest of the world. Further, he argued that the preferred narrative was driving a Chinese model that was leading to international confrontation.

Professor Sheng Hong of the beleaguered Unirule Institute has written tracts sympathising with this view. He also opined early in 2019 on the significance of institutions if China is to be a serious competitor in science and technology in the future. While acknowledging the role of 'Reform and Opening Up' in spawning scholarship, culture and advances in academic research and intellectual property, he was critical of the government's heavy-handed approach. He argues that intellectual property is a product of the institutional structure that nurtures it, and that structure is basically about the rule of law, which provides all of the institutional conduits for the production of knowledge and intellectual property. Without it, China's potential will be restricted, in spite of inherent advantages such as its capacity in imitation and adaptation, market size and national strategy policies.

Professor Xiang Songzuo of Renmin University published an essay in December 2018 assessing the state of China's economy, and insisting that while the government had the fiscal and monetary tools with which to stabilise the economy in a cyclical sense, the authorities were not addressing critical shortcomings and imbalances in the economy's structure, the serial violation of laws and regulations, or recurring speculation. He argued that the government's neglect of these matters was resulting in a loss of private sector confidence and dynamism, and that the key issues on the policy agenda should be how to restore and build trust in the government, comprehensive reform of the tax structure, and reforms to both political and state governance.

Criticism has not been confined to intellectuals. A few former officials have had their say too. Long Yongtu, China's former chief trade negotiator who took China into the WTO, openly criticised Beijing's trade war tactics in a conference in December 2018. And Lou Jiwei, former Minister of Finance from 2013–16, who subsequently became chairman of the National

Council for Social Security Fund, said in March 2019 as a delegate of the People's Political Consultative Conference that China's signature technology strategy, Made in China 2025, had been a waste of taxpayers' money, should have been left to the market and shouldn't have been tied to 2025 specifically. Soon after, he lost his job and was replaced.

It is easy to be dismissive of these criticisms as not being representative or even important, given that no one is challenging or standing up to the president himself. Yet they speak to a sense of disquiet that has already manifested itself in a softer rhetoric, at least as far as Made in China and the Belt and Road Initiative are concerned. The criticisms also address deeper issues of sensitivity about whether China is heading in the wrong direction.

One important and contentious area is the role that private enterprise, the backbone of China's economic eruption, should play in the future of China's economic development. It is noteworthy that in China 'private' doesn't always mean what it does in Western economies. Companies that register as private can, in practice, still be state-controlled, or file as collectively owned or cooperative companies, according to the National Bureau of Statistics. Some limited liability companies may have mixed private and public owners, and many may have layers of holding companies behind which is a state-owned enterprise. Over 70 per cent of private and foreign firms have Party representatives involved in operational management and senior executives know that if the interests of the Party and those of shareholders are not well aligned, those of the former always prevail.

In January of 2018, Zhou Xincheng, a professor of Marxism at Renmin University in Beijing, wrote a paper in which he argued for the abolition of the private sector. In August that year, a relatively obscure investment banker turned internet entrepreneur, Wu Xiaoping, wrote a paper arguing that the private sector had played its historical role and should now be phased out and merged back into the state sector. The paper went viral and was eventually deleted, but no senior Party official disowned it.

Private v Public

Partly to address this 'identity crisis' for private firms, President Xi has engaged with top entrepreneurs and urged high-ranking colleagues to assure them that the private sector is valued and has a critical role to play in China's development. Yi Gang, the governor of the People's Bank of China, is one of a few senior leaders who has invoked the European concept of 'competitive neutrality', according to which there should be no discrimination among state, private and foreign enterprises.

Yet verbal assurances alone, and exhortations to state banks to lend more to (riskier) private firms, are not going to cut the mustard, especially when the president and the government also regularly offer a full-throated defence of state-owned enterprises and the dominant roles they have been earmarked to play in the development of China's economy and technological prowess. Given this, it is hard to see how the government would ever create a genuinely level playing field in procurement, fiscal, competition and regulatory policies, for example.

Meanwhile, private firms remain under pressure. They have borne the brunt of heavy industry capacity reductions and have suffered much more than state enterprises from the deleveraging of the financial system pursued during 2017 and 2018 and the tightening of the Party's grip on the economy and influence on (or interference in) the company sector. Since they account for about 90 per cent of China's exports, they have suffered far more than state enterprises from the trade war.

They have also been experiencing rising levels of default in their bond financing and became ensnared in another equity market slump in 2018, where they were forced to pledge their shares as collateral for loans. According to stock exchange filings, roughly forty-six private firms had to sell large stakes back to state enterprises, with around half of them succumbing to reverse privatisation, in which they sold controlling stakes back to state firms.

All of this begs the question as to where China is with regard to reform, which everyone agrees is as essential in China as elsewhere. The problem is that the Chinese government and many of its economic observers have different ideas about what reform should involve. Critics argue that under Xi Jinping, China has backed away from market-oriented reforms to favour state-directed, top-down and bureaucratic reforms designed mainly to increase the efficiency and market position of state enterprises and to target the stability of economic growth.

Indeed, while it is true that China has markets in goods in which prices and other market mechanisms play an important role in terms of resource allocation, it is also true that the factors of production – land, labour and capital – that combine to produce goods are wholly or mostly controlled by, or aligned with, the state and Party. Further, the government has deeply conflicted roles in these markets, as I argue earlier in the book, as owner, participant and regulator. In a modern, advanced society, Western analysts think the state's role should be to focus on politically impartial regulation and on facilitating multiple objectives including industrial development, efficiency and modernity, innovation, fair income and wealth distribution, and a competitive and efficient tax system. In China, the Party-state has little interest in this rather limited role.

The uneven playing field between the public and private sectors does not look likely to be phased out any time that we can predict. Bureaucratic reform is commonplace, but not political or market-based reforms. Directives, restrictions and quotas determined by central political authorities are still prevalent and we are left to wonder if this model will be able to underpin the ideas, ubiquitous technologies and innovations, and modern services that we think private enterprise and initiative are better honed to sustain.

No one can argue that China's political model is not capable of producing extraordinary feats, as we have already seen in lunar exploits, genome sequencing, supercomputing, bio-medicine, electric vehicles and artificial intelligence. Nor that there won't be areas where China will catch up with the West in the future.

Yet China's capacity to continue along this path is really about how quick and efficient it will be with regard to two vital sets of reforms. First, the implementation of reforms that allow institutions to foster the productive application of new technologies across broad swathes of the economy. These reforms include, but are not limited to, certain freedoms, property rights, judicial independence, tolerance, openness and intellectual property protection. And second, the willingness to embrace more market-based reforms that transfer wealth and commercial responsibility to private enterprise, and enable the state to oversee sustainable policies of deleveraging, higher income equality and levels of social security, and long-term productivity growth.

These are not uncommon sentiments propagated by Western-trained economists, but they also resonate for some in China. Indeed, you need look no further than a report entitled 'The Phenomenon of Reform Obstruction in China: Performance, Origin and Solution' by the National Development and Reform Commission in 2017, which alleges that reform has fallen into a stalemate. Drawing attention to misconceived top-level design faults in policies, as well as problems among local officials and state managers, it laments, among other things, flabby state conglomerates and household registration rules that treat migrants as second-class citizens. Since the report, the state and Party have, if anything, become more top-down and controlling, and nothing has really changed to revitalise the overall effort to reform the economy and state. Xi has made public ownership and state control the cornerstone of Socialism with Chinese Characteristics. In an editorial in the *People's Daily* in February 2019, the president was quoted as saying 'the status of public ownership as the backbone of our economy must not be jeopardised, and the leading role of the state-owned economy must not be questioned'.

Economic twists, turns and traps

In the early months of 2019, China's economy was in a sort of 'no man's land'. It was neither decelerating as sharply as in the last few months of 2018, but neither did it appear to be expanding vigorously following the stimulus measures the government took to stabilise the economy over the winter. Although the resource and materials sectors improved, and industrial profits bounced back reflecting the policy boost to infrastructure spending, there was little in the way of relief from the weakness in manufacturing investment, property sales and starts, employment indicators, or the extraordinary year-long slump in car sales, which by May had fallen 30 per cent from their peak in 2016. Companies listed on stock markets had their worst year of earnings in 2018, with 452 of 3,602 firms listed on the Shanghai and Shenzhen exchanges reporting an annual loss, and double that number having to write down the value of goodwill in the light of the trade war and deleveraging policies.

To combat the sharp twist down in economic activity in the second half of 2018, following a milder decline earlier, the government adopted a number of stabilisation measures. It allowed credit growth to accelerate again, though not to levels previously experienced, and announced tax cuts of about 2 per cent of GDP. It said it would allow the narrowly defined fiscal deficit to rise to just over 3 per cent of GDP but, taking into account local governments, special funds, and an array of off-balance-sheet borrowing vehicles and funds, the so-called augmented fiscal deficit may rise to about 15 per cent of GDP in 2019. The government also allocated over RMB 2.5 trillion in new transportation spending, gave private companies relief from additional social security obligations, and announced a series of measures to ease home purchase restrictions, and to boost sales of automobiles and consumer durables.

The stabilisation of the economy in the first half of 2019 looked tenuous, and certainly vulnerable to a renewed deterioration because of the consequences of the trade war. Yet, from a broader perspective, as I have

argued, the short-term cyclical behaviour of the economy is almost inci-
dental. The real issue for the government is how it chooses to embrace
either policies geared mainly to achieve financial stability or those that
prioritise political stability.

Stabilising finance and debt, but for how long?

As I explained in Chapter 4, new and tougher 'macro-prudential' regulations in and after 2017 sought to dampen down or punish some of the
more egregious examples of risk-taking and financial engineering. These
involved wealth management products, for example less lending to so-called
non-banking financial intermediaries, and pressures on banks to bring back
on to their balance sheets a lot of financial activity that had been migrated
off-balance-sheet where the regulations were lighter and the costs lower.
Banks were also encouraged or obliged to lower the proportion of deposits
raised at very short maturities, for example in the interbank market.

The overall result was that shadow banking sector assets, which
amounted to about 87 per cent of GDP in 2017, dropped to about 68 per
cent of GDP in 2018. The growth in the regularly published aggregate of
credit creation, Total Social Financing, which had been growing at an
annual rate of around 17 per cent between 2015 and 2016, dropped to 12
per cent in 2017 and then little more than 8 per cent at the end of 2018,
before rising again to over 10.5 per cent in early 2019. Adding in local
government bond issuance, the total decline in credit growth was a little
sharper in 2017–18, but as the most recent policy initiatives allow local
governments to increase bond issuance significantly in 2019, we should
expect to see slightly faster credit expansion in 2019.

With credit growing around 2–3 percentage points faster than GDP,
China's ratio of debt to GDP will rise more quickly again, and with it come
a series of familiar problems. Rising levels of household debt, for example,
are already affecting many families. In general, the debt service ratio has
risen from 3 to 10 per cent of disposable income over the decade to 2018,
but this masks an extraordinary burden on many poorer families. Research
in the China Household Financial Survey for 2015 suggests debt service
ratios as high as 40 per cent for a significant proportion of families. I
imagine that debt burdens must have risen since then. Corporate and local
government debt burdens are also likely to rise again, and many borrowers
already have high ratios of debt to assets, and pressing cash flow and debt
service capacity issues.

These developments are quite likely, therefore, to undermine the progress Chinese banks have made in trying to deal with their non-performing loan problems. Even though there is no formal or credible recognition of the scale of the bad debts, the government has, for the last year or two, encouraged banks to acknowledge higher levels of bad debt and to pre-emptively, and in orderly fashion, write them down. The benefit of this policy is that the negative impact on GDP and bank profits can be absorbed better than if it is implemented in a downturn or in a crisis. However, it only works if the disposal of bad debt proceeds faster than the accumulation of new bad debt. That, though, is precisely what is unlikely to happen because of weaker growth and new, bank-financed infrastructure programmes.

It is worth noting the parlous state of finances among local governments – which deliver most of the infrastructure programmes – and their spending levels, which are about 40 per cent greater than their revenues. As a result they depend on obtaining revenues from local SOEs, land sales, and risky debt financing. Local governments officially had about RMB 19 trillion (or almost $3 trillion) of debt in March 2019, but an additional RMB 52 trillion of off-balance-sheet liabilities, 60 per cent of which were those of local government financing vehicles. Local and provincial government debt amounted to about 70 per cent of GDP in 2018. Former finance minister Lou Jiwei noted in 2014 that the entire tax and fiscal system in China was balkanised, opaque and poorly aligned with China's needs for social fairness and advanced levels of social security.

The drastic reform of the system he urged then hasn't happened. Although China has since relaxed the rules on local government bond issuance, introduced a three year loan-for-bond swap programme, brought a nationwide VAT system into being, and tried to get some local governments to repay certain liabilities and implicit debt, there is still only a vague prospect of a long-discussed national property tax, which would go a long way to bolstering the revenue base of local governments. There is little chance, moreover, of a more radical overhaul of the relationship between central and local governments, in which comprehensive tax reform and a legal division of responsibilities between these two tiers of government could find expression.

Is China developing a current account deficit?

A potentially significant development in China, with implications for the yuan and for global financial markets, was a slide in the balance of payments surplus in 2018. In the first quarter of the year, China recorded its first current account deficit for over 2 decades, amounting to 1.1 per cent of GDP. In the following quarter it was roughly balanced. This spawned a lot of discussion among China-watching economists on whether the country's balance of payments may finally have turned the corner and was headed into permanent deficit.

If that were indeed to happen, as I discussed in Chapter 5, China would need to be vigilant with its monetary policy, the yuan would become more sensitive to global currency demand flows and the economy would depend on capital inflows to finance the deficit.

It would, though, be a positive development for the rest of the world. We need China's demand impulse, which this would reflect, not its finance capital. And in the event it happened, we would know that the main driver was a marked fall in national savings relative to investment, suggesting also that Chinese demand was on a stronger trajectory as, for example, consumers would be saving less and consuming more.

In the end, though, the year ran out with the final two quarters registering surpluses of 0.7 and 1.5 per cent of GDP respectively. And, as I made clear in the book, the likelihood of China running a permanent current account deficit is pretty slim. The key to what happens is the relationship between savings and investment. Even though the investment share of GDP has slipped, savings have too, most likely reflecting lower corporate savings because profits have been under pressure and lower government savings as the fiscal deficit has risen. What we aren't really seeing is a material drop in household savings, which, at about a quarter of GDP, are relatively high.

While a number of medical insurance and pension schemes have been rolled out in the last 10–15 years and are an important work in progress, the social safety net is not all that generous – especially for migrant workers – and tends to keep savings high. High home ownership rates have the same effect. So do high levels of income and wealth inequality: China's Gini coefficient, a measure of income inequality, is one of the highest in the world. While the top and bottom income deciles had comparable shares of income in 1978 at about 27 per cent, these had changed to 41 and 15 per cent, respectively, by 2016. This keeps savings high, because the better off tend to save a high proportion of income, and the least well off have to save because of a weak social safety net and a low degree of progressiveness in the tax system.

Eventually, ageing China could be characterised by lower household savings, as we have seen, for example, in ageing Japan and a few other rapidly ageing countries. However, this might require China to first reach much higher income and consumption levels in relation to GDP, and that might lie a long time in the future.

Relentless ageing

In Chapter 6, I explained why China is suffering from rapid and premature ageing, and the significance of the phrase 'getting old before you get rich'. The consequences for China, as elsewhere, are more cumulative and glacial than sudden or shocking, but there is no question that they will have material economic, financial and social repercussions as the working age population declines, and old age dependency climbs inexorably.

According to the Chinese Academy of Social Sciences, China's population is on course to peak in 2029 at 1.44 billion, after which it will go into relentless decline reaching 1.17 billion by 2065. Some private forecasters think that the population is likely to peak slightly lower and as early as 2023. In any event, since the population will probably fall by 200,000–230,000 between 2029 and 2100, we can anticipate that population size will drop below 1 billion in the 2040s for the first time since 1980. The weakness of the fertility rate is the key factor in ageing societies and has prompted the government to not only use rhetoric such as 'have children for the country' but to look at extensions to periods of maternal leave, and to financial incentives to encourage couples to have second children.

Yet births data suggest that these methods aren't working. After 17.86 million births in 2016, the figure dropped to 17.2 million in 2017 and 15.2 million in 2018 – the third lowest rate after 1949 and the 1960–61 famine. If, as in other countries, lower fertility trends remain intact and if there's no change in the steady decline in China in the number of women of childbearing age, it is not hard to see the number of births continuing to slide over the coming years. The fertility rate is officially estimated to be 1.6 children per woman, but some private forecasters think the rate has been and is lower. One researcher, Yi Fuxian at the University of Wisconsin-Madison, thinks the rate could have been as low as 1.18 on average between 2010 and 2018.

The middle-income trap clock ticking

The middle-income trap discussion doesn't really tell us anything about whether a country has the capacity or potential to grow or to be innovative, but is very much about the risk to and possible failure of governance. In other words, it's about institutions and whether political elites can and want to implement policies and reforms to realise long-term improvements in productivity yielding benefits to all citizens. It is in this sense – plenty of innovation potential but weak governance – that I have expressed some doubts and reservations about Xi's China.

The key measure that we use to benchmark whether a country is making progress is total factor productivity, a term used to describe the efficiencies and technical progress that derive from the organisation of institutions. Empirical evidence in China demonstrates a strong correlation between high or accelerating total factor productivity and periods when market-oriented reforms have been pursued, and vice versa. Using company data, moreover, the evidence also shows that new technology firms with better total factor productivity potential have in the past often offset the effects elsewhere of capital misallocation, the willingness to sustain zombie companies and inefficient government intervention. However, this usually occurred in the context of liberalising reforms.

Although many reforms were announced in 2013, little has been accomplished, as suggested earlier. Indeed, the theme developed in the book is that the Party has no real interest in the kind of institutional and political change that Western minds think are important to realise the critical success factors necessary to jump the middle-income trap. There is no secret about what the Party believes to be important: the emphasis on control in every sphere of life and the centralisation of power; the primacy of the state sector; setting its own industrial and technological standards and building its own global brands; the goal of reducing dependence on foreign technology; and the political imperative to reduce the country's exposure to market and economic risks.

My argument is that these goals, and the policies that the government pursues to realise them, may not be sufficiently well crafted in the absence of institutional and political reform to deliver the total factor productivity performance necessary to escape the trap. Far from looking as though China might be inclined to learn the reform lessons from its own history of 'Reform and Opening Up', Xi's China looks to be doubling down on a more authoritarian, stricter and more stifling governance system.

Trade winds in a larger storm

When I submitted my original manuscript in early 2018, China and the US were still locked in an escalating trade war. Even though it was largely understood that the term 'trade war' was a catch-all for a wider commercial and technological conflict, few people thought then that the Sino–US relationship was starting to fray around its existential seam. And yet that is where things have ended up just over a year later, with at least some voices on both sides seeing virtue and advantage in 'decoupling' and in greater self-reliance. The economic interdependence on which this relationship was built and on which it flourished now seems to some to be a burden, from which the solution is to break free.

By the autumn of 2018, the US had imposed punitive tariffs on about $250 billion or half of the goods imported from China, threatened to raise most tariff rates to 25 per cent from 1 January 2019, and said it would also extend them to the other half of imports from China. In return, China matched America's tariff initiatives, but in doing so it was quickly running out of scope for this type of retaliatory action for the simple reason that it imports so much less from the US than the other way around.

Yet the winds of change in trade politics sometimes blow in curious and unexpected ways, and at the G20 Summit of world leaders in Buenos Aires at the end of November 2018, President Trump and President Xi Jinping agreed to a truce.

The US suspended further tariff increases for ninety days pending talks with China. The US wanted China to agree to increase its purchases from the US of agricultural goods, energy and aircraft, for example, but also to address the deeper frictions in the trade war. These were partly about increasing market access to US firms and easing operating conditions for them in China, but also about even more sensitive industrial and technology policy issues, including forced technology transfer, intellectual property protection and cybersecurity. These were and remain matters about which foreign firms in China have complained for some time, but the core role played by new technologies in the economic and military rivalry of the future moved them centre-stage.

Both sides had an incentive to pull back from an intensification of the trade war. President Trump, with one eye on the short-term performance of America's then faltering financial markets, and the other on voters in swing, especially agricultural, states ahead of the 2020 presidential campaign, was keen to reach a deal. Higher tariffs, moreover, would feed through cumulatively and negatively into US high street prices, corporate earnings and business confidence. For China the impact of tariffs and trade disruption was sharper still and more menacing, especially if President Trump's threats of expanding punitive tariffs were going to be validated. It is clear that

America's relentless prosecution of the trade war, until that point at least, had wrong-footed President Xi and stirred disquiet in China about his approach to foreign policy in general and the US in particular.

The ninety-day deadline passed without incident as both sides expressed optimism about the trade negotiations. By early May, they seemed relatively confident about the chances of reaching an agreement, even if some of the more sensitive matters might have been fudged or left unaddressed. President Trump referred to the prospect of 'an epic trade deal' after several weeks in which high-powered delegations had flown back and forth between Beijing and Washington.

Following a random and unexpected tweet by President Trump, however, things suddenly deteriorated rapidly. On 10 May, with Chinese negotiators in Washington, Donald Trump authorised the hike in punitive tariffs on $200 billion of Chinese goods imports, which had originally been set for the start of the year, from 10 to 25 per cent. He later said that the US would extend these tariffs to the other half of goods imports ($300 billion) not hitherto affected. The US said that China had reneged on certain commitments that it thought had been agreed. China disagreed, saying there were simply disagreements over the text of a deal. It responded to the immediate tariff hike by subjecting $60 billion of imports from the US to tariffs of 20–25 per cent, bringing the total affected to $110 billion – almost all US imports. Other forms of retaliation in the future might include the cessation of purchases of specific products, such as Boeing aircraft, or a clamp down on US service industry providers, or regulations to make commercial life more difficult for US firms.

In time, we may learn why, some four months after the Buenos Aires truce, the talks faltered. Perhaps it was a misunderstanding somewhere in the language of trade diplomacy. It might have been a miscalculation by China about the weakness of the US negotiating position and economy. It could even have been a last minute pushback by China against US demands for possible changes in China's policies to be codified or legislated as a means of assuring compliance with stated commitments.

This last interpretation was supported by a press conference given by China's chief negotiator Liu He to the Xinhua News Agency in Washington before he left to go home. Apart from wanting the US to remove tariffs and to be realistic about the volume of imports China might additionally buy from the US, he insisted that the text of any agreement should be balanced and ensure dignity. This was very likely China recoiling from the perceived threat of the US intruding into what China regards as its sovereignty, and a stark reminder of China's long standing aversion to what it regards historically as 'unequal treaties' and interference by foreigners.

Moreover, China's willingness to take steps to boost intellectual property protection and address other US demands does not extend to the issuance of formal statements and agreements, let alone amending domestic laws that might then be in conflict with other laws and the Party's core philosophy. Its preferred modus operandi is to communicate via ad hoc regulations and State Council directives. The US, though, views these – with cause – as insufficient, and as hostage to Chinese regulations and conditions, often laid down by local and provincial governments, which tend to dilute or thwart vaguely worded and ambiguous policy statements.

In some ways, then, the US is chasing shadows. Even if laws are changed or introduced, there is no guarantee that they would be effective, especially since the rule of law does not exist. The new Foreign Investment Law, for example, approved in March 2019, ostensibly offers equal treatment to and support for foreign firms, eliminates the requirement to transfer proprietary technology and introduces a punitive damages mechanism to protect against intellectual property infringement. Yet its wording has been criticised by lawyers as vague and ambivalent. The law does not address low-level and local government regulations that protect domestic firms and industries, or protect against political interference, or address the deep-rooted problems of surveillance and commercial espionage.

When President Trump met President Xi Jinping at the G20 Summit in Osaka, Japan, at the end of June 2019, low expectations for a breakthrough in the trade talks were validated. They agreed to resume negotiations. The US also shelved its proposal to extend punitive tariffs to the other half of imports from China and, in what looked like a major concession to China, said it might relax the restrictions facing the Chinese tech company Huawei. In a separate forum, China announced additional ways in which it treatment to extend ownership and access opportunities to foreign companies. The apparent rapprochement at the G20 in Osaka may not, however, be any more productive than that at Buenos Aires six months earlier, or even last as long.

While trade diplomacy and politics might always throw up the prospect of one side backing down, or both sides agreeing to a weak deal to appease domestic audiences, it certainly seems that the US and China are digging in for protracted trade friction, which will span commercial and technological exchanges affecting the sale and purchase of goods and components and investment abroad by companies.

The trade war is already having profound consequences for the way the world system works. It is leading to more sluggish growth in the volume of world trade. It is causing global and Chinese firms to rethink their China-centric supply chains, as they look elsewhere for certainty and the ability to compete effectively. Some surveys published by large banks and the American and EU Chambers of Commerce in China in 2019 reported that between a fifth and third of companies surveyed had already moved some supply chain operations to other nations, with comparable proportions indicating that they planned to do so in the future. The trade war also represents confirmation for China that, faced with a more hostile US, it needs greater self-reliance when it comes to sourcing technologies and components abroad. The Made in China 2025 strategy provided for this anyway, but the trade war has emphasised the urgency.

Whichever way the trade winds blow, it is clear that a corner has been turned. The US National Security and Defence Strategies have already used remarkable language in thinking about China. Congress passed the National Defence Authorisation Act 2019, calling for a 'whole of government' pushback against China's economic, security and political challenges. The Committee on Foreign Investment and other agencies and commit-tees of the US government are increasingly focused on China's activities inside and outside the US, notably with Russia. As if to validate US concerns, President Xi attended the St Petersburg Economic Forum in June 2019, combining with it his twenty-ninth summit meeting with President Putin since 2013 at which both leaders reached high-level polit-ical and commercial agreements in the face of a now common American adversary.

Deals or no deals, it certainly seems now that commercial and other tensions will be a permanent feature in the relationship between China and the US, and the West. The challenge will be to find ways to engage regard-less and to restrain the potential for these tensions to spill into other areas.

Until relatively recently, the EU's China focus was principally on economic and trade matters, including the so-far unsuccessful pursuit of a bilateral investment treaty since 2013, which the EU sees as a route to improved access to Chinese markets. The EU is China's largest trade partner, and the EU is China's second largest partner. Bilateral trade in 2018 amounted to a little over €600 billion, or nearly double the level a decade earlier. Direct investment by EU companies in China amounted to about €60 billion in 2018, with just over €17 billion going the other way, though this was half what it had been in 2016.

China has strong commercial interests in the EU but its courting of political interests is no less significant, capitalising on US–EU tensions and, to a degree, on disunity within EU member states and across the bloc. To this end, it has nurtured deeper relations with the so-called 16+1 group of central and eastern European countries, including eleven EU member states, and in 2019 it gained a much valued endorsement from Italy for the Belt and Road Initiative, the first G7 country to do so, much to the chagrin of Italy's EU peers.

There was little warning though of how quickly the EU's approach to China was about to change. At the EU–China summit in 2018, both sides celebrated the fifteenth anniversary of their 'competitive strategic partnership'. Just one year later, a certain frisson hung over the visit of Premier Li Keqiang and the Chinese delegation following a publication by the EU Commission in March 2019 called 'EU–China – A Strategic Outlook'. In the report, China was deemed to be an 'economic competitor in pursuit of technological leadership and a systemic rival promoting alternative models of governance'. This abrupt shift took place against a changed policy backdrop in which tighter screening of Chinese investment in EU member states at both national and supranational levels had become more widespread. Moreover, while the EU strategy document looks to engagement and cooperation with China in several areas, it also provides for or anticipates a tougher approach to anti-trust rules, telecommunications including 5G, industrial strategy, artificial intelligence, reciprocity and the large EU procurement market.

Any way for Huawei?

It is worth emphasising that America's concerns over industrial policy, technology and security matters are shared. Its allies in the so-called Five Eyes intelligence alliance – Australia, Canada, New Zealand and the UK – have all had occasion in the last year to probe, investigate and opine on the security-sensitive aspects of engagement with Chinese tech companies, in particular in the telecommunications industry given the central role played by Chinese tech giant Huawei. The EU and member states have also been drawn into this increasingly sensitive and important discussion.

Huawei has become both the substance and a symbol of Sino–Western divisions. While there is considerable focus on whether its current activities and engineering quality in rolling out the new 5G telecommunications networks represent a threat to security, the broader issues centre more on its ownership structure, its relationship to the Party and state in China, and whether it or its peers merit our trust in the future.

Huawei has been involved in relatively minor controversies since the early 2000s, but for the most part these concerned intellectual property and regulatory market issues. Over the last five to seven years, it became the subject of more security-related matters in which Australia, for example, banned the company from its national broadband network. Things escalated quickly, however, from 2018 as the trade war between the US and China escalated. Huawei came under much closer regulatory scrutiny, along with another Chinese tech firm called ZTE Corporation, in relation to charges of breaking the Iran sanctions regime. A US court fined ZTE in 2017, and a year later the government banned US companies from exporting to it, threatening its very existence. The ban was lifted when the company agreed to replace its senior management and allow its compliance to be monitored. In 2018, Australia banned the purchase of Huawei equipment, and all members of the so-called Five Eyes security and intelligence alliance undertook closer surveillance of or took actions against Huawei.

When Meng Wanzhou, Huawei's chief financial officer and daughter of the founder and CEO of the firm, was arrested in Canada upon a request from the US in December 2018, a sort of Rubicon was crossed. She was later charged with financial fraud by the US, which sought her extradition pending due process. China responded by arresting two Canadians and later charged them with espionage and incarcerated them.

In May 2019, with the trade talks faltering, the US government upped the ante as President Trump issued an executive order giving the US government the power to block US firms from buying foreign-made telecommunications equipment deemed to be a national security risk. The move was largely symbolic because such equipment supplied by Huawei is hardly used by major US telecommunications carriers. Yet it was a signal to other nations about US intent, it was an appeal for support, and its language was broad enough to cover a wide range of information technology goods and services supplied by persons 'subject to the jurisdiction or direction of a foreign adversary'.

More importantly, though, the Department of Commerce announced it would add Huawei and seventy affiliates to an 'Entity List', comprising companies banned from buying components from US firms without government approval. This was more harmful because Huawei and other Chinese firms still depend significantly on purchases of complex microchips and other products and software from US firms. Huawei's benchmark smartphone, for example, sources components from thirty-three US firms, including Google, Qualcomm, Broadcom and Intel, among other foreign suppliers. Such is the impact of this move, that the Department of Commerce quickly announced, in deference to US firms, it would grant a temporary license to enable some companies to continue supplying existing networks and devices.

Further, a bill was introduced in the Senate which, if passed, would place all fifteen top priority tech sectors in China's Made in China 2025 strategy on the US export control list, in effect banning sales to relevant Chinese firms. The cross-party consensus in Washington has embraced the Pentagon and security services' warning – and rejected Huawei's firm denial – that Chinese firms might be able to control networks, intercept data and shut down infrastructure, mobile phone networks and gas pipelines among other things.

These developments suggest that Chinese firms will try even harder to develop their own operating systems and components if they can, and that the balkanisation of the digital age is underway. Where once we thought of the tech industry as global and with deep roots in supply chains and inter-national trade, a new bifurcated industry is developing with consequences we cannot yet foretell.

People have referred to a new technological wall being erected between China and the West, more colloquially known as the 'Splinternet'. The idea is that we may be moving towards one system that works in China and another in the West. Each will work in aligned countries and both will compete with one another in third countries. Apart from being less effec-tive and efficient, parallel technological universes will necessitate a reboot of supply chains, trade and much else.

Belt and Road bumps

The Belt and Road Initiative was defined in Chapter 9 as President Xi Jinping's signature foreign policy. It matters a lot to him, to China and to the rest of the world. It serves China's national economic and geopolitical interests much more than it is an alternative model for global development as Xi Jinping has argued. In the last year or two, the Belt and Road has come in for criticism, the rhetoric has been dialled back and the scale of expansion has slowed.

In the last week of April 2019, Beijing hosted the second Belt and Road Forum. It was attended by thirty-six heads of state, including nineteen from Asia and Africa and twelve from Europe. New signatories who completed a memorandum of understanding or otherwise showed support for the Belt and Road included Italy, Austria, Djibouti, Egypt, Portugal, Thailand, the UAE and Singapore, making for a total of 126 nations, and 29 international organisations. Of these countries, the number actually involved in Belt and Road projects is 115, almost twice and many as 5 years ago. Yet, the Belt and Road universe is also highly skewed: about 40 per cent of contracts signed are with ten leading recipients of financing – Bangladesh, Egypt, Indonesia, Iran, Laos, Malaysia, Nigeria, Pakistan, Russia and the UAE.

China announced at the forum that $64 billion in new deals had been signed – though it is standard practice at this sort of venue to mention many already announced deals and contracts, including those that may take years to deliver. The Forum also announced a list of 283 so-called 'deliverables', or results, initiatives or cooperation mechanisms proposed or launched by China.

The Belt and Road is no stranger to swagger and hyperbole. Since its inception, it has been surrounded by an industrial size public relations effort that has inflated its scale from hundreds of billions of dollars to as much as $5 trillion. By the end of 2018, though, the total of Chinese-led Belt and Road contracts agreed since 2013 – of which about two-thirds were financial and a third direct investment – may have amounted to close to about $600 billion. The largest volumes were booked in 2016 and 2017.

Yet in spite of the plaudits that the Belt and Road has received, and the success it has enjoyed in many countries, it has also been the target of a rising chorus of criticism, to which China has become quite sensitive. While the number of Belt and Road contracts has continued to rise overall, several countries have cancelled or renegotiated specific contracts. Since 2018, for example: Pakistan cancelled a $14 billion dam project amid debt problems that entailed having to go to the IMF for a $6 billion assistance programme; Montenegro complained about the cost of building a highway that threatened to devour the small state's budget; Kenya became sensitive to rising indetbtedness with China as the country's biggest lender and to the strong presence of Chinese workers that left little scope for local job creation; Tanzania suspended construction of the $10 billion Bagamayo port project indefinitely, citing onerous financial conditions established by China, and balking at the demand for a ninety-nine-year lease and a ban on the development of other port facilities, including at Dar-es-Salaam; Uganda, Kenya, Ethiopia and Zambia all became embroiled in financial disputes and or construction defect issues; Malaysia negotiated a one-third cut in price of the East Coast Rail Link, complaining about corruption; Nepal cancelled a costly hydroelectric dam due to concerns over cost: Myanmar cancelled a dam project and scaled back a major port construction initiative; and the Maldives asked to renegotiate contracts following an election in which corruption figured prominently.

Although some critics, including a few in the US administration, have seized on an Indian commentator's idea that China is pursuing 'debt-trap diplomacy' – that is, using debt as a lever with which to gain control of infrastructure assets and exercise political leverage – there has really been only one example of a Chinese creditor taking control of a financially stressed borrower, which was the Sri Lankan port of Hambantota. Indeed, there have been a number of other cases where China has rescheduled or renegotiated loans.

Rather it seems that most pushback against the Belt and Road has been as a result of China's attitudes and practices. The Belt and Road, properly considered, is less a carefully crafted strategy radiating out from Beijing than a catch-all for the sometimes chaotic and uncoordinated activities of state-owned enterprises, local governments, ministries and special leading groups – not dissimilar, in fact, to the state enterprise, local government and special funds infrastructure financing model at home, though with the addition of foreign governments.

A lack of transparency and accountability is a common refrain. There is no register or database of projects, funds raised and lent, or loan standards, terms and covenants. The first six years of the Belt and Road have thrown up examples of ineptitude, inefficiency, weak lending standards and governance, poor risk and project management ability, and inadequate attention to the cost, debt and debt service capacity situation in recipient countries. There have been complaints about China's penchant for building coal-fired power capacity in the Belt and Road and for not pursuing other climate change-friendly policies, and complaints about corruption, not so much as a local by-product of individual deals but as a structural feature at the highest level of engagement.

At the forum, Xi Jinping certainly seemed to acknowledge some of these issues, at least rhetorically. The communiqué issued at the end of the forum stressed diversified and sustainable financial support for Belt and Road projects, as well as the need for debt sustainability, environmental protection and stamping out corruption. Xi himself said that China would look more to multilateral lending institutions and financial centres such as the UK and Switzerland to help diversify the financing of the Belt and Road, and appealed for more countries – presumably the US, India, Japan, Germany and France – to participate in the future. He also said the Belt and Road would be implemented according to 'internationally accepted rules, standards and best practices'.

Yet he also said that any changes in the implementation of the Belt and Road would have to be 'in line with our national legislation, regulatory frameworks, international obligations, and applicable international norms and standards'. And there is no question that these are increasingly in conflict with international rules and standards. The new approach announced by President Xi sounds constructive and interesting, but we should be cautious.

Changing the Belt and Road's governance system is not a matter of presentation and fine-tuning, and China has not had a road-to-Damascus conversion about the SOE–local government–state bank infrastructure model, which is the DNA of the Belt and Road, and which exists to serve China's interests. The Belt and Road is a China-centric economic, commercial and security construct that seeks to bind countries to China in a twenty-first century form of tribute – the dynastic arrangement under which ancient China regulated trade and diplomacy. Support for – and defence of – the Belt and Road strategy is welcomed and rewarded with contracts and market access, but these can be threatened or withdrawn in the event that support falters or disputes arise.

Geopolitics for our time

At the first Belt and Road Forum in 2017, President Xi Jinping said: 'We will not follow the old way of geopolitical games during the push for the Belt and Road Initiative, but create a new model of win-win and cooperation. It will not form a small group undermining stability, but is set to build a big family with harmonious co-existence.' As I have argued, though, Belt and Road rhetoric and reality do not always align well.

Eager followers of contradictions like this will also recall President Xi's significant speech to the Davos elite in 2017, in which he presented China as the new guardian of globalisation, free trade and openness, when many in the audience will have been keenly aware that China's own practices and behaviour are at best ambivalent. The core industrial strategy, Made in China 2025, for example, has at its heart government-backed initiatives to protect domestic firms and encourage them to attain high domestic market shares in AI, robotics, electric vehicles and other advanced tech sectors over the medium-term. China's willingness to allow foreign firms to set up and produce in China in some sectors is matched by a steadfast refusal to open up in others, or allow them to compete effectively with local firms.

President Xi also speaks about 'working together to build a community of shared future for mankind' based around ideas of partnership, security, growth, international exchanges and the building of a sound ecosystem. Like other high-level goals and visions, this is perfectly laudable 'motherhood and apple pie'. The trouble is that it doesn't sit well alongside Xi Jinping's condemnation of Western values, such as judicial independence, civil society institutions, constitutional democracy and a free press. Xi's China is instead trying to cultivate a Chinese culture that strengthens the Chinese Communist Party, and its capacity to shape China at home and its influence abroad.

It does not gel either with a more domestically targeted rhetoric of 'foreign hostile forces' often accused of fomenting trouble. These forces are cited generally in the Chinese media for undermining or spreading rumours about China and have been mentioned specifically in connection with China's #MeToo movement, the treatment of Uighurs in the western province of Xinjiang, and the Hong Kong protests against the contentious extradition bill in 2019.

It certainly doesn't go down well with most of the citizens of Taiwan, who know that Xi Jinping would like as part of his legacy the reunification of their country with the mainland. The Taiwanese are watching developments in Hong Kong very closely especially ahead of presidential elections in January 2020, the result of which may pull Taiwan further away from China's objective. This puts America's own presidential and congressional elections at the end of 2020 in an additionally important context as the outcome may well influence Beijing's subsequent thinking about Taiwan.

In a nutshell, Xi's China is bolting on an ideological and historical mission to a long-standing ambition to substitute Chinese values and institutions for Western ones. Throw in the additional frisson of the centralisation and consolidation of power that no leader has enjoyed since Mao, and you can see that we have arrived at a crucial juncture in China's relations with the West.

This is why I think President Trump, whatever we may think about him, has struck a chord by calling for a reset of the China relationship. It is the only issue which unites US Democrats and Republicans in Congress, and one of few issues about which the US and its allies in Europe and Asia agree in principle. Quite how that relationship will be reset, and the policies pursued to realise it, is more contentious. While it is commonly assumed that global stability requires some form of engagement and cooperation, it is noteworthy that both sides of this relationship have their own protagonists of 'decoupling' and 'self-reliance' which, in extreme forms, speak to a much more distant and dangerous construct.

Readers should ponder what the current misalignment of interests between China and the West means for the world economy and global integration. How might the global system work differently? Even though levels of economic and business interdependence between China and the West are high, how should our politicians and companies respond to Chinese politics that propagate belief and value systems that are in many ways inimical to our own? Assuming we do try to engage with China in different ways, where do we need to draw lines and how? How will we emphasise and defend those things that we still hold dear, such as democratic government, human and property rights, diversity, fairness and the rule of law?

These are some of the trenchant questions of our time in a geopolitical environment that is the most challenging since the Cold War. In this book, I have tried to present a picture of China that will hopefully help to inform and shape this discussion. We must recognise both its many accomplishments and capacities but also the sometimes daunting economic challenges that are coalescing for the 2020s. We cannot leave out of our calculations and speculation the Communist Party's political and survival interests or the prevailing governance system, but neither should we assume that these lead to pre-determined and unalterable outcomes.

In the geopolitical challenge that now looms over us, America and many other Western countries are still trying to come to terms with turbulent conditions inside their post-financial crisis bunkers, and looking with angst or trepidation from the battlements at the outside world and most especially China. There is now, though, a growing urgency to recognise new realities in the global system. The US government should work harder to re-establish unanimity of purpose with its allies, instead of picking petty fights, and we must collectively establish new ways of engaging with China in which we can also assert our own values and principles.

ENDNOTES

Preface to the Paperback Edition

1 Andrew J. Nathan, 'The New Tiananmen Papers', *Foreign Affairs*, 30 May 2019.

Introduction

1. There are few better insights into Deng Xiaoping than *Deng Xiaoping: Portrait of a Chinese Statesman*, ed. David Shambaugh, Oxford University Press, 1995.
2. Henry Kissinger, *On China*, Penguin Books, 2012, p. 443.
3. The first foreign company to set up in Shenzhen in 1981 was a joint venture between a Thai agricultural company, Charoen Pokphand Group, and Continental Grain of the US. See 'Company 0001, the first foreign company in Shenzhen', Nikkei Asian Review, 18 December 2016, <https://asia.nikkei.com/Business/Dhanin-Chearavanont-18-Company-0001-the-first-foreign-company-in-Shenzhen>.
4. Peter Nolan, *Re-Balancing China*, Anthem Press, 2015, p. 32.
5. Goldman Sachs, 'Building Better Global Economic BRICs', <http://www.goldmansachs.com/our-thinking/archive/archive-pdfs/build-better-brics.pdf>.
6. Xinhua News, <http://news.xinhuanet.com/english/2007-03/16/content_5856569.htm>, 16 March 2007.
7. 'China's "Authoritative" Warning on Debt: People's Daily Excerpts', Bloomberg, 9 May 2016, <https://www.bloomberg.com/news/articles/2016-05-09/china-s-authoritative-warning-on-debt-people-s-daily-excerpts>.

1 Echoes

1. 'What Does Xi Jinping's China Dream Mean?' BBC, 6 June 2013, <http://www.bbc.co.uk/news/world-asia-china-22726375>.
2. 'China's New Party Chief Xi Jinping's Speech', BBC, 15 November 2012, <http://www.bbc.co.uk/news/world-asia-china-20338586>.
3. Angus Maddison was a British economist whose specialisation was quantitative macro-economic history, and the measurement and analysis of economic development around the world going back to AD 1.
4. 'A Not-So Golden Age', *The Economist*, 17 June 2017.
5. Ian Morris, *Why the West Rules – For Now*, Profile Books, 2010, p. 384.

6. Tim Marshall, *Prisoners of Geography: Ten Maps That Tell You Everything You Need to Know about Global Politics*, Elliott & Thompson, 2015, pp. 35–6.

7. Angus Maddison, *China's Economic Performance in the Long Run*, 2nd edition, OECD, 2007, p. 27.

8. Ryan Patrick Hanley, 'The Wisdom of the State: Adam Smith on China and the Tartary', *American Political Science Review*, vol. 108, no. 2, May 2014.

9. Adam Smith, *An Inquiry into the Nature and Causes of the Wealth of Nations*, cited in Andre Gunder Frank, *ReORIENT: Global Economy in the Asian Age*, University of California Press, 1998, p. 279.

10. Eric Midthun Brooks, 'The Enlightenment European Perception of China', BA thesis, Haverford College, 2009, pp. 25–6, <https://scholarship.tricolib.brynmawr.edu/bitstream/handle/10066/3597/2009BrooksE.pdf?sequence=2&isAllowed=y>.

11. Ibid., p. 55.

12. Angus Maddison, 'China in the World Economy: 1300–2030', *International Journal of Business*, vol. 11, no. 3, 2006, p. 243.

13. Henry Kissinger, *On China*, Penguin Books, 2012, p. 36.

14. Robert Bickers, *The Scramble for China*, Penguin Books, 2012, p. 37.

15. Maddison, *China's Economic Performance in the Long Run*, p. 54.

16. Margaret MacMillan, *Peacemakers: Six Months That Changed the World*, John Murray, 2001, p. 343.

17. Bickers, *The Scramble for China*, p. 6.

18. Albert Feuerwerker, *The Chinese Economy 1870–1949*, Center for Chinese Studies, University of Michigan, 1995, pp. 76–83.

19. Stephen C. Thomas, 'Chinese Economic Development from 1860 to the Present: The Roles of Sovereignty and the Global Economy', p. 7, <http://forumonpublicpolicy.com/archive07/thomas.pdf>.

20. Maddison, *China's Economic Performance in the Long Run*, p. 54.

21. An expert account is Rana Mitter, *China's War with Japan, 1937–1945: The Struggle for Survival*, Allen Lane, 2013.

22. 'Xi Jinping Invokes Opium Wars at the Inauguration of Hong Kong's New Leader', *Quartz*, 1 July 2017, <https://qz.com/1019826/hong-kong-handover-xi-jinping-invokes-opium-wars-at-the-inauguration-of-hong-kongs-new-leader/>.

23. Jonathan Fenby, *Will China Dominate the 21st Century?*, Polity Press, 2014, p. 16.

24. Mitter, *China's War with Japan*, p. 386.

25. Barry Naughton, *The Chinese Economy: Transitions and Growth*, MIT Press, 2007, p. 48.

2 From Mao to Modernity

1. Alain Peyrefitte, *The Collision of Two Civilisations: The British Expedition to China 1792–4*, HarperCollins, 1993, pp. xx–xxi.

2. Frank Dikötter, *The Tragedy of Liberation: A History of the Chinese Revolution 1945–1957*, Bloomsbury, 2013, p. 158.

3. Isabel Hilton, 'The Environment in China and the Return of Civil Society', The China Story, <https://www.thechinastory.org/2013/04/the-environment-in-china-and-the-return-of-civil-society/>.

4. Frank Dikötter's *The Tragedy of Liberation* is a highly respected source.

5. Angus Maddison, 'Historical Statistics of the World Economy: 1–2008 AD' <www.ggdc.net/maddison/historical_statistics/horizontal-file_02-2010.xls>.

6. Barry Naughton, *The Chinese Economy: Transitions and Growth*, MIT Press, 2007, p. 60.

7. Angus Maddison, *China's Economic Performance in the Long Run*, 2nd edition, OECD, 2007, p. 72.

8. Naughton, *The Chinese Economy*, p. 70.

9. Kimberley Singer Babiarz, Karen Eggleston, Grant Miller and Qiong Zhang, 'An Exploration of China's Mortality Decline under Mao: A Provincial Analysis, 1950–80', *Population Studies*, vol. 69, no. 1, March 2015, pp. 39–56.

10. This is explored in more detail in Chapter 8, Middle-Income Trap.

11. Naughton, *The Chinese Economy*, p. 81.
12. Julian Gewirtz, *Unlikely Partners*, Harvard University Press, 2017, p. 20. Gewirtz notes that over time this metaphorical cat would change colour from yellow to white.
13. Henry Kissinger, *On China*, Penguin Books, 2012, p. 333.
14. Maddison, *China's Economic Performance in the Long Run*, p. 70.
15. Gewirtz, *Unlikely Partners*, pp. 26–7.
16. This aside, according to Julian Gewirtz, Kornai's most important contribution was to articulate the idea that a market economy could still be regulated or managed by the government through indirect means, e.g. the fiscal and monetary policies used in Western economies, rather than the direct planning of socialism.
17. Z. Yang and J. Chen, *Housing, Housing Affordability and Housing Policy in Urban China*, Springer, 2014, pp. 15–43.
18. Jonathan Fenby, *The Penguin History of Modern China*, Penguin Books, 2008, p. 646.
19. Kissinger, *On China*, p. 441.
20. China Labour Bulletin, 'Reform of State-Owned Enterprises in China', 19 December 2007, <http://www.clb.org.hk/en/content/reform-state-owned-enterprises-china>.
21. Gewirtz, *Unlikely Partners*, p. 263.
22. Ross Garnaut, Ligang Song and Yang Yao, 'Impact and Significance of State-owned Enterprise Restructuring', *China Journal*, vol. 55, January 2006, pp. 35–65.
23. Daniel Berkowitz, Hong Ma and Shuichiro Nishioka, 'Recasting the Iron Rice Bowl: The Reform of China's State-Owned Enterprises', 17 May 2016, <http://www.econ.pitt.edu/sites/default/files/working_papers/WP16-004.pdf>.
24. Victor Shih, Luke Qi Zhang and Mingxing Liu, 'What the Autocrat Gives: Determinants of Intergovernmental Transfers in China', Northwestern University, <http://faculty.wcas.northwestern.edu/~vsh853/papers/shih_zhang_liu_autocratgives08.pdf>.
25. 'China Onshore Insights', HSBC Global Research, 19 October 2017.
26. 'China's New Premier Pledges Reform, Sees Risks', Reuters, 17 March 2013, <http://uk.reuters.com/article/us-china-parliament-idUKBRE92G02M20130317>.
27. 'Rethinking Financial Deepening: Stability and Growth in Emerging Markets', IMF Discussion Note, 2015, <https://www.imf.org/external/pubs/ft/sdn/2015/sdn1508.pdf>.
28. Naughton, *The Chinese Economy*, p. 461.
29. David Sanger and Michael Wines, 'China Leaders' Limits Come into Focus as US Visit Nears', *New York Times*, 16 January 2011.
30. Andrew Jacobs and Jonathan Ansfield, 'China's Premier Admits Failings but Defends Image', *New York Times*, 4 March 2013, <http://www.nytimes.com/2013/03/05/world/asia/china-leader-wen-is-regretful-but-defensive.html>.
31. Elizabeth Economy, 'What Hu Jintao Leaves Behind', *Diplomat*, 10 November 2012, <http://thediplomat.com/2012/11/what-hu-jintao-leaves-behind/>.

3 The End of Extrapolation

1. Oru Mohiuddin, 'China Still Lucrative for Business, Despite Rising Wage Rates', 13 March 2017, <http://blog.euromonitor.com/2017/03/china-still-lucrative-businesses-despite-rising-wage-rates.html>.
2. See, for example, Nicholas Lardy, *Sustaining China's Economic Growth After the Global Crisis*, Peterson Institute for International Economics, 2012.
3. 'The 13th Five-Year Plan', US–China Economic and Security Review Commission, Washington DC, February 2017, p. 4.
4. Technically, this measure is known as the incremental capital-output ratio (ICOR), and this is the estimate according to the National Bureau of Statistics. The IMF, and some private sector analyses, though, reckon that while the ICOR has risen sharply, it is a little lower, at 7–8.
5. Sally Chen and Joong Shik Kang, 'Credit Booms – Is China Different?', IMF Working Paper, January 2018.
6. 'Xi Jinping's Dream City Xiongan May Turn Out to be China's Biggest Public Works Project Ever', *South China Morning Post*, 13 April 2017.

7. 'China's Zombie Factories and Unborn Cities', BBC, 23 February 2017, <http://www.bbc.com/future/story/20170223-chinas-zombie-factories-and-unborn-cities>.
8. Atif Ansar et al., 'Does Infrastructure Investment Lead to Economic Growth or Economic Fragility? Evidence from China', *Oxford Review of Economic Policy*, vol. 32, no. 3, 2016, pp. 360–90.
9. 'China Anti-Corruption Campaign Backfires', *Financial Times*, 9 October 2016, <https://www.ft.com/content/02f712b4-8ab8-11e6-8aa5-f79f5696c731>.
10. Barry Naughton, 'Shifting Structures and Processes in Economic Policy-Making at the Centre', in China's Core Executive, Merics Papers on China, no. 1, June 2016.
11. 'Made in China 2025', State Council, Beijing, 2016, <http://english.gov.cn/2016special/madeinchina2025/>.
12. 'Second Child Policy Increases Births by 7.9 Per Cent', China.org.cn, <http://www.china.org.cn/china/2017-01/23/content_40158434.htm>.
13. Yasheng Huang, *Capitalism with Chinese Characteristics*, Cambridge University Press, 2008.
14. IMF, 'Global Financial Stability Report', October 2016, p. 104.
15. 'China's State-Owned Zombie Economy', *Financial Times*, 29 February 2016, <https://www.ft.com/content/253d7eb0-ca6c-11e5-84df-70594b99fc47?mhq5j=e2>.
16. For a good review of the contradictions and confusion surrounding the stall or backward steps in SOE reform, see Barry Naughton, 'Two Trains Running: Supply-Side Reform, SOE Reform and the Authoritative Personage', Hoover Institution, July 2016, <https://www.hoover.org/research/two-trains-running-supply-side-reform-soe-reform-and-authoritative-personage>.
17. T.S. Lombard, 'China Reform Watch: Xi Pushes for Bigger SOEs', 29 June 2016.
18. 'China Watch: State Sector Reform Continues to Underwhelm', Capital Economics, 31 July 2017.
19. 'Reinstatement', *The Economist*, 22 July 2017, <https://www.economist.com/news/finance-and-economics/21725293-outperformed-private-firms-they-are-no-longer-shrinking-share-overall>.
20. Fu Chengyu, interview with Xinhua, cited by Andrew Batson, 'Fu Chengyu's Frank Talk on SOE Reform', Andrew Batson's blog, 20 March 2017, <https://andrewbatson.com/2017/03/20/fu-chengyus-frank-talk-on-soe-reform/>.
21. 'Concerning Signs in SOE Reform', Credit Suisse, China Market Strategy, *Asian Daily*, 8 June 2016.
22. 'Walled In: China's Great Dilemma', Goldman Sachs Investment Strategy Group, January 2016.
23. 'Urban China', World Bank and Development Research Center of the State Council, 2014, p. 17.
24. 'Migrant Workers and Their Children', China Labour Bulletin, <http://www.clb.org.hk/content/migrant-workers-and-their-children>.
25. Charles Parton, 'China's Acute Water Shortage Imperils Economic Future', *Financial Times*, 27 February 2018, <https://www.ft.com/content/3ee05452-1801-11e8-9376-4a6390addb44>.
26. 'Will China's Children Solve Its Crippling Water Shortage Problem?', *Guardian*, 22 March 2017, <https://www.theguardian.com/global-development-professionals-network/2017/mar/22/children-china-crippling-water-scarcity>.
27. 'China debt-fueled stimulus may lead to recession – People's Daily', Reuters, 9 May 2016, <http://www.reuters.com/article/us-china-economy-trend-idUSKCN0Y003W>.
28. Yanrui Wu, 'China's services sector: the new engine of economic growth', *Eurasian Geography and Economics*, vol. 56, no. 6, 2015.
29. China Family Panel Studies, University of Beijing, 2010, cited in Zheping Huang, 'China's 1 percent owns one-third of the country's wealth – but it is still more equal than the US', Quartz, <https://qz.com/595389/chinas-1-owns-one-third-of-the-countrys-wealth-but-it-is-still-more-equal-than-the-us/>.

4 Debt Trap

1. 'Strengthening the Banking System in China: Issues and Experience', Bank for International Settlements Policy Papers, no. 7, October 1999, <http://www.bis.org/publ/plcy07.pdf>.
2. Shinjie Yao and Minjia Chen, 'Chinese Economy 2008: A Turbulent Year Amid World Financial Crisis', China Policy Institute, University of Nottingham, February 2009.
3. Victor Shih, 'Financial Instability in China: Possible Pathways and Their Likelihood', Mercator Institute for China Studies, 20 October 2017.
4. 'China's Continuing Credit Boom', Liberty Street Economics, Federal Reserve Bank of New York, 27 February 2017, <http://libertystreeteconomics.newyorkfed.org/2017/02/chinas-continuing-credit-boom.html>.
5. 'People's Republic of China, Article IV Consultation', IMF Country Report no. 16/270, 2016.
6. BIS Quarterly Review, March 2018, <https://www.bis.org/publ/qtrpdf/r_qt1803.pdf>.
7. Gan Li, 'The Growing Mortgage Crisis Facing China's Poor', Sixth Tone, 3 February 2017, <http://www.sixthtone.com/news/1884/the-growing-mortgage-crisis-facing-china's-poor>.
8. Shih, 'Financial Instability in China'.
9. World Bank, 'Budget Reform at the Local Level in China: Issues and Prospects', Beijing seminar, 13 March 2017.
10. Olivier Blanchard and Adam Posen, 'Reality Check for the Global Economy', Peterson Institute for International Finance, March 2016, and European Parliament, Directorate General for Internal Policies, 'Non-performing loans in the Banking union', March 2016.
11. 'China Banks Guru Warns of Bad Debt Reckoning', Barrons, 15 August 2016.
12. IMF, 'Global Financial Stability Report', April 2016, pp. 16–18.
13. Charles W. Calomiris and Stephen H. Haber, *Fragile by Design: The Political Origins of Banking Crises and Scarce Credit*, Princeton University Press, 2014, p. 4.
14. I heard the term Minsky Moment first in 1998 from a UBS colleague at the time, Paul McCulley, opining on the Asian crisis.
15. Moritz Schularick and Alan M. Taylor, 'Credit Booms Gone Bust: Monetary Policy, Leverage Cycles and Financial Crises 1870–2008', *American Economic Review*, vol. 10, no. 22, April 2012, pp. 1029–61.
16. S&P Global Market Intelligence, 'The World's 100 Largest Banks', 11 April 2017.
17. Jon Anderson, 'There is No Reform Agenda (Part 2)', Emerging Market Advisors, 3 August 2017, and 'The China Crisis Handbook', Emerging Advisors Group, 28 October 2016.
18. The term 'shadow banking' was also coined by Paul McCulley, this time when he was at PIMCO. See, for example, Paul McCulley, 'The Shadow Banking System and Hyman Minsky's Economic Journey', PIMCO, May 2009, <https://www.pimco.com/en-us/insights/economic-and-market-commentary/global-central-bank-focus/the-shadow-banking-system-and-hyman-minskys-economic-journey>.
19. Torsten Ehlers, Steven Kong and Feng Zhu, 'Mapping Shadow Banking in China', Bank for International Settlements, February 2018, <https://www.bis.org/publ/work701.pdf>.
20. Brookings Economic Studies, 'Shadow Banking in China: A Primer', March 2015. Conversions made at $1 = RMB 6.5.
21. Moody's, 'Quarterly China Shadow Banking Monitor', 8 May 2017.
22. Engen Tham, ' "Ghost Collateral" Haunts Loans Across China's Debt-Laden Banking System', Reuters, 24 May 2017, <http://www.reuters.com/investigates/special-report/china-collateral-fake/>.
23. 'Shadow Lending Threatens China's Economy, Officials Warn', *New York Times*, 18 March 2017.

24. Federal Reserve Bank of San Francisco, 'The Growing Importance of China's Money Market', 15 September 2016, <https://www.frbsf.org/banking/asia-program/pacific-exchange-blog/china-money-market-growth/>.
25. China Banks, 'China WMP Reforms: A Blessing in Disguise?', UBS Global Research, 14 March 2017.
26. 'Four Fresh Worries About China's Shadow Banking System', Bloomberg, 6 September 2016.
27. IMF, 'Global Financial Stability Report', April 2017, pp. 35–8.
28. China Banks, 'Facing a Funding Crisis?', UBS Global Research, 15 June 2017.
29. 'China Crackdown to be Intensified After Xi Meeting, Nomura Says', Bloomberg, 28 April 2017, <https://www.bloomberg.com/news/articles/2017-04-28/xi-meeting-shows-china-crackdown-to-be-intensified-nomura-says>.
30. 'China Focus: Financial Reform Plans Unveiled to Serve Real Economy in Sustainable Manner', Xinhuanet, 17 July 2017, <http://news.xinhuanet.com/english/2017-07/16/c_136446619.htm>.
31. China Banks, 'China's Interbank Market: A Conduit for Contagion?', UBS Global Research, 30 June 2017.

5 Renminbi Trap

1. Cited in Rudolf Richter, 'European Monetary Union: Initial Situation, Alternatives, Prospects – In the Light of Modern Institutional Economics', University of Saarland Economic Series 9908, May 1999.
2. A more moderate version in English by the governor, Zhou Xiaochuan, 'Reform the International Monetary System', 23 March 2009, can be found at <http://www.bis.org/review/r090402c.pdf>.
3. 'Think Twice Before Declaring War on Chinese Currency', People's Daily, 27 January 2016, <http://en.people.cn/n3/2016/0127/c98649-9010063.html>.
4. Eswar S. Prasad, 'China's Economy and Financial Markets: Reforms and Risks', Testimony to US–China Economic and Security Review Commission, Hearing on China's 13th Five-Year Plan, 27 April 2016.
5. Michael Pettis, 'The Titillating and Terrifying Collapse of the Dollar. Again.', Seeking Alpha, 16 May 2016, <https://seekingalpha.com/article/3973009-titillating-terrifying-collapse-dollar>.
6. 'China's Stock Market Woes Could Determine Communist Party's Fate', The Epoch Times, 5 July 2015,
7. 'Beijing's Pyrrhic Victory Over the Equity Rout', China Centre for Economics and Business, The Conference Board, July 2015.
8. Arthur Kroeber, 'Making Sense of China's Stock Market Mess', Brookings, 13 July 2015, and Sara Hsu, 'China's Volatile Stock Market and Its Implications', China Policy Institute, Paper no. 7, University of Nottingham, 2015.
9. 'Goldman Estimates China's " 'National Team' " Stock Rescue at $144bn', Financial Times, 6 August 2015, <https://www.ft.com/content/ec29a8b2-3bf8-11e5-8613-07d16aad2152>.
10. 'China Spent $470bn to Maintain Confidence in Renminbi', Financial Times, 13 June 2016, <https://www.ft.com/content/26484358-308d-11e6-bda0-04585c31b153>.
11. 'In China's Alleyways, Underground Banks Move Money', Wall Street Journal, 27 October 2015, <https://www.wsj.com/articles/in-chinas-alleyways-underground-banks-move-money-1445911877>.
12. 'Xi's Sign-Off Deals Blow to China Inc's Global Spending Spree', Wall Street Journal, 23 July 2017, <https://www.wsj.com/articles/chinas-latest-clampdown-on-overseas-investing-has-president-xis-approval-1500802203>.
13. A useful discussion on this topic is 'Making China's FX Reserves Feel Inadequate', Financial Times, 26 August 2015, <https://ftalphaville.ft.com/2015/08/26/2138542/making-chinas-fx-reserves-feel-inadequate/>.

6 Demographic (Ageing) Trap

1. 'A Model of Family Planning, Rudong County Takes Brunt of Aging Society', *Global Times*, 20 January 2016, <http://www.globaltimes.cn/content/964697.shtml>.
2. George Magnus, *The Age of Aging: How Demographics Are Changing the Global Economy and Our World*, John Wiley & Sons, 2008.
3. See, for example, Martin King Whyte, Wang Feng and Yong Cai, 'Challenging Myths About China's One-Child Policy', *China Journal*, vol. 74, 2015, pp. 144–59, <https://scholar.harvard.edu/files/martinwhyte/files/challenging_myths_published_version.pdf>.
4. 'China Has World's Most Skewed Sex Ratio at Birth – Again', *South China Morning Post*, 27 October 2016, <http://www.scmp.com/news/china/policies-politics/article/2040544/chinas-demographic-time-bomb-still-ticking-worlds-most>.
5. 'China May Have 90 Million Fewer People Than Claimed', *South China Morning Post*, 23 May 2017, <http://www.scmp.com/news/china/policies-politics/article/2095311/china-population-much-smaller-you-think-researchers-say>.
6. Harry X. Wu, Yang Du and Cai Fang, 'China's Premature Demographic Transition in Government-Engineered Growth', in *Asymmetric Demography and the Global Economy*, ed. José Maria Fanelli, Palgrave Macmillan, 2015, pp. 187–212.
7. Hukou, discussed in Chapter 4, is the registration system according to which citizens are classified as rural or urban.
8. Shuaizhang Feng, Yingyao Hu and Robert Moffitt, 'Long Run Trends in Unemployment and Labour Force Participation in China', National Bureau of Economic Research, August 2015.
9. Xin En Lee, 'Unemployment in China: Degree to Nowhere?', China Household Survey, 21 July 2014, <http://knowledge.ckgsb.edu.cn/2014/07/21/employment/unemployment-in-china-degree-to-nowhere/>.
10. 'Wages and Employment', China Labour Bulletin, 2017, <http://www.clb.org.hk/content/wages-and-employment#%E2%80%8BUnemployment>.
11. BBC, 'Foxconn Replaces 60,000 Factory Workers with Robots', 25 May 2016, <http://www.bbc.co.uk/news/technology-36376966>.
12. 'China's Robot Revolution', *Financial Times*, 6 June 2016.
13. Mitali Das and Papa N'Diaye, 'Chronicle of a Decline Foretold: Has China Reached the Lewis Turning Point?', IMF Working Paper 13/26, 29 January 2013.
14. 'China's Rural Poor Bear the Brunt of the Nation's Aging Crisis', Bloomberg, 5 January 2017, <https://www.bloomberg.com/news/articles/2017-01-05/china-s-rural-poor-bear-the-brunt-of-the-nation-s-aging-crisis>.
15. 'China Plans Immigration Agency to Lure Overseas Talent', Bloomberg, 18 July 2016, <https://www.bloomberg.com/news/articles/2016-07-18/china-said-to-create-new-office-to-lure-overseas-work-talent>.
16. 'China 2030', World Bank and Development Research Center of the State Council, 2013.
17. Carmen M. Reinhart and Kenneth S. Rogoff, *This Time Is Different: Eight Centuries of Financial Folly*, Princeton University Press, 2009.
18. IMF, 'Older and Smaller', Finance and Development, vol. 53, no. 1, March 2016.
19. IMF, Fiscal Monitor, October 2016.
20. Hu Jiye, China University of Political Science and Law, cited in Wynne Wang, 'The Silver Age: China's Aging Population', Cheung Kong Graduate School of Business (CKGSB) Knowledge, 17 October 2016.
21. Steven Barnett and Ray Brooks, 'China: Does Government Health and Education Spending Boost Consumption?', IMF Working Paper 10/16, January 2010.
22. China Labour Bulletin, 'China's Social Security System', June 2016, <http://www.clb.org.hk/content/china's-social-security-system>.
23. OECD, 'Economic Survey of China 2017'.
24. 'China 2030', World Bank and Development Research Center of the State Council, p. 332.
25. World Health Organization, 'Deepening Health Reform in China', 2016.

7 Middle-Income Trap

1. Daron Acemoglu and James Robinson, *Why Nations Fail: The Origins of Power, Prosperity and Poverty*, Crown Publishers, 2012.
2. 'With Greater Efforts, There's Still Time to Avoid Middle-Income Trap', *China Daily*, 17 March 2016, <http://www.chinadaily.com.cn/opinion/2016-03/17/content_23903667.htm>.
3. Greg Larson, Norman Loayza and Michael Woolcock, 'The Middle-Income Trap: Myth or Reality?', Research & Policy Briefs, March 2016, <http://documents.worldbank.org/curated/en/965511468194956837/pdf/104230-BRI-Policy-1.pdf>.
4. Barry Eichengreen, Donghyun Park and Kwanho Shin, 'Growth Slowdowns Redux: New Evidence on the Middle-Income Trap', NBER Working Paper 18673, January 2013.
5. Ruchir Sharma, 'Broken BRICs: Why the Rest Stopped Rising', *Foreign Affairs*, November/December 2012.
6. Pierre-Richard Agenor, 'Caught in the Middle? The Economics of Middle-Income Traps', Fondation pour les études et recherches sur le développement international, May 2016, p. 6, <http://www.ferdi.fr/sites/www.ferdi.fr/files/publication/fichiers/wp142_agenor-upadte_version-2016-05.pdf>.
7. World Bank, 'World Development Report 2017'.
8. Jesus Felipe, 'Tracking the Middle-income Trap: What Is It, Who Is in It, and Why?', Levy Institute, Working Paper no. 715, April 2012.
9. Paul Krugman, 'The Myth of Asia's Miracle', *Foreign Affairs*, November/December 1994.
10. Indermit S. Gill and Homi Kharas, 'The Middle-Income Trap Turns Ten', Policy Research Working Paper no. 7403, World Bank, August 2015.
11. Asia Productivity Databook 2016, Asia Productivity Organisation, 2016.
12. 'Unproductive Production', *The Economist*, 11 October 2014.
13. Dani Rodrik, 'Getting Institutions Right', Harvard University, April 2004, <https://drodrik.scholar.harvard.edu/files/dani-rodrik/files/getting-institutions-right.pdf>.
14. 'Xi's Signature Governance Innovation: The Rise of Leading Small Groups', CSIS, <https://www.csis.org/analysis/xis-signature-governance-innovation-rise-leading-small-groups>.
15. Mancur Olson, *The Rise and Decline of Nations*, Yale University Press, 1982.
16. 'China Economic Update', World Bank and the State Council Development Research Center, June 2015, <http://documents.worldbank.org/curated/en/526971468001756352/pdf/97901-WP-PUBLIC-Box391490B.pdf>.
17. 'World Bank Removes Critical Section from China Report', *South China Morning Post*, 6 July 2015, <http://www.scmp.com/news/china/economy/article/1833253/world-bank-removes-critical-section-china-report>.
18. 'China Economic Update', formerly p. 28.
19. James McGregor, 'China's Drive for Indigenous Innovation', US Chamber of Commerce, 2010, <https://www.uschamber.com/sites/default/files/documents/files/100728chinareport_0_0.pdf>.
20. 'The 13th Five-Year Plan (2016–2020)', Central Compilation & Translation Press, Central Committee of the Communist Party of China, <http://en.ndrc.gov.cn/newsrelease/201612/P020161207645765233498.pdf>.
21. Samm Sacks, 'Disruptors, Innovators, and Thieves', CSIS, January 2018, is a good technical guide to Chinese technology developments.
22. 'Biting the Bullet', *The Economist*, 23 September 2017, <https://www.economist.com/news/finance-and-economics/21729442-its-record-industrial-policy-successes-patchy-china-sets-its-sights>.
23. 'Study Emphasizes Foreign Investment's Role in Chinese Economy', *Wall Street Journal*, 1 December 2016, <https://blogs.wsj.com/chinarealtime/2016/12/01/study-emphasizes-foreign-investments-role-in-chinese-economy/>.
24. Paul Triolo and Jimmy Goodrich, 'From Riding a Wave to Full Steam Ahead', New America DigiChina project, 28 February 2018, <https://na-production.s3.amazonaws.com/documents/20180228-DigiChina-TrioloGoodrich-ChinaAI.pdf>.

25. Jeffrey Ding, 'Deciphering China's AI Dream', Future of Humanity Institute, University of Oxford, March 2018.
26. Dennis Normile, 'One in Three Chinese Children Faces an Education Apocalypse: An Ambitious Experiment Hopes to Save Them', *Science*, 21 September 2017, <http://www.sciencemag.org/news/2017/09/one-three-chinese-children-faces-education-apocalypse-ambitious-experiment-hopes-save>.
27. Zhu Tian, 'Will China's Educational System Strangle Economic Growth?', *Forbes Asia*, 16 May 2016, <https://www.forbes.com/sites/ceibs/2016/05/16/will-chinas-educational-system-strangle-economic-growth/#49a2592b430c>.
28. 'Workforce Skill Gaps Loom Large for Made in China 2025', The Conference Board, 28 June 2017.
29. 'Education at a Glance 2016', OECD, 15 September 2016, <http://www.keepeek.com/Digital-Asset-Management/oecd/education/education-at-a-glance-2016_eag-2016-en#.WVOes2W-zSU>.
30. 'New Records Set in Global Filings of Patents, Trademarks, Industrial Designs in 2016', World Intellectual Property Organization, 6 December 2017, <http://www.wipo.int/pressroom/en/articles/2017/article_0013.html>. See also 'International Patenting Strategies of Chinese Residents', Economic Research Working Paper no. 20, World Intellectual Property Organization, 2014.
31. 'The People's Republic of China – Avoiding the Middle-Income Trap', OECD, September 2013.
32. 'Global Innovation Index 2017', World Intellectual Property Organization, 2017.

8 Trade Dogs of War

1. Edward Luttwak, 'From Geopolitics to Geo-Economics: Logics of Conflict in the Grammar of Commerce', *National Interest*, Summer 1990.
2. Simon Tisdall, 'China Syndrome Dictates Barack Obama's Asia-Pacific Strategy', *Guardian*, 6 January 2012, <https://www.theguardian.com/commentisfree/2012/jan/06/china-barack-obama-defence-strategy>.
3. 'President Xi's Speech to Davos in Full', World Economic Forum, Davos, 17 January 2017, <https://www.weforum.org/agenda/2017/01/full-text-of-xi-jinping-keynote-at-the-world-economic-forum>.
4. Anna Wong, 'China's Current Account: External Rebalancing or Capital Flight?' International Finance Discussion Papers 1208, Federal Reserve Board, 15 June 2017, <https://www.federalreserve.gov/econres/ifdp/files/ifdp1208.pdf>.
5. Simon Evenett and Johannes Fritz, 'Will Awe Trump Rules?', 21st Global Trade Alert Report, 3 July 2017, <http://www.globaltradealert.org/reports/42>.
6. Design of Trade Agreements Database, <https://www.designoftradeagreements.org>.
7. Chad P. Brown, 'Trump's Threat of Steel Tariffs Heralds Big Changes in Trade Policy', *Washington Post*, 21 April 2017, <https://www.washingtonpost.com/news/monkey-cage/wp/2017/04/21/trumps-threat-of-steel-tariffs-heralds-big-changes-in-trade-policy/?utm_term=.9e0cd000312a>.
8. 'The People's Republic of China', Office of the United States Trade Representative <https://ustr.gov/countries-regions/china-mongolia-taiwan/peoples-republic-china>.
9. The Rhodium Group, 'Two-Way Street: 25 Years of US-China Direct Investment', November 2016, <http://rhg.com/wp-content/uploads/2016/11/TwoWayStreet_ExecutiveSummary_En.pdf>, and for latest estimates, <http://rhg.com/interactive/china-investment-monitor>.
10. The Rhodium Group, 'Chinese FDI in the US in 2017: A Double Policy Punch', 17 January 2018, <https://rhg.com/research/chinese-fdi-us-2017-double-policy-punch/>.
11. 'Globally, More Name U.S. Than China as World's Leading Economic Power', Pew Research Center, 13 July 2017, <http://www.pewglobal.org/2017/07/13/more-name-u-s-than-china-as-worlds-leading-economic-power>.

12. A good discussion on how the US has accommodated the global economy, and why China should but probably won't, can be found at Michael Pettis, 'China Financial Markets: A US Retreat on Global Trade Will Not Lead to a Shift in Power', Carnegie Endowment for International Peace, 16 December 2016, <http://carnegieendowment.org/chinafinancialmarkets/66485>.

9 The East Wind Prevails Over the West Wind

1. 'The East Wind Prevails Over the West Wind', Selected Works of Mao Tse-tung, 17 November 1957, <https://www.marxists.org/reference/archive/mao/selected-works/volume-7/mswv7_480.htm>.
2. 'All Aboard the China-to-London Freight Train', BBC News, 18 January 2017, <http://www.bbc.co.uk/news/business-38654176>.
3. Peter Cai, 'Understanding China's Belt and Road Initiative', Lowy Institute, Center for Strategic and International Studies, March 2017, <https://www.lowyinstitute.org/publications/understanding-belt-and-road-initiative>.
4. Guy de Jonquières, 'Xi Jinping's Long Road to Somewhere? China's OBOR Initiative and How Europe Should Respond', May 2016, <http://ecipe.org/publications/xi-jinpings-long-road-to-somewhere/?chapter=all>.
5. Mahathir Mohamad, leader of the new Malaysian government, announced in 2018 that he would pull out of the Kuala Lumpur-to-Singapore link for budgetary reasons.
6. Asian Development Bank, 'Meeting Asia's Infrastructure Needs', <https://www.adb.org/sites/default/files/publication/227496/special-report-infrastructure.pdf>, May 2017.
7. Bank Credit Analyst, 'China's Belt and Road Initiative: Can It Offset a Mainland Slowdown?', Emerging Markets Strategy, BCA Research, 13 September 2017.
8. About 20 per cent of financing has come from the so-called policy banks, including China Development Bank, and Export Import Bank of China. The rest comes from the Silk Road Fund, launched by the government in 2014 with initial funding of $40 billion and backed by the China Investment Corporation, China's sovereign wealth fund, and the State Administration for Foreign Exchange. The Asian Infrastructure Investment Bank is also a supplier of financing but in 2017 its outstanding loans disbursed to BRI countries were around $2 billion.
9. David Dollar, 'Yes, China is Investing Globally – But Not So Much in Its Belt And Road Initiative', Brookings, 8 May 2017, <https://www.brookings.edu/blog/order-from-chaos/2017/05/08/yes-china-is-investing-globally-but-not-so-much-in-its-belt-and-road-initiative/>.
10. CNBC, 'China pledges more than $100 billion in Belt and Road projects', 14 May 2017, <https://www.cnbc.com/2017/05/14/china-pledges-more-than-100-billion-in-belt-and-road-projects.html>.
11. Bank Credit Analyst, 'China's Belt and Road Initiative: Can It Offset a Mainland Slowdown?'.
12. Yu Jie, 'China's One Belt, One Road: A Reality Check', LSE IDEAS Strategic Update, 24 July 2017, <http://www.lse.ac.uk/ideas/research/updates/one-belt-one-road>.
13. 'Li Vows to Protect Rights of Chinese Working Abroad', China Daily, 10 May 2014, <http://www.chinadaily.com.cn/world/2014livisitafrica/2014-05/10/content_17497900.htm>
14. Peter Cai, 'Understanding China's Belt and Road Initiative'.
15. Brook Larmer, 'Is China the World's New Colonial Power?', New York Times, 2 May 2017, <https://www.nytimes.com/2017/05/02/magazine/is-china-the-worlds-new-colonial-power.html>.
16. John Hurley, Scott Morris and Gailyn Portelance, 'Examining the Debt Implications of the Belt and Road Initiative from a Policy Perspective', Center for Global Development, Policy Paper 121, March 2018, <https://www.cgdev.org/sites/default/files/examining-debt-implications-belt-and-road-initiative-policy-perspective.pdf>.

17. '5 Things About Fishing in the South China Sea', *Wall Street Journal*, 19 July 2016, https://blogs.wsj.com/briefly/2016/07/19/5-things-about-fishing-in-the-south-china-sea/

18. 'How China Rules the Waves', *Financial Times*, 12 January 2017, <https://ig.ft.com/sites/china-ports/>.

19. 'Beijing Rejects Tribunal's Ruling in South China Sea Case', *Guardian*, 12 July 2016, <https://www.theguardian.com/world/2016/jul/12/philippines-wins-south-china-sea-case-against-china>.

20. 'Priority Policy for Development Cooperation FY2017', Ministry for Foreign Affairs, April 2017, <http://www.mofa.go.jp/files/000259285.pdf>.

21. 'China–Pakistan Economic Corridor Unacceptable to India: Shivshankar Menon', *Indian Express*, 22 April 2017, <http://indianexpress.com/article/india/china-pakistan-economic-corridor-unacceptable-to-india-shivshankar-menon-4623185/>.

22. 'American Dad Explains Benefits of "One Belt, One Road" to His Daughter as Bedtime Story', Shanghaiist, 11 May 2017, <http://shanghaiist.com/2017/05/11/one-belt-one-road-bedtime-stories.php>.

23. Full text of President Xi's speech at opening of Belt and Road forum, *Global Times*, 14 May 2017, <http://www.globaltimes.cn/content/1046925.shtml>.

24. Henry Kissinger, *On China*, Penguin Books, 2012, p. 12.

25. 'Less biding and hiding', *The Economist*, 2 December 2010, <http://www.economist.com/node/17601475>.

26. Zbigniew Brzezinski, 'A Geostrategy for Eurasia', *Foreign Affairs*, vol. 76, no. 5, September/October 1997, <https://www.foreignaffairs.com/articles/asia/1997-09-01/geostrategy-eurasia>.

27. 'Asia Welcomes Clinton, and Renewed Attention', *New York Times*, 5 November 2009, <http://www.nytimes.com/2009/02/15/world/asia/15iht-clinton.4.20197943.html?mcubz=3>.

28. Michael Green, *By More Than Providence: Grand Strategy and American Power in the Asia Pacific Since 1783*, Columbia University Press, 2017, p. 5.

SELECT BIBLIOGRAPHY

Acemoglu, Daron and Robinson, James, *Why Nations Fail: The Origins of Power, Prosperity and Poverty*, Crown Publishers, 2012

Bank for International Settlements, Basel, Quarterly Reviews and various reports

Bickers, Robert, *The Scramble for China*, Penguin Books, 2012

Brookings Economic Studies, 'Shadow Banking in China: A Primer', March 2015

Cai, Peter, 'Understanding China's Belt and Road Initiative', Lowy Institute, Center for Strategic and International Studies, March 2017

Chatham House, 'The Critical Transition: China's Priorities for 2021', ed. Kerry Brown, February 2017

Collier, Andrew, *Shadow Banking and the Rise of Capitalism in China*, Orient Capital Research, 2017

Dikötter, Frank, *The Tragedy of Liberation: A History of the Chinese Revolution 1945–1957*, Bloomsbury, 2013

Ding, Jeffrey, 'Deciphering China's AI Dream', Future of Humanity Institute, University of Oxford, March 2018

Ehlers, Torsten, Kong, Steven and Zhu, Feng, 'Mapping Shadow Banking in China', Bank for International Settlements, February 2018

Fenby, Jonathan, *The Penguin History of Modern China*, Penguin Books, 2008

Fenby, Jonathan, *Will China Dominate the 21st Century?*, Polity Press, 2017

Gewirtz, Julian, *Unlikely Partners*, Harvard University Press, 2017

Gill, Intermit and Kharas, Homi, 'The Middle-Income Trap Turns Ten', Policy Research Working Paper no. 7403, World Bank, August 2015

Hanley, Ryan Patrick, 'The Wisdom of the State: Adam Smith on China and the Tartary', *American Political Science Review*, vol. 108, no. 2, May 2014

Hoover Institution, China Leadership Monitor, <https://www.hoover.org/publications/china-leadership-monitor>

IMF, 'People's Republic of China' (annual report)

IMF, 'People's Republic of China, Financial System Stability Assessment', December 2017

Kissinger, Henry, *On China*, Penguin Books, 2012

Kroeber, Arthur, *China's Economy: What Everyone Needs to Know*, Oxford University Press, 2016

Lardy, Nicholas, 'Sustaining China's Economic Growth after the Global Crisis', Peterson Institute for International Economics, 2012

McGregor, James, 'China's Drive for Indigenous Innovation', US Chamber of Commerce, 2010, <https://www.uschamber.com/sites/default/files/documents/files/100728chinareport_0_0.pdf>

McGregor, Richard, *The Party: The Secret World of China's Communist Rulers*, Allen Lane, 2010

Maddison, Angus, *China's Economic Performance in the Long Run*, 2nd edition, OECD, 2007

Magnus, George, *The Age of Aging: How Demographics Are Changing the Global Economy and Our World*, John Wiley & Sons, 2008

Magnus, George, *Uprising: Will Emerging Markets Shape or Shake the World Economy?*, John Wiley & Sons, 2011

Marshall, Tim, *Prisoners of Geography: Ten Maps that Tell You Everything You Need to Know about Global Politics*, Elliott & Thompson, 2015

Mercator Institute for Chinese Studies, 'China's Core Executive', June 2016

Mitter, Rana, *China's War with Japan, 1937–1945: The Struggle for Survival*, Allen Lane, 2013

Morris, Ian, *Why the West Rules – For Now*, Profile Books, 2010

Naughton, Barry, *The Chinese Economy: Transitions and Growth*, MIT Press, 2007

Nolan, Peter, *Re-Balancing China*, Anthem Press, 2015

OECD, 'The People's Republic of China: Avoiding the Middle-Income Trap', September 2013

OECD, 'Economic Survey, China', 2017

Pei, Minxin, *China's Crony Capitalism*, Harvard University Press, 2016

Pettis, Michael, 'China Financial Markets: Will China's New "Supply-Side" Reforms Help China?', <http://blog.mpettis.com>, 2016

Pieke, Frank N., *Knowing China: A Twenty-First Century Guide*, Cambridge University Press, 2016

Ringen, Stein, *The Perfect Dictatorship: China in the 21st Century*, Hong Kong University Press, 2016

Shambaugh, David, ed., *Deng Xiaoping: Portrait of a Chinese Statesman*, Oxford University Press, 1995

Shih, Victor, 'Financial Instability in China: Possible Pathways and their Likelihood', Mercator Institute for China Studies, 20 October 2017

'Silk Road Bottom Up: Regional Perspectives on the Belt and Road Initiative', ed. China-Programme/Stiftung Asienhaus, 2017

Wuttke, Joerg, 'A Practitioner's Perspective on Organizational Behaviour in China', in *Handbook of Chinese Organizational Behaviour: Integrating Theory, Research and Practice*, ed. Xu Huang and Michael Harris Bond, Edward Elgar Publishing, 2012

Yasheng Huang, *Capitalism with Chinese Characteristics: Entrepreneurship and the State*, MIT Press, 2008

INDEX

Unattributed entries, for example *geography*, refer to the book's metatopic, China.

Printed and bound by CPI Group (UK) Ltd, Croydon, CR0 4YY

28/11/2023

08196939-0001